P9-DMX-222

PLAYING PERIOD PLAYS

FIG. 1. Farandole Dance of the Twelfth to Fourteenth Century

PLAYING PERIOD PLAYS

by

LYN OXENFORD

FORMERLY PROFESSOR, GUILDHALL SCHOOL OF MUSIC
AND DRAMA, AND STAFF TUTOR,
THE BRITISH DRAMA LEAGUE, LONDON

illustrated by

BERNICE CARLILL

J. GARNET MILLER LTD
129 St. John's Hill, London, SW11 1TD
England

THE COACH HOUSE PRESS INC.
53 West Jackson Boulevard, Chicago
Illinois 60604, U.S.A.

FIRST PUBLISHED IN ONE VOLUME BY
J. GARNET MILLER LTD
IN 1958

SECOND IMPRESSION, 1959
THIRD IMPRESSION, 1966
FOURTH IMPRESSION, 1969
FIFTH IMPRESSION, 1974
SIXTH IMPRESSION, 1984

•

PRINTED IN GREAT BRITAIN BY
A. WHEATON AND CO. LTD.
EXETER

ISBN 0 85343 549 9

CONTENTS

PART I

MEDIEVAL AND EARLY TUDOR PERIOD

CHAP. PAGE

I. THE SPIRIT OF THE PLAYS 1

Spirit of the medieval period—Development of plays and place of performance—Style of acting—Conventions of setting—Progression into early Tudor plays and playing—List of reference books, genuine period plays and modern period plays, both one-act and three-act

II. MOVEMENT IN COSTUME 14

Outline of costume from 1066 to 1550—Movement in costume—List of costume accessories for movement for each century and fashion of make-up—List of costume books—List of artists from each century who sum up the visual aspect of the period

III. OCCUPATIONS 34

Occupations and amusements of the period for stage, arena or pageant production—Classified list for each century: men, clerks, servants, monks, ladies, pages, etc.—List of useful books

IV. MANNERS AND DANCES 43

Manners and customs—Bows and curtsies—Dances for each period, Caroles—Farandole, Branles and Pavane—List of gramophone records and reference books on dances

V. MUSIC 62

Musical forms of the periods—Instruments used—List for each century of instruments and composers, modern stage equivalents and possible gramophone records and useful books

VI. PRACTICE SCENES 73

Suggested scenes from plays for practice in period movement—Mime scenes for each century with suggestions for gramophone records as music

PART II

ELIZABETHAN AND JACOBEAN PERIOD
(*including Masques*)

CHAP. PAGE

VII. THE SPIRIT OF THE PLAYS 81

Spirit of the periods—Development of plays and place of performance—Progression from Elizabethan to Jacobean and Stuart playing—List of reference books, period authors, and genuine period plays and modern period plays, both three-act and one-act

VIII. MOVEMENT IN COSTUME 95

Outline of costume from 1558 to 1630—Movement in costume—List of costume accessories for movement for each period—List of costume books—List of artists for each period, who sum up the visual aspect of the times

IX. OCCUPATIONS 114

Occupations and games and amusements of the periods for stage, arena or pageant production—Classified list for each period: servants, tradesmen, ladies, etc.—Useful book

X. MANNERS AND DANCES 130

Manners and customs—Bows and curtsies—Dances for each period, Galliard, Coranto, Canaries, La Volta—List of reference books on dances

XI. MUSIC 153

Musical forms of the periods—Instruments used and their modern stage equivalents—List for each period of composers, instruments and suggested gramophone records

XII. PRACTICE SCENES 162

Practice scenes from plays suggested—Mime scenes

PART III

RESTORATION AND GEORGIAN PERIOD

CHAP. PAGE

XIII. The Spirit of the Plays 169

Spirit of the Restoration plays—Development of plays and place of performance—Style of acting—The Georgian theatre and its setting—Regency audience and plays—The modern producer's problems—List of reference books, genuine period playwrights and modern period plays, both one-act and three-act

XIV. Movement in Costume 180

Outline of costume from 1668 to 1820—Movement in costume—List of costume accessories for movement and hair-styles for each period—List of costume books—List of artists who sum up the visual aspects of the periods

XV. Occupations 200

Occupations, sports and amusements of the periods for stage, arena and pageant production—Classified list for each period: ladies, gentlemen, outdoor servants, indoor servants, cottage-dwellers, tradesmen, etc.—List of useful reference books

XVI. Manners and Dances 217

Manners and customs—Bows and curtsies—Dances for each period, Gigue, Allemande, Gavotte and Minuet—List of suggested dance music and reference books on dances

XVII. Music 235

Musical forms of the periods—Instruments used and modern stage equivalents—List of composers, instruments, and useful reference books

XVIII. Practice Scenes 240

Suggested scenes from plays for practice in period acting—Mime scene for Restoration movement with music and poetry

PART IV
VICTORIAN AND EDWARDIAN PERIOD

CHAP. PAGE

XIX. The Spirit of the Plays 249

Spirit of the periods—Development of plays and places of performance—Style of acting—Conventions of setting—List of reference books, playwrights and modern period plays, both three-act and one-act

XX. Movement in Costume 260

Outline of costume from 1827 to 1910—Movement in costume—List of costume accessories for movement and hair-styles for each period—List of costume and other books—List of artists who sum up the visual aspect of each period

XXI. Occupations 281

Occupations and amusements of the periods for stage, arena and pageant production—Classified list for men, ladies, servants, tradesmen, etc.—List of useful books

XXII. Manners and Dances 294

Manners and customs—Bows and curtsies—Dances for each period, Waltz, Polka—List of reference books on dances

XXIII. Music 307

Musical forms of the period—Instruments used—List for each period of composers, instruments and suggested music for atmosphere

XXIV. Practice Scenes 311

Suggested scenes from plays for practice in period acting—Mime scene for practice in period movement, with music

Index 317

Readers are advised to consult *British Books in Print* (Whitaker, London) or *Books in Print* (Bowker, New York) at their public library to check the availability of titles mentioned in *Playing Period Plays*.

LIST OF ILLUSTRATIONS

PART I

FIG.

1. Farandole Dance of the Twelfth to Fourteenth Century *Frontispiece*

PAGE

2. Lady Showing Dress Looped Over Forearm 21
3. Lady Showing Alternative Way of Holding up Dress 23
4. Man Showing Thumb Ring 25
5. Man Fingering Chain of Office 27
6. Man (Tudor) Fingering Beard 49
7. Branles Dance of the Twelfth to Sixteenth Century 55
8. Man Playing Pipe and Tabor 63
9. Man Playing Trumpet on Cleft Stick 65
10. Lady Playing Lute 66
11. Man Playing Hand-organ 68
12. Lady Playing Dulcimer 70

PART II

13. Ballad Sheet Pedlar 103
14. Jacobean Masque. Man 105
15. Jacobean Masque. Lady 105

FIG. PAGE

16. Lady Making Beauty Potion 116
17. Boy (Jacobean) with Hornbook 116
18. Stuart Gentleman Consulting Surgeon 127
19. Stuart Servant Arranging Wall Hangings 127
20. Stuart Curtsy 133
21. Elizabethan Pavane (End) 139
22. Elizabethan Galliarde 141
23. Courante, Stuart Period 149

PART III

24. Restoration Lady 181
25. Restoration Man 184
26. Georgian Man Fencing 189
27. Valet Adjusting Wig on Stand 202
28. Maid Snuffing Candles 202
29. Lady Serving Chocolate 208
30. Woman Selling Rabbits 214
31. Washerwoman 214
32. Country Fair Showman 215
33. Gavotte 228
34. Minuet 231
35. Georgian Lady Playing Harpsichord 237

PART IV

FIG. PAGE

36. VICTORIAN MUSIC HALL ARTISTE 252

37. EDWARDIAN TENNIS PLAYER 263

38. EDWARDIAN PICNIC 266

39. VICTORIAN DANDY 273

40. VICTORIAN CHILD PLAYING DIABOLO 286

41. LADY WITH WATERING CAN 286

42. LADY'S MAID THREADING RIBBON IN PETTICOAT—LATE VICTORIAN OR EDWARDIAN 288

43. VICTORIAN LADY PLAYING CROQUET 288

44. FLOWER WOMAN—LATE VICTORIAN OR EDWARDIAN 290

45. ITALIAN STREET VENDOR WITH ONIONS 292

46. COACHMAN—BOTH PERIODS 292

47. VICTORIAN POLKA 304

By the same Author

DESIGN FOR MOVEMENT

PART ONE

THE MEDIEVAL AND EARLY TUDOR PERIOD

CHAPTER I

THE SPIRIT OF THE PLAYS

Spirit of the medieval period—Development of plays and place of performance—Style of acting—Conventions of setting—Progression into early Tudor plays and playing—List of reference books, genuine period plays and modern period plays, both one-act and three-act

THE medieval play is the perfect antidote to Sartre. It surges along exuding vigour, hope and commonsense. The dramatic moments are clearly signposted, the comedy quite unmistakable and the audience is left in a state of exhilarated satisfaction.

These early plays were written for amateurs and they demand the qualities of freshness and sincerity that are the assets of the amateur. As they were originally played in the open air they rely on broad effects rather than a polished technique. They are admirably suited to casts whose voices and accents are more notable for variety than beauty. Lovely voices are not wasted, they can be used for angels (pure convention, as who can say with any accuracy how an angel speaks?).

Audibility, broad gestures and comic invention are demanded from the players. A cast who have been broken in with exercises in Improvisation will hail the parts with delight, as there are endless opportunities for ingenious stage business. All the plays are based on the shattering assumption that it is the actor's job to act and that he can be trusted to do so. The producer, who has an essential role nowadays, is not, irreverent as it may seem, an important medieval figure.

This part is intended for anyone embarking on such plays who, for various reasons, cannot do the necessary research for the purpose. It also covers the early Tudor period up to 1550. The next part covers the Elizabethan and Jacobean plays and masques from 1550–1640.

Examples have been chosen for their dramatic possibilities. The Period play is, perhaps, the most difficult in which to create the illusion of reality because the details which are correct historically are, in many cases, not effective theatrically. Many absorbing historical books of reference have nothing which it is feasible to use in a play. Most medieval records are concerned with law and order rather than with manners and customs. They reveal a vista of lurid sanitary and hygienic arrangements which do not lend themselves to stage presentation to an unsuspecting audience.

The chapters in this book are composed of selected examples of each subject which, it is hoped, will help to bring the plays to life again. All the information has been selected from reliable sources, but nothing has been included that is impracticable to stage.

The mimes at the end are intended to give the cast a chance to work in a concentrated way on period movement, using period music, acting in the style of the period as a preparation for the script of the period. These, with improvisation and experiment in acting historical incidents or folk songs, will be found a firm basis for period playing. The cast will find it considerably easier to bring out the true flavour of the play if rehearsals are not confined to the script.

Medieval plays fall into four categories: Liturgical,

Mystery, Miracle, and Morality. The Liturgical plays, based on the Liturgy and its responses, were performed in churches by the nuns, the monks, and the choir boys. They are in Latin and can only be regarded as an act of worship, produced under the direct guidance of a priest, even if a translation is being used. These plays were so popular that the churches could not contain the audience and the play moved out into the churchyard, which was the beginning of secular drama. Later on they moved into the market places and inn courtyards. By then the plays had developed in a way far removed from the original idea of drama as a form of worship, and were fast becoming a form of entertainment for the mob, not the congregation. Although there was still interest in and reverence for the religious message, the audience relished the comic interludes in the vernacular which were increasing in number. No one author wrote these plays; they grew with each production and different towns added local allusions. The fact that the early players were dedicated nuns and monks naturally restricted the themes of the plays.

The Mystery plays have themes taken from the Bible, and the cycle of plays, that some towns like Chester and Coventry possessed, started with Genesis and went on to the Resurrection. Other towns had short plays of episodes in the Old Testament. In the fourteenth century the Guilds took over these plays and used carts as stages, so that they could take them all over the town. The Guilds took the plays that were suitable to their craft; the Mariners had the Flood, and the Goldsmiths chose the Adoration as they could obviously provide most lavish "props". Thus the Craft Mystery plays refer to the Guild, not the subject of the play.

The Miracle plays were about the lives of the saints and were performed in the same way. Although little or no scenery could be used on the carts, the costumes were often very gorgeous and most expensive. As the cast all had to be members of the Guild they were naturally all men, so that the actress disappeared for three hundred years. Young boys whose voices had not yet broken played the parts of women.

The Morality plays started in the fifteenth century and had symbolic characters—Vanity, Gluttony and so forth—and told a highly moral story. It is surely a pure coincidence that these were the first plays to have professional actors in them. They are very easy for a modern audience to appreciate and lend themselves to any size of stage.

The Farces were peasant humour at its broadest and have as their climax either the trickster caught in his own schemes and discomfited, or a free fight in which the villain is the only one to escape unharmed. The sense of humour is that of a small boy who is ecstatic at the success of his booby trap.

It is quite fascinating to trace the growth of sophistication by first reading a thirteenth-century play and then a sixteenth-century one. The fourteenth-century Liegoise play of the Nativity is, perhaps, the most touching example of its period, and is a lovely blend of charm, innocence and piety. Any effort involved in producing these plays is worth while, as the experience is a most rich and rewarding one. They have a special quality that occurs in no other period; this is impossible to describe, but makes itself felt in no uncertain manner to everyone concerned in the project.

Modern medieval plays, while interesting in many ways, do not weave this spell. The ones suggested in the list at the end of this chaper are all interesting examples of various periods with strong characterisation and varied setting. If, by any chance, Lionel Hale's *She Passed Through Lorraine* is chosen, it is to be hoped that the producer will remember that the apple harvest is the most important thing in the life of the farm, and must permeate the play. Whether modern or medieval, the basic necessities of life dominated the existence of the peasants and this must not be ignored in the drama of the times.

The successful producer of a medieval play must achieve three things; an understanding of the spirit of the age, an appreciation of the outline in costumes and decor symbolic of the age, and a knowledge of the music that conveys the rhythm and pace of the age. He must select the particular examples of the period that evoke an instant reaction in the audience. Any audience has a vague impression of every period, based largely on pageants. It is moderately broadminded about accepting period customs it has not met before, but it is easily upset to the point of muttering loudly if it is given unfamiliar shapes and sounds. The producer must concentrate on the fact that his object is to create for the audience that basic quality in the play that has made it survive through centuries. If it is a modern play written about the period his task is easier, because the author is subconsciously writing for a modern audience.

The details that make a play come to life for an audience are the occupations of the characters, whether these are their work or their amusements. Emotional scenes form a comparatively small part of a play, they must be offset by scenes of ordinary life. In modern times the changes are rung on smoking, drinking, ironing, etc. The period plays suffer too often from a lack of this background. The curtain rises on a lovely picture (people who choose such plays have a strong pictorial sense) which dwindles into a number of people in fancy dress. They seem to have nothing to do and nowhere to go. They would clearly be much happier in a series of tableaux rather than in a play, demanding characterisation and a presentation of life. Life, indeed, is what so many of these productions lack; this is so wrong, because Life, abundant, leaping and springlike, is the special quality that colours the medieval plays. They are simple and straight to the point whether tragic or comic. Issues are boldly set, characters are clear cut, decisions are firmly made. The plays have a beginning, a middle and an end. Any form of dawdling destroys the impact. The pace and rhythm, however, are not so simple. Scenes must not either dawdle or rush. The progress must flow like a brook, bubbling along with occasional waterfalls, serene little pools, but no treacherous depths. Simplicity is vital both for the producer and the actors. Sincerity and attack must be the aim of everyone concerned with the play. They must leave gentility to the Victorians. Clear speech without "elocution" is needed for the words, and broad gestures for the movement. One warning; no actor can put across the humour if he has a niggling suspicion that it is not really funny. He should resign and seek a more congenial period.

The players will encounter two tempting pitfalls in the comedies. The first is for the actor to play them in a music hall manner which is too broad. A style that is essential to put across an act that lasts five minutes has a bludgeoning effect on an audience when it is sustained in a play for a couple of hours.

The second pitfall lies in wait for the actress, who is tempted to adopt an ever-so-coy-and-winning manner. The hall mark of this is the forefinger and or little finger held rigid, the eyes opened very widely and the mouth pursed. When nuns acted there was a sense of taking part in a service, so naturally they displayed simplicity and sincerity. There is no place for affectations either mental or physical in Mystery plays. In the Miracle and Morality plays there is a wide variety of types and the playing can have as many facets as any other type of play. Originally, men played the women's parts in these, so it is still as well to avoid coyness and daintiness.

Real characterisation is demanded from all the cast of either a Mystery or Miracle play, as the dialogue is clear-cut and individual. The Morality play needs actors who can take advantage of the symbolic nature of their costumes for their gestures. Wings, tails, and skulls all lose effect if their owners look embarrassed at having to handle them. The verse must be neither chanted nor droned, but spoken with commonsense and clarity. There are no purple patches that have had to be learnt at school, and the cast are therefore spared that hideous moment of knowing that the whole audience are following the speech, word for word, in a breathy whisper. While every producer will cling to his own ideas, there are some conventions of the plays of the Middle Ages which ought to be known. They can either be used or discarded; to contemporary audiences they had more significance than nowadays.

When the early plays were performed in churches there was, of course, no stage curtain to drop. Processions were an important part of the scene and added greatly to the dramatic effct. This has to be realised with regard to timing, especially if the company has graduated from the Parish Hall stage of 10 feet by 12 feet.

Heaven and Hell were presented in a stylised way; Heaven was always stage right and Hell was stage left. Only the Mouth of Hell needs to be shown, the audience ought to be lured into imagining untold horrors for themselves. Incidents on the Earth took place stage centre. Heaven was on a higher level than Earth whenever possible, although Hell and Earth could be on the same level. In this way sinners could be pushed into Hell quite unsuspectingly, while if Hell was placed under a trap-door they could drop down with satisfying screams. Devils could pop up with useful tridents for prodding those who struggled against their deserved fate. A good time was had by all.

When the Guilds took the various episodes round the town on carts, each cart would represent a locality. On a small stage the use of reversible book flats is a practicable method of setting the very short scenes, as often scene 1 recurs as scene 6, 8 and 10.

All these plays were performed in the open air and this must be borne in mind and adjustments made if the play takes place in a small hall. Aisles should still be used for anything that needs a procession, and different levels introduced however much effort is needed to achieve them.

The Voice of God or the Voice of Moses should never in any circumstances be female.

There is a wealth of description and accounts (paid and unpaid) of the costumes worn in many medieval manuscripts which the cast would find amusing to hear. There was a convention that Adam and Eve wore pink leather combinations.

Traditionally the Vigin's robe is blue and Judas's hair is red, devils can be black or red, and angels robes and wings can be any or all colours.

Whether the production is realistic or stylised, there is scope for far more variety in decor than is usually seen. The scenes which take place in "a room in the Castle" need not have a nondescript baronial aura. After the twelfth century the castle was divided into rooms, many of which were set aside for special occupations. This was necessary for the functioning of daily life when everything was hand made. The armoury, the stillroom, the harness room are all possible stage sets, although these occupations *can* take place in the hall. Peasants' huts normally had only one room and little furniture, so it is wise here to introduce colour by lighting. Shafts of sunlight, a sunset seen through the open door, or leaping firelight can take the place of an elaborate set.

Details of interior decoration, such as mirrors, tapestries and table appointments, are listed at the end of Chapter III, linked with the servants whose task it was to keep them in order. This is done to save space and to make it clear that the designing of sets is not included in this book. The artists of the Medieval and Tudor periods should be studied, and these together with the architecture and woods used in each century are listed on pages 26, 28 and 33.

The paintings help the actor to visualise the scene of the time. Even if the subject of his play is different from the picture there is always a wealth of detail in the background that can be studied to conjure up the life of that day into instant reality.

The early Tudor plays (1500–58) carry on from the Morality plays, gradually assuming more of a modern shape, with more human themes and with single authors now coming to the fore. They are often very long-winded and need careful cutting. Puns are creeping in, and a malicious cast could make out a watertight case against acting the plays if they chose to pick out all the worst bits and read them consecutively. The audience of that time doubtless evolved methods of getting through moments of boredom and relished the local and topical jokes, which now have only an academic appeal.

The plays are divided into acts nominally, but to say they meander along is a British understatement. The modernised versions of the plays of Hans Sachs and Pierre Patelin are an excellent example of how such plays can be streamlined.

There are many modern one-act plays written about Henry VIII and one or other of his wives, and other plays deal with Mary Tudor, Lady Jane Grey and the young Princess Elizabeth. The producer has plenty of choice, if he particularly wants to present this era.

It is not until later that the play, as we know it now, comes on the scene. Intrigue, murder for gain, and historical events, as distinct from the Bible stories, are treated in these plays. Characters cease to be symbolic, although a moral is often drawn. Some of the plays are more interesting to read than to perform. It is the February before the April of the Elizabethan Age flowered into its wonderful season.

Modern dramatists have written several plays about Henry VIII and Mary Tudor that are better suited to the amateur than the genuine plays would be. Any list soon becomes out of date, so the producer interested in choosing a play taking place between 1500 and 1550 would be better to consult the latest publishers' catalogues. The British Drama League's library is an invaluable help in any dilemma, and will give knowledgeable advice in case of doubt. The reference library has the most complete collection of theatrical books in the world, including many prompt copies of famous producers and authors (not, of course, before the eighteenth century, although the plays themselves may have been written about the medieval period.) It is obviously much easier for all concerned if a play by a modern author is chosen, as the speech is in the contemporary idiom and the cast will not only find it easier to learn but easier to play. It will probably be in three acts so that the actors will have to sustain the parts only for the length of time to which they are normally accustomed. This makes the producer's task much simpler, although there is not such a thrill as when working on a genuine historical text.

List of Useful Books

The Miracle Plays in England	S. W. Clarke	(William Andrews)
Masks, Mimes, and Miracles	Allardyce Nicholl	(Harrap)
British Drama	Allardyce Nicholl	(Harrap)
English Drama from Early Times to the Elizabethans	A. P. Rossiter	(Hutchinson)
The Drama of the Medieval Church	K. Young	(O.U.P.)

The Production of Religious Plays E. Martin Browne (S.P.C.K.)
Scenes and Machines on the English Stage During the Renaissance L. B. Campbell (C.U.P.)

Some Genuine Plays
from the 10th to the 16th century

Chief Pre-Shakespearean Drama edited by J. Q. Adams (Harrap)

Volume I. Sources and the liturgical drama.
Volume II. Liturgical plays dealing with the Life of Christ.
Volume III. Liturgical plays dealing with miscellaneous biblical stories, and with the legends of the Saints.
Volume IV. The introduction of the vernacular.
Volume V. The Craft Cycles, dealing with Old and New Testament.
Volume VI. Non-Cycle Plays.
Volume VII. Moralities: Everyman, Castle of Perseverance, Mankind, etc.
Volume VIII. Folk Plays: Robin Hood, St. George's Play, etc.
Volume IX. Farces: The Four P.P., The Play of the Wether.
Volume X. School Plays: Ralph Roister Doister, Gammer Gurton's Needle.
Volume XI. Inns of Court Plays: Gorbaduc, Supposes.

The York Cycle edited by C. Purvis (S.P.C.K.)
The Three Estates David Lindsay, 1490– (Heinemann)
Seven Shrovetide Plays Hans Sachs (Deane)
Five Pre-Shakespearean Comedies edited by F. S. Boas (O.U.P.)

There are other editions of all these plays and many of the plays are published singly.

The British Theatre Association, 9 Fitzroy Square, London W1P 6AE, has a play library, and gives advice and information to all its members; books can be borrowed singly as well as in sets for play-reading.

RaDiuS, St. Paul's Church, Covent Garden, Bedford Street, London WC2E 9ED, specialises in advice and help on religious drama to all its members.

Some Modern Plays about these Two Periods

Three-Act

The Zeal of Thy House †	Dorothy L. Sayers	(the building of Canterbury Cathedral)	(Gollancz)
She Passed Through Lorraine	Lionel Hale		(Deane)
Richard of Bordeaux	Gordon Daviot	*Richard II*	(French)
The Kingmaker (in *The Heritage of Literature Series*)	Margaret Luce	15th Century	(Longmans)
The Lady's Not for Burning	Christopher Fry	15th Century	(O.U.P.)
The Rose Without a Thorn	Clifford Bax	16th Century	(French)

One-Act

Godstow Nunnery	Laurence Binyon	12th Century	(J. Garnet Miller)
Little Plays of St. Francis	Laurence Housman	13th Century	(Sidgwick & Jackson)
The Rose and the Cross	Clifford Bax	14th Century	(Heinemann)
There's Rue for You	Margaret Turner	16th Century	(French)

Love in a French Kitchen	C. Clements and J. M. Saunders		(French, U.S.A.)
Two Saints Plays	Robert Gittings and L. Lehman	St. Chad and St. Richard	(Heinemann)
The Devil Among the Skins	E. Goodwin	14th Century	(French)
The York Nativity Play	arr. and ed. by E. Martin Browne		(S.P.C.K.)
The Farce of the Devil's Bridge	Henri Ghéon trs. by Barry Jackson		(J. Garnet Miller)
The Pie and the Tart	Hugh Chesterman		(Deane)
Pierre Patelin	Anon.		(French, U.S.A.)
The Fountain (in *Great God, Brown*)	Eugene O'Neill		(Cape)

CHAPTER II

MOVEMENT IN COSTUME

Outline of costume from 1066 *to* 1550*—Movement in costume —List of costume accessories for movement for each century and fashion of make-up—List of costume books—List of artists from each century who sum up the visual aspect of the period*

EVERY effort, short of murder, should be made to build up an adaptable wardrobe for the company. It is heartbreaking how often carefully planned grouping is ruined by hired anachronisms. If the costumes have to be hired, then as many details as possible should be made, and rehearsed with. The correct accessories, shoes, belts, hats, jewellery, weapons, can transform the whole show. At the end of this chapter will be found a list of books on costume of this period for the stage, with practical instructions for suitable materials, patterns and methods of making, not only costumes but also armour, weapons and jewellery.

There is also a list of accessories for each century which can be used for characteristic movement; in the same way that cigarettes, powder compacts or lipsticks can be used in a modern play, to point lines.

The outline of the early medieval robes lend themselves admirably to stage pictures, either still or in movement. They look delightful for swift movement and fall in lovely folds whether the players are standing, sitting or kneeling. The tight sleeves give a clean line to an outflung arm, and emphasis to dramatic hand gestures. The head-dresses, because they are close-fitting, simplify grouping. They have no horns, as in the later period, to break into the profile. The wimple, which outlines the entire face, focusses the attention on the actress's expression. The men's costumes have the same quality. The long robe, reaching to the feet, falls in good lines and the shorter tunic, knee length, gives freedom for striding and leaping with vigour. Man's life was largely taken up with physical activities, and the clothes were designed with this in view.

The later medieval clothes are much more elaborate and the clean line is now distorted in many different ways. Men's clothes start getting fantastic in the early fifteenth century, the hats and shoes first, then the sleeves and tunic.

Women followed suit, but they started, at the same period, by wearing horned, wired head-dresses, and at the end of the fourteenth century bodices were heavily trimmed and skirts had so much material in them that they had to be lifted to show an elaborate underskirt.

When Henry VII was on the throne, in the early sixteenth century, the outline had quietened down again and women had a dress, with bodice, skirt and sleeves all in one colour, and a simple draped head-dress, while the older men had a long fur-trimmed robe and a plain hat. The young men had the well-known square outline, padded shoulders, knee-length tunic and square-toed shoes, an unmistakable Henry VIII figure. This is a very brief description of the changes in outline during the period from the eleventh century to the mid-sixteenth century.

The producer has a wide choice of accessories and hand properties which not only add decoration to the grouping, but also help the audience to recognise the status of the characters.

Each trade and profession had its distinctive dress, but, as nowadays an audience would not know many of these uniforms, only those useful for stage purposes have been given.

In any medieval crowd there were people such as pilgrims and scribes and monks, and they immediately give an authentic look to the stage scene.

For a market scene, each tradesman had his apron tied to show he sold his particular goods. It is sufficient for stage purposes if each trade *has* a differently tied apron, which gives variety instead of uniformity. Pilgrims had a long robe, a script which was like a school satchel, slung over the shoulder and which holds bread, a water bottle of leather either round and flattened in shape or like a thermos bottle. The cockle shell, if they had gone the Compostello pilgrim's way, is worn in the hat.

Monks' habits have not changed through the centuries, but it is wise to discover if there was a local monastery (near the town) and which Order it was. The same rule applies to nuns.

Scribes in the fourteenth century had sheets of parchment, quills and horn-rimmed spectacles. (Leave this out if the actor normally wears them or else make them outsize, in cardboard.)

Women in the market wore an apron and a white handkerchief either round the shoulders or tied over their head. They sold bundles of herbs and vegetables, not potatoes, but peas, beans, turnips and cabbages.

A man peasant would have a spoon stuck in the band of his hat so that he need never refuse an unexpected meal.

Women peasants carried their baskets on the arm, on the head, or on the back with the arms put through the handles each side of the basket.

A tradesman's wife brought him his dinner wrapped in a white cloth.

Ladies carried small round baskets holding wool to wind, small square workboxes holding silks to embroider the bands trimming the tunics and sleeves, or large workbags mounted on handles made of rings of willow.

Every man habitually wore one dagger if not two. If he had been hunting he had a bow and arrow.

Long bows were used from Saxon times and cross

bows, which take far less space, from the twelfth century, for fighting, not for hunting or sport. If the men had been hawking, a heavily gauntleted glove was worn on the left hand. The little bells were actually worn by the falcon, but it is better to dispense with the bird and let someone carry and jingle the bells.

Lepers, who were not allowed to come into a town or crowded place, can look dramatic hovering on the edge of the scene, and they provide interesting sound effects. They were forced to wear a robe, gloves and a hood; blind lepers had no eye-holes in their hoods. They carried a bell or clappers, two pieces of wood that they had to clap together to give warning of their approach. They had to carry their own mug and bowl. Many walked on crutches.

The important thing to remember when moving in period clothes, is that it must appear to the audience perfectly normal and natural. If the actor does not get his costume until the dress rehearsal he will find that one wearing is not enough to accustom his body to totally strange garments, which restrict him in unexpected places. It is essential for him to discover at an early stage of rehearsal the type of costume he is expected to wear and whether it has any special accessories or pitfalls. He must also ask the producer whether there are any hand props—and if the producer replies in the negative, he is strongly advised to find some for himself. These must, of course, be in keeping with the character, and must be capable of being used dramatically. (Dogs do not come under this heading.) If the costume has any features that are markedly different from modern wear, then something resembling the garment must be used in which to practise. This understudy garment may be so ridiculous that it would upset the rehearsal to wear it in public, in that case the practice must take place in the bedroom, the oftener the better. The tights worn under the short tunic of Richard II are an obvious example of this type. These emphasise the legs so much more than modern trousers, every angle needs to be studied, and experiments tried in walking and standing. Attitudes should be struck in front of a long mirror, bows and flourishes watched from a critical standpoint, and any shame-faced huddling together of the knees firmly checked.

Probably the best view is obtained by wearing bathing trunks, which would be too cold in the usual rehearsal room. Bedroom slippers help to give the actor the feel of the walk, provided they have not been trodden down at the heel for more than two years.

The main difficulty for the actress concerns the fourteenth century skirt, as there is so much fullness in it that it is too cumbersome to drag it to every rehearsal. She can also practice in her bedroom with two sheets draped around her which will give approximately the amount of yardage she must learn to manage gracefully. She should also wear bedroom slippers of a solid kind. These give a grip round the ankles that helps the walk far more than the glovelike ballet slippers which, too often, are worn. High-heeled mules will sabotage any period walk.

The walk should be normal and comfortable with the head poised to balance the head-dress and the body upright. The foot movement is the same as in modern walking with the heel touching the ground first and then the ball and toe. The men take athletic strides, unless it is mentioned in the script that they have ridden day and night to reach the castle; then they can ring the changes on saddlesore staggers. Since every man could ride, hunt, shoot and fish, this must show in the bearing of the body when the cast are playing the parts of average men. On the other hand, courtiers of Richard II would deliberately cultivate a languid and drooping manner of an affected kind. This is not the same as a modern slouch; the modern equivalent may be observed in the photographs of interior decorators in the glossy magazines. Ungainly slouching and sagging look out of place in period clothes except as character work. The ability to lounge gracefully and to prowl languidly is an asset to any player.

The actress also has to cope with a rigid belt worn under the dress before corsets came into fashion, and a head-dress that pulls her head slightly backwards. This means that she must keep a trim waist line, with her shoulders held well back. Her walk comes more from her knees, a hockey stride looks ludicrous. If the fullness is at the front of the skirt then it is lifted at the front when walking or curtsying. If the fullness is at the sides then it is spread out to the sides on the sinking movement of the curtsy and dropped on the rise. Above all, it must be clear that the dress is lifted because it is in the way not because it is a "pretty period gesture". When she sits the skirt should be smoothed under her, and the surplus folds draped gracefully; when she gets up again the folds are rearranged to allow freedom of movement. If this is not done the luckless wench will rise with a large crumpled bunch poised behind her, spare folds wound round her legs, and a bleak prospect of freeing herself by a series of pettish kicks.

An actress, unused to coping with the amount of material to be handled in medieval robes, has a tendency to move slowly and heavily except when speed is clearly indicated, when she rockets off like a sack of potatoes on roller skates. This is because she does not control her waist firmly enough, slumps in the middle and strides from the thighs.

It is essential to control the waist and diaphragm for all movements quick or slow and a quick walk can easily be done if the steps are kept fairly small and the skirt held away from, not above, the knees. The variety of pace is most important; too many players either move very slowly, or very quickly, which gives an odd effect of hiccups. Any stage movement is changed by period costume, either to more significance or less, according to amount of drapery involved; therefore it is doubly important to use pace carefully.

It is obvious that the same basic gesture will look quite different according to the outline of the garment. A circular move could have a weight and significance in a fifteenth-century costume of full skirt, lifted away from the underskirt, puffed sleeves, and horned head-dress with wired veil, that it would entirely lack in the soft stripped line of the twelfth century (*See* Fig. 2).

Positions of the hands

Portraits and pictures of the period should be studied and ideas refreshed from time to time by the actors themselves, but here are some suggestions for suitable positions of the hands, and a warning about some that look completely out of place. The list of costume details and accessories has been compiled largely with a view to helping with variety of movement. While at first glance it may seem to suggest that the cast will spend most of their time dressing and undressing themselves, this is not the intention of the list. The possiblities for individuality and characterisation in buttoning or lacing up shoes will be at once realised when one remembers the famous description of Irving in *The Bells*, in the book *Henry Irving* by Edward Gordon Craig.

Ladies. (Not serving women or peasant women.)

When in repose the hands can be clasped on the girdle whether this is worn low on the hips or just under the bust. The left hand can hold the elbow of the right arm, while the right hand rests against the right shoulder or holds the locket on the neck chain, or rests against the left shoulder.

Both hands can hold the skirt clasped against the waist

FIG. 2. Lady Showing Dress Looped Over Forearm

(it is otherwise easier to hold the skirt either draped over the wrist or forearm so that the hands are free) or the hands may lie lightly folded on top of each other at waist level. (*See* Fig. 3.)

When sitting the hands may be dropped at the side resting in the folds of the skirt or laid on the lap crossed at the wrists; or folded with the hands clasping the forearms, not the elbows, or the hands can rest on the arms of the chair. The positions to be avoided by the ladies are the ones that are suitable for serving wenches and peasant women.

These are: standing with the hands clasped behind the back, crossing the arms with the hands clutching the elbows, patting or poking the hair or face and (a favourite modern stance) sagging all over with one or both hands on the hips.

When a peasant woman sits she may spread both knees wide apart and put her hands like starfish on them, or she can lean forward with hands clasped between her knees. She can stride more freely than the ladies, but a Hollywood hip wriggle is better left out. A young maid can use a good hip swing if it is in character, when men are around, but she must use it with discretion, always remembering that the mistress had authority to have her whipped for unseemly behaviour.

Hand and arm positions *for men* should combine common sense with a sense of decoration. For instance, take a simple stance with the legs slightly apart and the hands holding the belt. If the belt has a decorative buckle and the sleeves are plain, the thumbs can be tucked into the belt just behind the hips. If the sleeves are the most showy part of the costume and are embroidered with flashing jewels, the hands are better moved to clasp the buckle centre front. If the sleeves are a vivid colour with long hanging scallops it is an opportunity to leave one hand

FIG. 3. Lady Showing Alternative Way of Holding up Dress

at the side of the hip and bring the other one to clasp it, so that both sleeves are visible in all their glory. If wearing a ring on the thumb, the actor can hold his collar, turning his hand to show the ring, hold his belt with the fingers inside and the ring turned outwards, or clasp his dagger and finger it. (*See* Fig. 4.) The arms can be folded with either fingers or the thumbs showing, according to which have the best rings. If heavily embroidered gloves are worn then the hands can be clasped around the knees when sitting, grip the arms of a chair, rest side by side on a table, or be laid across the body with the little fingers resting on the belt and the thumbs on the ribs. The fact that there are no pockets in which to hide the hands need not paralyse the actor, it can be a chance for him to use his hands in a way impossible in modern plays.

A chain of office was sometimes worn; this can be touched to emphasise an order. (*See* Fig. 5.) A signet ring or important jewel can be used in the same way. When in a temper the actor can toy with his dagger or sword to show that words can lead to deeds.

A cloak must never hang in a dispirited way as if the owner felt awkward, a long cloak must swirl and a short cloak must swing and poise over the arm which is bent with the hand on the hip. It is a curious thing that the best period movement is often seen off stage when the cast are hurrying to their dressing rooms. They run gaily up the stairs, dealing with their garments in the best way to accommodate them to their movements, and looking perfectly at home in them. Yet on the stage these same people are to be seen hamstrung and unhappy, wondering if they can bow without something coming unstuck. This seems to prove that it is the attitude of mind that is really important. On stage they think nervously of period costumes, off stage they take the clothes for granted and therefore the clothes look as if they belonged to the actors instead of the other way round.

Fig. 4. Man Showing Thumb Ring

When men had all these gorgeous shapes and colours from which to choose, they could obviously have such fun with their clothes that they enjoyed wearing them, so the actor should enjoy himself too. Women are much better usually at coming to terms with their costumes because their own clothes are meant to be displayed and admired. The actors' problems are mental, the actresses' physical; neither are really difficult to solve.

Accessories for Movement

11th Century

Canute the King.	1017
Edward the Confessor.	1042
William I.	1066
William II.	1087

Oak used for furniture, settles, tables, stools. Saxon and Norman architecture for churches and castles.

Men. Long cloak may be fastened by drawing through leather brooch and knotting the ends.
Long trousers may be cross gartered all the way up.
Berets and Phrygian caps may be worn or tucked in belts.
Lances used for fighting: Saxons without pennants.
Normans with pennants.
Long bows used.

Hair. *Men.* Long hair combed back from the forehead.
Women. Long hair parted in the middle and hanging in two plaits or twisted into two ropes or coiled under a coif.

12th Century

Henry I.	1100	Tournaments introduced. Crusades undertaken.

FIG. 5. Man Fingering Chain of Office

Stephen.	1135		Painting on glass. Tiles.
Henry II.	1154	French Queen.	Windmills. Gothic architecture.
Richard Coeur de Lion.	1189		Oak used for furniture.
John	1199		

Women. Sleeves can unbutton from the shoulder to give knights for tournaments favour.
Flowers can be taken from head wreaths for the same purpose.
Small squares of cloth can be embroidered with pearls for the same purpose.
Rectangular cape can be worn with cord to be threaded through eyelets.

HAIR. *Men.* Shoulder length can be curled usually, but for Kings or people of high office can be arranged in four tight curls, two hanging behind and one each side of the face.
Short beard can be curled and occasionally a moustache.
Women. Hair can be braided with pearls or ribbons, the ends enclosed in a metal case, or the braids may be rolled up each side of the face, or the hair may be coiled up under a coif.

13*th Century*

Henry III. 1216.
Edward I. 1272.

Dominicans, black habits; Franciscans, grey habits; Carmelites, white habits. Order of the Garter.

Men. Helmet with movable visor, surcoat embroidered in many colours, black worn for mourning.
Crusaders: Knights of St. John used a white cross on a black surcoat; Knights Templars, a red cross on a white

surcoat; Teutonic Knights, a black cross on a white surcoat. Untried knights, who wore a green surcoat, could change into the surcoat of one of the above Orders after they had won their spurs. Spurs were three pointed. A leather belt may be worn low on the hips, holding the sword with its hilt in the shape of a cross to show it was dedicated. A dagger may be worn for the left hand as well as the right. A ring of gold on the finger.

A 10-foot lance with a lozenge-shaped point may be carried.

Women. Gold net caul to draw over hair.

Oblong cloak to fasten with brooch.

Frock to lace up the back.

Gloves to carry or tuck in belt.

The hands can be put through the openings in the skirt to lift the fullness.

Rosaries may be worn or carried.

Short walking sticks with heads of animals or birds may be used.

Cloak may be drawn round neck with cord.

Chatelaine holding keys, scissors, etc., hanging from belt may be used.

HAIR. *Men's* hair can be cut short to just below the ears and puffed out at the sides. Short beards may be trimmed from chin to ear.

Women's hair may be confined in a head-dress, young girls' hair may be combed and brushed loosely with a chaplet of flowers or metal.

14th Century

Edward II.	1307
Edward III.	1327
Richard II.	1377 (French Queen).

Men. May wear two daggers or may carry a long staff.

For hand gestures or positions—Ring on thumb, chain round neck, belt on hip, pouch hanging from belt with writing materials, mirror and comb in it.

Cloak with hood to pull up or high collar to pull down.

Armour to put on—steel plates on arms, legs and feet.

Shoes with 6-in. points to chain to knee.

Gloves of great elegance can be carried or worn.

Women. Monogram of the Virgin or family badge to embroider.

Handbag (like a Dorothy bag) to carry with a book of devotion in it to read.

Rings, charms, and jewelled girdles to adjust.

Shoes to buckle across instep, lace at the sides, or to button at the sides.

HAIR. *Men's* hair can be cut square across the forehead and either cut short all round or rolled under to look short.

Face can be clean-shaven or with a small moustache.

Women's plaits to be coiled up at the side of the head or wound round head or enclosed in the head-dress.

Young girls brush hair loosely and bind with a fillet.

15th Century

Henry V.	1413.	French Queen.	
Henry VI.	1422.	English Queen.	
Edward IV.	1461.	,,	,,
Edward V.	1483.	,,	,,
Richard III.	1483.	,,	,,
Henry VII.	1485.	,,	,,

Men. Turbans and round hats to be arranged.

Parti-coloured hose on each leg which must be shown off with a flourish in the bow.

Bishop sleeves very long which may be pushed up into

folds and into which letters, poison bottles, charms, may be concealed or produced.

Complete armour to be put on—no surcoat, only a tabard like the knave of hearts.

Women. Belt on the hips holds purse.

Full trains and fullness in front of skirt over stomach to be held up and arranged.

Horned head-dresses affect head movement.

HAIR. *Men.* Part the hair and brush it across the forehead or cut a fringe. Shave the face clean if a young man, a small pointed beard to be worn if an older man.

Women. Eyebrows to be plucked to a fine line, hair to be shaved or pulled back to make a high forehead.

16th Century

Henry VII.	1485.	English Queen.	
Henry VIII.	1509.	Katherine of Aragon.	Spanish.
		Anne Boleyn.	English.
		Jane Seymour	,,
		Anne of Cleeves	Dutch.
		Katherine Howard.	English.
		Katherine Parr.	,,
Edward VI	1547.		

Men. Hose may be gartered below or above the knee or may be knotted and cross gartered.

Hose may be laced all the way up the back of the leg.

Doublet can be fastened up the front with buttons or lacings.

Sleeves of the jerkin can be attached by pieces of ribbon which lace into the armholes of the jerkin or doublet called "points".

Rosettes can be fastened on to the shoes.

Face can be entirely clean-shaven. Hair can be arranged

in a long bob until 1530, when a short bob came into fashion.

Beards of churchmen to have a cathedral cut, judges a formal cut, soldiers a spade beard, older men a round beard, other characters can have a small pointed beard and a small moustache.

Wide linked chain can be put on around the shoulders with a pendant or Order hanging from it.

Chains hanging low in front with miniatures can be worn.

Jewelled brooches can be fastened in the cap, jewelled rings, rosaries, gloves and daggers can be worn. (The jewels were emeralds, rubies, diamonds, sapphires and pearls.)

Women. Sleeves can be fastened by points to the arm-hole of the bodice.

Several petticoats can be put on under the skirt.

Cloak with hood attached can be worn outdoors.

Hair can be parted in the middle, waved and knotted at the back under the cap.

Split sleeves may be fastened together with small gold clasps at intervals all the way up.

Necklaces, brooches, buckles, rings, cap ornaments, and chain girdles may be adjusted.

Pomanders, metal balls with charcoal inside as hand warmers, rosaries and reticules may be carried.

Leather or metal corset to be laced into.

Eyebrows to be plucked, powder and rouge used.

List of Useful Reference Books

Dressing the Play Norah Lambourne (Studio)

This gives materials, details of patterns in vogue for stencilling dresses, ways of dyeing materials for dresses, tapestries, banners, stained-glass windows, etc. How to make jewellery, armour, weapons, and how to plan an adaptable wardrobe. Also how to design and plan the costumes for an entire production for each period.

English Costume of the Early Middle Ages Iris Brooke (Black)
English Costume of the Later Middle Ages Iris Brooke (Black)
Two books with charming pictures of the costumes to stimulate the designer in the use of colour.
Dressing the Part F. P. Walkup (Harrap)
Survey of costume from the Roman times to present day, with small drawings showing details of shoes, head-dresses, hair-dressing, under garments, etc. No actual patterns of how to make them, although some details drawn showing cut of coats, etc.
Adaptable Stage Costume for Women Elizabeth Russell (Garnet Miller)
Basic bodice and skirt with additions and accessories for each period from Saxon to Victorian. Detailed patterns and sewing instructions.

List of Artists of the Period

Study of these pictures is most stimulating when the production is being planned.

11th and 12th Centuries. The Bayeux Tapestry. Penguin Book.
13th Century. Cimabue. Giotto. Guido of Sienna.
14th Century. Fra Angelico. Paolo Uccello. Orgagna. Taddeo Gaddi.
15th Century. Fra Filippo Lippi. Botticelli. Ghirlandaio. P. della Niccolo. Francesca. Perugino. Mantegna. Donatello di Nicollo. L. della Robbia. Leonardo da Vinci. H. and J. van Eyck. Memling. Massys.
16th Century up to 1550. Michelangelo. Raphel. Andrea del Sarto. Giorgone. El Greco. Antonio Moro.

All these artists are represented in England and postcards can be obtained of examples of their work.

CHAPTER III

OCCUPATIONS

Occupations and amusements of the period for stage, arena or pageant production—Classified list for each century: men, clerks, servants, monks, ladies, pages, etc.—List of useful books

MEDIEVAL life was crammed to overflowing with both work and play; everything had to be hand made and as time went on the liking for decoration became a passion. As travelling became more general with Crusades, wars, foreign Queens to import and English Princesses to export, new ideas for interior decoration and fashion flowed into England.

Different servants had special duties and, although it is not necessary to stick to rigid domestic distinctions, these are listed to help to give small parts to a large cast. There was no strong feeling for privacy, therefore minor scenes can be played downstage while the work of the house goes on upstage. The banquet can be elaborately laid in full view of the public without holding up the playing time of the script; the feeling of bustling life and crowds of retainers establishes the atmosphere perfectly.

The amusements are full of gusto and mostly decorative and must be worked into the texture of the play. Certain games were obviously played more by men than by women, some were more popular with the peasants than with the lords and ladies. Income can be a rough guide to this, just as nowadays some people's finances run to polo and some salaries cope better with shove halfpenny.

English children have always had games and toys, and often when a foreign Queen arrived she brought new games as well as fashions, customs and dances. Unless specifically stated in the list at the end of this chapter, the materials for games are the same as nowadays.

The occupations should be treated from a production and a character viewpoint, just as they are nowadays, and movements should be well contrasted. If several servants are on the stage doing niggling work such as chasing spurs and tipping arrows, the audience must be given the chance to take this in first, and then it can settle to watch the important part of the scene. It is also practical for the servants to group themselves downstage if working in an unusual occupation, so that the audience is given a clear view, and then transfer themselves upstage when the focus has to be on the speaking characters.

Work can be an opportunity for variety in static groups. If four ladies in waiting are working at a standing tapestry frame, one can sit on a low stool embroidering the lowest corner of the picture, one can perch on a high stool doing the opposite corner, one can sit on the ground and work horizontally across the border of the picture, and one can stand and work vertically down the border furthest from the first girl. If two girls conspire in a plot, they can move behind the frame ostensibly to finish off the thread. These moves must be carefully planned to give the effect either of a stylised pattern or an emotional one, as they can too easily look like a game of Tom Tiddlers' Ground. Whips can be mended while the actor sits on the table, with the whip, cord, knife, etc., spread out on it; or while he sits on the floor, or stands with one foot on a stool, the whip resting on his knee, or stands at the table. If he is a Knight who is fussy about his gear, he can sit in an arm chair with two pages to hand him his gear, and another page to clear up, and a lady to admire the finished result.

These examples are given to stress the fact that individual characterisation is the important point; it must not be lost in period movement but blended with it. Chess and cards may be played cautiously, recklessly or moodily, with personal mannerisms such as drumming with the fingers, or humming a tune, or any other trick the actor feels the character would use.

There were also well-trained servants and careless ones. Some castles had almost military discipline and others allowed the staff great liberty. Minstrels were normally kept firmly in their place, while troubadours were accorded a higher position. Clerks were trained in the monastries and their positions varied very much; some were treated as one of the family, some as inferiors. Pages may be impudent and privileged or snubbed and cuffed.

There are two points worth mentioning which are better treated theatrically than truthfully. Medieval records are bursting with furious denunciations of giddy and frivolous nuns who persisted in wearing their coifs at an alluring angle. Nuns should be presented on the stage with dignified and controlled bearing.

In Edward III's sumptuary laws there was an edict that fur-trimmed dresses were only to be worn by ladies whose lives were blameless. The producer is advised to ignore this; although the rest of these laws give valuable insight into the customs of the period, and help the producer to know what was allowed to be worn by commoners and what was not. The Guild and Craft Rules for apprentices have some interesting pointers for behaviour and bearing which are essential to show in a scene with apprentices in it.

In the early Tudor days England was settling down; it was worth while collecting lovely things to put in the manors when it was certain that no other knight would ride over and sack the place.

Fairgrounds were a riot of noise and colour, with all kinds of freaks and other entertainments. There was an entrance fee and the ground was fenced around. The gate was guarded by men with large biceps all ready to fight gate-crashers. The audience at the play was rowdy and vociferous in its comments on the hapless actor who disappointed it. Improbable as it may seem no one ever queued. Crowds ramped and cavorted when pleased and they stamped and kicked when displeased. Pedlars coaxed customers and pleaded with them to buy their wares, tradesmen urged goods on their patrons, and took pains to show their merchandise off in the best way. Everything and anything was eaten in the streets and on the fair-ground—bought from the booths and the Tudor equivalent of "Stop me and buy one". Eating was practically a hobby in those days, yet the modern producer ignores this, he will produce a banquet or nothing. Things such as sticks of striped sugar, toffee apples, meat pies, and roasted crabs are all colourful and easy to provide for a fair or market scene, and certainly give an air of informal enjoyment to the party.

As the manor house was a dwelling-place rather than a fortress ready for small sieges, other changes took place. Gardens became extremely popular and flowers and herbs were grown in them as well as fruit trees and vegetables. They had a formal pattern of beds, which were edged with box or lavender. There were lavender hedges and hawthorn hedges. Bushes were clipped into fantastic shapes, and bowers were popular with courting couples.

Linen was bleached from early times on the grass in the sun, and herbs hung up to dry. Rose leaves and petals were collected to dry and to make into beauty potions. The single roses, striped red and white, are the earliest known variety, then came red roses and white roses and the pink wild rose as it is known now. These all grew against walls rather than as standard bushes, if one wants to be a stickler for accuracy, but such pedantry is not really necessary. Dovecots and beehives were used in a decorative way. Ornamental pools and little fountains were very much favoured by the wealthier ladies and at the palaces. Gardeners, as distinct from farm hands, were beginning to become the important people they are to-day.

12TH AND 13TH CENTURY OCCUPATIONS

An asterisk indicates that the work or play may be used in succeeding centuries and in plays of a later date.

Servants

Men. Cleaning hearth in the middle of the *Hall* and placing fire-dogs and logs ready for fire. Sharpening hunting knives, daggers, swords and spears. *Plaiting whips and making handles and tips for them. Polishing the body belts used by the knights, pressing the tunics and cleaning the boots and sword-belts. Curling the hair and beard with curling tongs. Offering drinking horn to chief guests.

Armourers. Forging swords, chasing spurs and armour, polishing glaves.

Clerks. Taking notes with roman, stylus type pencil on jointed ivory tablets or writing evidence on parchment for trials, or doing accounts in very long narrow account books.

Women. Sweeping, polishing household goods, turning the hour-glass, sorting feathers for cushions (white) or for arrow tips (dark)—this is useful for a comedy scene—cooking on open fire and stirring the pot hung on tripod, teasing wool.

Ladies. *Carding wool on board with bent pins to pull it through, using a spindle held in the hand, weaving on a small frame; making-up herb medicines and beauty recipes (show the difference by tasting the first and applying the second), which includes pounding with pestle and mortar, mashing and straining, either through cloth or a wooden strainer, measuring by spoon and mixing the ingredients which can then be heated. Weaving wreaths and garlands; flowers of this period are primroses, peri-winkles, pennyroyal, daisies, irises, lily of the valley, lilies, and small roses striped red and white and single; making these flowers into favours to throw to knights in tournaments.

Amusements. Hunting with bows and arrows, spears, horns; or hawking. Dancing (*see* Chapter IV) and *dicing with dice carried in small bags, *betting on how far a stone would roll, *singing a round.

14TH CENTURY OCCUPATIONS

Pages. *Laying the table with knife, spoon, napkin, trencher and salt for their masters; serving long loaves of bread wrapped in a white towel twisted into a sling, so that all the company can help themselves by tearing off the piece they want, serving special dishes to their master. All serving to be done on bended knee. *Standing behind their master's chair at meals and whenever needed, brushing link mail free of dust and seeing that no link was loose, polishing the joints of armour gloves.

Servants. *Laying the table with tablecloths, drinking vessels of metal, horn, wood, or silver, according to the status of the house or castle, placing the chief ornament of the table, a large silver salt cellar, to show the division between the nobles and the other ranks; carrying round the large model of a ship which held the spices for diners to flavour their food; lighting and placing the dark yellow candles or torches for table and walls, putting logs on the fire and brushing up the hearth with twig broom.

Minstrels. Blowing trumpets for grace, playing, singing, or reading aloud (this for a quiet meal when the Lord of the Manor was away).

Kitchen servants. *Turning the spit, cooking with saucepans, frying pans, cauldron, using chopping board and knife, and grater for breadcrumbs from long loaf.

Servants or Pages. *Before and after dinner taking ewer, of wood, silver, or gold, according to whether it is manor, castle or palace, to each diner, holding it while the hands are washed, and handing the towel afterwards so that the hands can be dried; serving bowls or dishes of peas, beans, cabbages, meat and cheese and fish, serving wine and water in earthenware jugs, *putting glass candlesticks and goblets on table if it is a luxurious setting.

Clerks. *Making inventories on long scrolls, *entering sums of money and using a tally to count the money, *writing and then sealing the letters with large seal and wax, making quill pens (paper was used in this century but parchment looks better on the stage. *If paper is used it must not be pure white.)

Amusements. *Walking on stilts, *bobbing for apples, *forfeits, guessing games, *leapfrog, *wrestling games, *quoits, *backgammon, *ball games, and *building blocks for children, brightly coloured.

15th Century Occupations

Servants. Strewing rushes on the floor, cleaning convex mirrors, *hanging freshly picked branches and tasselled strings of beads on the walls, *painting the walls, *carving the walls, cupboards, chests, chairs and screens, *painting screens, and *polishing the linenfold carving on walls.

Pages and Household Servants. *Lighting the hanging lamps of Roman type, *closing the shutters or lattices, *serving oranges, apples, cherries, jars of ginger, shelling walnuts and almonds, serving large dishes of rice dyed with saffron to a brilliant yellow, tying bright pennants on lances for jousts, cleaning swords and maces for tourneys.

Monks. *Making books, looking after bees, *painting texts on ivory to hang on walls, *gardening of all kinds including clipping bushes into fantastic shapes.

Women. *Covering books with silk and velvet, *tending pots of growing flowers (not arranging them in vases yet),

*watering pots of herbs which stand on windowsill, *crushing petals to make scent which is poured into small round bottles which can be held in the hand or hang from the belt.
Amusements. *Puppets shows, *chess, *hide-and-seek, *cards. These cards were 7 by 4 inches large, and had pictures of emperors, loves, stars, etc., painted on the back.

16TH CENTURY OCCUPATIONS. 1500 TO 1550

All the starred ones listed in the previous centuries.
Dentists carrying equipment for tooth pulling, fomenting swellings, bandaging hurt limbs, and leeches for bleeding.
Barbers carrying razors for shaving, soap in mug, and towels which were warmed in front of the fire.
Furriers with samples of their wares.

These three occupations can be carried on in a shop, but a nobleman would have a visiting dentist, barber and furrier who came to the house.

Beggars. These increased in number during this period.
Bear leaders with dancing bears on a chain with bells round their necks.
House servants. Polishing the coloured leather boots for men. Polishing the wooden staircases that were coming into the house instead of stone ones. Laying the table with cloth, knives, spoons and trencher and loaves in a flat shape to fit the trenchers. Taking round the basin and towel after dinner for the guests to wash their hands after grace.
Women Servants. Putting flowers in pots and bowls for the window-sill and mantelpiece.

Sowing and watering the small herb and flower gardens that came into fashion in the more settled times, using foxgloves, carnations, marigolds, snapdragons, sweet williams, stocks, lilies and pansies, rosemary, thyme, mint and veronica.

Amusements. Hunting and hawking, bowls, tennis (indoor), golf, hockey, football, torchlight processions, the playhouse, fighting with quarter staff, fishing and netting fish, quoits, backgammon, cards; children's toys were alphabet blocks, balls, hoops, tops and mechanical wooden toys made in the shape of animals which walked.

List of Useful Reference Books

Life and Work of the People of England — D. Hartley and M. E. Allen (Batsford)

This gives details of all specialised costumes, e.g., tradesmen, pilgrims, clerks, merchants, religious, etc., with diagrams for making them and the tools of their calling.

Mediaeval Life — E. Power (Penguin Series)

This is a most fascinating description of the way of life of peasants, merchants and other people in England and other countries.

Cooking Through the Centuries — J. R. Ainsworth Davies (Dent)

Exactly what the title promises.

CHAPTER IV

MANNERS AND DANCES

Manners and customs—Bows and curtsies—Dances for each period, Caroles—Farandole, Branles and Pavane—List of gramophone records and reference books on dances

THERE are many vivid descriptions and denunciations of "modern" manners even in the ninth century, so that those who sigh for the bygone courtly ways would get a rude shock if they actually met them. Actors are concerned only with the broad outline of such things, and there is a stage convention that the best manners are shown for period plays and assumed to be normal. After all, it would take a medieval woman to know that a nun was showing a giddy nature when she wore her veil pushed up to reveal her forehead.

In the early Middle Ages there were a number of rules to be observed, as well as rigid class distinctions, but the stage producer can afford to ignore most of the minor ones. The plays are full of action, and this must not be held up by a pedantic accuracy that conveys nothing to the modern mind. There are, however, three forces that dictate many of the plots, and these also govern the actions of the characters, so that the producer must reckon with them.

The Church was enormously powerful, both in a spiritual and a secular way, so that there must always be most respectful greetings for church dignitaries; a curse was a thing that might easily come true, so the gesture of crossing oneself was automatic, and any supernatural appearances, although perhaps not usual, were not incredible and were greeted politely, with due respect.

The second force was the nobles, who had the power of life and death in fact, if not always legally, over most of their domain. Serfs, servants, pages could be most unpleasantly punished and therefore took good care to be affably subservient to their masters.

Children were the possessions of the parents, they had to behave themselves in a most respectful way not only to father and mother but to almost anyone of the older generation. The manners and greetings given in this chapter must all be stressed and intensified if they are directed towards the Church, the nobles or the old. Greetings in early times were quite simple. The family, which includes cousins, aunts, uncles, guardians, kissed each other if women, or if of the opposite sex. Knights often kissed each other, but this is a case where it is better not to be authentic as the audience will certainly giggle. It is hardly necessary to say that the kiss bestowed by a knight on his aunt differs in kind and degree from that which he lavishes on a comely peasant wench.

It was a time when it was difficult to know who was friend or foe, or even how long anyone would be either, so the men's greeting reflects this attitude. Approaching each other warily the men would simultaneously grasp each other with both hands gripping above the elbows tightly. This ensured that one was not stabbed first, as no hands were free to reach the dagger. There was no ban on killing after the greeting was over, it was just a point of honour not to be taken unawares in the first moment. This fashion lingered some time after it was always necessary; in fact there is no actual date when it is possible to say that one set of manners stopped and the next began.

The older generation and the country man and woman would use the manners of a previous time and the Court would use the most up-to-date ones, almost certainly with the influence of whatever the nation was from which the Queen came. French, Italian, Spanish, Portuguese, German, Dutch and Danish customs thus all came to England in due course and made variety in the dances, bows and curtsies of each successive reign. Almost the only habit unchanged for more than six centuries was the Englishman's firm addiction to wearing a hat except when he was in bed. He uncovers for the King, his overlord, a lady, and in church, and then he quickly puts his hat on again; he uncovers if he comes into the hall after dinner has started, but he puts his hat on if he is going to eat. He takes it off for the passing of a Holy relic in a procession, but only briefly.

The later period had a bow for a man which showed off the pleasant fashion of wearing one leg lemon and one chocolate coloured. The hat is taken off and held in the left hand, either swept back or close to the hip, with the inside held next to his body. The left foot is taken back as if he is about to kneel on it, while the weight is still on the front foot. After a half bend both knees are straightened. This bow can be done, with variations, from the fourteenth century onwards to men, and from the eleventh century to ladies. If there is no hat but long dragged sleeves, then both arms can be swept backwards, if the shoes are elaborately pointed, a little flourish can be done with the right foot on rising. The ladies curtsy for the entire medieval period is very simple, the style only varies from simple to sophisticated as times goes on. The basic movement is a bend of both knees, the depth of the bend governed by the rank of the character to whom the curtsy is being made; without either bending or lowering the head. The skirt is held as its fullness dictates. When the head-dress is the simple Early-Medieval type, the head is inclined to one side, or may even be drooped. When the head-dress is elaborate and stiffened, the head is inclined and a small shoulder movement should be used. The right shoulder can be taken forward on the bend, the head inclined toward the right, the left shoulder brought forward on the rise as the head is straightened. It is charming if rather theatrical, to cross the hands lightly on the breast during the curtsy; perhaps this gesture could be used when the lady is supposed to be a minx.

When curtsying to a king or overlord, the arms can be swept back with the palms of the hands facing front, to show submission. This gesture would be suitable for Katherine in a production of *The Taming of the Shrew* dressed Renaissance.

Curtsies must be as individual as a modern handshake, and must show the social differences of the characters, ranging from the raw country debutante to the polished woman of the world.

Weapons all had to be cleaned and kept, and as stage business can be done by servants, although there would always be keen sportsmen fussing over their own pet gadgets. Sporting dogs, falcons or other livestock should never be seen, they unsettle the audience. "Noises off" must appreciate that not every breed of dog says, "Bow wow"—and highly-born ladies had their own pet dogs.

Actions that occur in Shakespeare's plays—*Richard II*, etc.—such as swearing allegiance, being knighted, paying homage, and taking seizen, are simple but must be done slowly. In order to kiss the sovereign's hand, the subject must kneel, and putting out his right hand, palm downwards, raise the sovereign's right hand, balancing it on the back of his wrist and then place his forehead on the back of the sovereign's hand. He then stands and bows before backing away. Paying homage is also done in a kneeling position; here the King takes both hands of the subject between both his, all the palms facing inwards, while the subject repeats the oath. When a character has knighthood conferred on him he takes out his sword with his right hand, then holding the centre of the blade with his left, he offers it to the monarch (the hilt is now resting on his right forearm), who takes it and touches it lightly to the knight's left shoulder. The knight accepts the sword again, between his two hands, stands up and resheathes it.

To "take seizen" means to receive a piece of earth as token of land held, and rents paid often took odd forms such as lobsters or sacks of flour.

These are all English customs. When a French Queen appears all the manners have a little extra flourish, the entertainments have an air of sophistication. The bearing of the courtiers in front of the King and Queen is respectful but gay and easy. When a Spanish Queen is at Court the etiquette is more rigid. The bows and curtsies are deeper and more often used to precede speeches. The bearing of the courtiers is more unbending and utterly correct and an atmosphere of formality pervades the palace.

All pictures and descriptions of movement are capable of being interpreted in several different ways. All period movement is, to a certain extent, guesswork. The pictures give a working basis, taken together with the limitations the costume automatically imposes. All manners are in accordance with the person, the mood and the situation. A bad-tempered bow takes less time than a conciliating one.

Social distinctions and family and personal relationships are vitally important to present convincingly, and the manners should be a means to this end.

The early Tudor manners present no particular difficulties. The dress is not inordinately full and can be held at the sides for the curtsy, which is still a gentle bend of the knees, with the head bent slightly. The women kissed each other in greeting if friends, sincerely or the reverse, curtsied to people of higher rank than themselves or to the men. Henry VIII's wives sped by with such disastrous haste that they had little influence on manners, with the exception of Katherine of Aragon. For the twenty years of her reign the Spanish customs were noticeable in the meticulously correct bearing of her own ladies-in-waiting and entourage, but the King and his gentlemen obstinately ignored these foreign ways.

Their greeting can be a hand clasp (not a shake) for special friends and a bow for everyone else. The hat is taken off and put on again, using both hands as it is tricky to adjust. The cloak is swung jauntily, the hand kept ready on the sword (just in case) and the other hand can finger the large neck chain. There is a useful little beard to stroke in thought or to tug in fury. (*See* Fig. 6.) The breeches are padded all round so that the walk is more of a straddle. The bow is made by taking the right foot forward into almost a fencer's lunge, taking off the hat which is held either at the side or across the body, and bending both knees while keeping the head erect. On rising, the hat is put on again, the back leg drawn up to the front one and the body relaxed. The well-known stance with both legs wide apart merely demonstrates the masculine gift for finding the most comfortable position in the most unpromising circumstances.

Many of the fans that the ladies carried had tiny mirrors in the centre of the feathers so that they could admire themselves. The gentlemen borrowed them occasionally but for an entirely different reason, of course, simply to note that all was in order with beard, eyebrows, ruff, etc. This is the type of action that can be used to show the degree of intimacy between characters. A sister might show her brother her mirror with a terse mutter about the state of his hair, while a lover might hold the fan in front of his lady's face so that he could gaze fondly on two images of her.

The pomander was used (and needed) at this time by both sexes. Spitting is a custom that gives authenticity to the scene and a nasty temper to the stage-hands.

FIG. 6. Man (Tudor) Fingering Beard

When a gentleman leads a lady either out to dance or out for a walk he holds her hand quite naturally as children do, but when he leads a Queen, he holds out his hand at a higher level and she places her hand on his wrist. The King would do as he liked.

Jesters still existed but as there were now professional actors, they were expendable. If they come into a play of any period their movement must be that of a trained dancer. This is often impossible with an amateur cast, so that actors had better learn a few stylised positions and realise that coy skips, winsome prances, and an arch fore-finger would never have won a place on the pay-roll as a jester, although they are seen embarrassingly often on the stage in such a part. Jesters were funny, in the correct sense of the word, otherwise they ceased to be jesters. Pedlars appear to be the natural successors to the jesters when the scene is laid in the country. They have an easy manner, freer than the town-folk but not as rough as the countrymen.

Dancing bears were popular and should be played for comedy. Cockfighting was another amusement, the cocks may be off-stage, but the actors should be able to place bets rowdily and win or lose with raucous vigour.

The social scale was still obvious, servants neither be-haved like their masters nor wished to, as the result would have been a beating. The servants' bows and bobs are quick and automatic, so are the tradespeoples', inn-keepers', and clerks'.

Dancing has always been both a popular amusement and a social programme; therefore the dances of any period are ruled by what the dancer wears and where the dance takes place. Accurate footwork and fine points of ballet technique never occur when the skirts sweep the floor and the work would be wasted. The pattern of the dance depends on social conditions, where the hearth is or where the important people sit. In early times there was not very much room, even in the great halls, to dance, so the Farandole was a typical open-air dance. As the halls were built on a larger scale, so the dance came indoors and the Branles were danced round the hearth, which was in the middle of the floor. Later still the fireplace moved up to the end of the room. Then a dais was built for the head table, where the most important people sat, both to eat and be entertained. So the dances, which began by rambling all over the place, next took the form of a circle, and finally became a procession which moved up the room to the top table and then retreated. In the beginning the dancers were all linked together, then they were joined in a ring which could be broken, and then paired in twos and put behind each other in a line moving up and down. After this the dance began to break out and to experiment in all directions, in steps, in figures, and in grouping.

The early medieval dances are altogether charming and not at all difficult to do. There are simple steps and patterns and no problems about equal numbers of men and girls. All the early dances take it for granted that the dancers sing while they dance, so this is a measure of the light-hearted air that pervades the whole thing.

Caroles, as the dances are called, include several varieties of rhythm, and different formations.

The Farandole is a most useful dance as it takes any number of people, can be done in a small space or a large one, and is simple and decorative. For a small stage it is done in one linked line. (*See* Fig. 1, facing title) For a large stage or a pageant as many lines can be used as the producer wishes. These lines work independently, so that either there can be one line to each stage area, or each line can be allowed the freedom of the field and taught what to do to avoid head-on collisions when it meets another line. It is ideal for arena production, as the weaving of the line gives everyone a chance to see and be seen.

The more dancers there are the better the song sounds. It may be necessary nowadays to have singers, who do not dance, laid on to swell the sound; but the dancers should join in occasionally as it is in the essential spirit of this dance.

The line forms for a Farandole by everyone holding hands, the leader having her left hand free and the last on the line having her right hand free. It does not matter if the sexes alternate or not. If the group is short of men, or if they have baulked at dancing in public, one man can alternate with three or four women.

The line skips (step, hop), following the leader wherever she wants to go, up and down, in and out, across the stage and back. As the dance was originally intended for the open air, because the small halls were cramped and had not much room, every advantage should be taken of an open-air setting. The line can skip in and out among the trees of a woodland setting, up banks and round bushes. This figure is called "The Meander" and the track could be thus:

1. A complete circle round the stage travelling from left to right.
2. Weaving back and forwards like a snake travelling upstage and down.
3. Weaving in the same way but travelling parallel with the footlights.
4. Travelling round the stage making a square by turning each corner sharply. If the line is long there will be a moment when this figure will be seen in its entirety, so each person must be responsible for going right up to the corner, and for not letting it merge into a circle.

During all this time the dancers skip steadily, not high in the air but with a lilt. The ladies can tuck their skirts into their girdles, and with flower garlands in their hands and wreaths on their heads, epitomise the spirit of the age.

"The Snail" can be the next figure. When a change of figure is imminent, or a more difficult figure, the leader drops into a walk. This is a great help to novices as it gives them time to think.

To make "The Snail" the line is led in a large circle and then, going in the same direction, in smaller and smaller circles until there is no room to make another circle. The leader then, by giving a sharp tug with her right hand, indicates that the second dancer must go under the arch made by the leader's right arm. The other dancers follow the second dancer, and they all walk through until there is a line again to begin the next figure. It is absolutely vital that no one lets go of anyone else's hand.

A figure that is a little more difficult but satisfactorily showy can now be introduced. The leader drops into a walk to warn her troupe that something is now going to happen and that they must pay attention. Everyone now holds up their arms, still holding hands, so that the line now looks like a pergola. The first dancer leads the second dancer under the arch made by the arms of the second and third dancers. She is now looking at the back of the line. She threads through the arch made by the third and fourth dancers and continues in and out until she has been through all the arches. The line follows, never letting go of each other's hands and naturally as each couple goes under so that arch disappears. The only snag here is that the dancers are apt to anticipate the movements. They *must* let the threading happen before they try to go through the arch themselves, otherwise they will find their arms dragged out of the sockets. Practise this very slowly at first and it is easy; try to rush it and there will be strangled or dislocated dancers.

"Oranges and Lemons" or "Threading the Needle" is

a very old figure. The first and second dancers stop skipping and raise their arms to make an arch. Now the third can release her left hand and go through the arch pulling the line with her. When the last one is through she holds out her right hand to the leader who takes it and gives her right hand to the second dancer who is now the end of the line.

"The Hey" is a figure the actors will probably know if they have done Square Dancing. It can be a charming variation when there is plenty of room to display it. Two lines of dancers advance towards each other (this is one time when they can let go hands). As they meet they pass their opposite number on the right and join hands again when the lines have passed.

The music for this dance can be practised by singing "Summer is a'coming in", and it can be done to the following record: Columbia DB2282.

The Caroles were team dances and did not depend on individual performers. The Round, which is done in a circle, is also called the Branle, and the typical movement is a swaying one. (*See* Fig. 7.) When this dance is done with a crowd, separate circles can be formed, and these can either mark social distinctions, or there can be a lively circle of youngsters and a decorous circle of the middle-aged.

It is important in the Branle to keep exact time and to keep the step with an easy sway. The dancers stand in a circle holding hands. The circle must travel towards the left so that the steps going to the left are larger than the steps going to the right.

Beginning with the left foot, walk three paces (left, right, left) and close the right foot to the left on the pause. The body is slightly turned so that the dancers can see where they are going. Then turning slightly to the right, they pace right, left, right, close the left to the right. This sequence of three steps and close is called a Double. The

FIG. 7. Branles Dance of the Twelfth to Sixteenth Century

whole dance consists of a Double to the right and a Double to the left, the circle moving slowly round until the dancers are back in their original places.

The music for the Branles has a short phrase which is repeated for as long as is wanted, like Sir Roger de Coverley.

It helps the cast if it is first practised to Peter Warlock's Branle in the Capriole Suite, as they will probably be familiar with it. A pipe record that is recommended is Columbia DB2608.

When in the twelfth and thirteenth centuries the Troubadours spread romantic notions wherever they went (and they went everywhere) they insisted on the dancers pairing off in couples. This in turn meant that the music ceased to be vocal and the accompaniment became instrumental. The dance was called "The Estampie" and is interesting because it was the beginning of the development of music as an independent art. Instrumental music, although for some centuries it continued to be written in dance form, had started to exist on its own.

In the fourteenth century the fireplace moved from the centre of the hall to the side wall and there was usually a dais at the top of the hall where the Lord of the Manor, important guests and the family sat. This is the origin of the Top Couple referred to even in nineteenth-century dances. Clothes were now stiffer and heavier and the women's head-dresses made it expedient to stop doing skipping steps.

The Processional dances now came into fashion with the Salterelle and Almain. The fifteenth century brought in the Basse dances with rather more springy steps, but still processional dances. They are more set and formal than the earlier dances but some of the rules are exceedingly helpful to uncertain novices. For instance, that the first step forward must be taken on the left foot and that the first step backwards must be taken on the right foot.

Steps are grouped together in Measures, and often the Measures alternated with each other so that when one was finished, the other started and then the first was repeated again. In Europe there were many dances and variety of steps as the great families intermarried from country to country.

England did not progress very fast with dance and was still dancing thirteenth-century dances in the sixteenth century, although some new ones were creeping in. The music in the Basse dances can be very tricky for the dancers, and it is better to embark on them under the eagle eye of a qualified dance teacher. They are fully described in Miss Wood's book in the list at the end of this chapter, but here there is only space enough to describe dances that are typical of their period and easy and theatrically useful.

The sixteenth century brought many changes and England gained a splendid reputation for magnificent dancing. The Pavane, the Galliard and the Tordion were all popular and La Volta and the Coranto are of this period. Dancing in cross rhythms was very much in vogue but in dealing with a modern cast "that way madness lies". The Branles were still danced in various forms; from now onwards the dance is fully documented and set down with great precision.

The English Pavane started with the partners standing beside each other, holding hands. It must here be stated that all this holding of hands was done at a low angle both in the Caroles and the Branles. Sometimes the hands were laid back to back in a processional dance where it was easy to stay side by side without actually clutching each other.

The lady turns towards her partner and curtsys, bending both knees, inclining her head, and holding her skirts. (Four counts.) At the same time the gentleman is taking off his hat with his left hand, taking a step back with his right foot and bending his right knee. He holds his hat either against his hip or lower down. (Four counts.) He then steps forward on the left foot, closes the right foot to the left, put on his hat, kisses his hand to the lady and offers it to her. (Four counts.) At the same time the lady is rising from her curtsy, kissing her hand and offering it to the gentlemen. (Four counts.)

This bow and curtsy took eight slow counts before the music started. The lady has less to do but must finish at the same time as the gentleman, which is why the instructions are written in two counts of four. This, it is hoped, will help them to see where they synchronise. The steps used in the Pavane are the Double (as in the Branles only forward) and half a Double, which is a Simple. This is one step forward on either foot and close the other foot up to the first, the whole taking two bars of the music. Doubles and Simples recur through the centuries as names for dance steps, but do not by any means apply to the same thing. In the same way, the Reprise sometimes means the same step done travelling backwards, and sometimes means a totally different step. The books of period dances never mention this hazard but leave the reader with the impression that each dance consists of the same steps only arranged in different figures. This is very far from fact and accounts for the difficulty the average actor finds when trying to work out the dance from instructions in a book When it says "2Ss; 2Ds" it certainly means two simples, two doubles, but *which* simples depends on which century the dance was made for.

The Branles simples travelled sideways in the circle with the steps going to the left larger than the steps going to the right. The Pavane simples travel forwards and are the same length whether started on the left or the right foot. The Spanish Pavane has more figures and more steps than the English.

The important style in the Pavane is the great dignity

that must be shown. This is helped by the slow music and the fact that there is a rise and fall in the steps. The steps forward or backwards are done on the toes and the drop on the heels comes whenever the feet are closed.

The dance travels up the room and back again, with the dancers facing the same way all the time. The steps are arranged thus. Start with the left foot and do a Simple forward with the left, a Simple forward with the right, and a Double forward with the left. This sequence, two Simples and a Double, is then repeated starting with the right foot. When these have been done as many times as is necessary to take the dancers to the top of the room, they can do them travelling backwards. This is the point where it can turn into a shambles, and the producer will find that only half his troupe know with certainty which is their left foot. The dance finishes with the same bow and curtsy.

In Henry VIII's time the custom was to finish the dances with the men giving the women a hearty kiss on both cheeks. If this is done (and it does give the lusty feel of the Tudor age), then it must be properly rehearsed, and no genteel pecks allowed.

The Pavane is in 2/4 time and there are three good records to choose from. The Fauré one is a later version, but the singing is so delightful that it is included here as it is in accord with the spirit of the age.

Although the Pavane is slow it must never be dreary or dragging. It needs immense dignity in the carriage of the head and arms, and the ability to hold the pause without causing the audience to wonder if the dancers have forgotten the next step. These dances have been simplified, to a certain extent, for stage purposes, the style and spirit have been emphasised, but technical details omitted. If an absolutely correct dance is needed, a teacher must be consulted. Such dances take a great deal of rehearsing and because they were originally social are not effective on the stage except in a schools' programme.

Records for Period Dances

Farandole

Roundelay (four short pieces)	Col.	DB2278
Melody (four short pieces)	Col.	DB2279
"Fools' Jig"	H.M.V.	B9577

Branles

"Capriole Suite". Warlock	H.M.V.	C4218
Scottish Air, etc.	Col.	DB2281
Salterelle	Col.	DB2278
"Ding, Dong, Merrily on High"	Col.	2608

Pavanes

Earl of Salisbury	Col.	5712
Pavane. Fauré	Col.	DX1369
Pavane "Capriole Suite". Warlock	H.M.V.	C4218
"Pavane pour une Infante Defunte" Ravel	H.M.V.	DB21553

Four Records with music for all these dances:

History of Music in Sound	H.M.V.	Vol. 2, sides 9–10
History of Music in Sound	H.M.V.	Vol. 7, sides 15–16

See also pp. 71–2.

Useful Reference Books

Historical Dances from the 12th to the 19th Century M. Wood (C. W. Beaumont)

This gives historical background and reasons for the development of the Dance, descriptions of the steps and dances taken from manuscripts of the period, but is not concerned with stage arrangement. It is scrupulously accurate if a documentary programme is needed or if the dances are to done purely for the dancers' own amusement, but the dances are not very easy to work out in a hurry without tuition. Music is included.

Manners and Movements in Costume Plays I. Chisman and H. E. Raven-Hart (Deane)

Excellent legal, military and religious ceremonial section and a special chapter on duelling, fighting and wrestling.

Orchesography Arbeau (C. W. Beaumont)
One of the most famous books on dance written by a seventeenth-century dancing master. This should be read not only for knowledge but also for amusement.

The Imperial Society of Teachers of Dancing, Historical Dance Branch, Euston Hall, Birkenhead Street, London WC1H 4AJ, will supply a list of teachers qualified in this subject.

CHAPTER V

MUSIC

Musical forms of the periods—Instruments used—List for each century of instruments and composers, modern stage equivalents and possible gramophone records and useful books

MOST medieval music sounds so doleful to modern audiences that unless the desired effect *is* unutterable misery, it is better left alone. The list at the end of this chapter gives period composers and moderns who have written in the style of different periods, also gramophone records and modern equivalents of period sound.

Two things are apt to be overlooked. Firstly, that twenty years usually elapse between the date of birth and the first piece of music written. Secondly, once the music has been written it can be used at any succeeding time. Thus a modern play could have the first act introduced by a Chopin prelude, the second by Purcell, and the third by Byrd.

Music mirrors society to an extraordinary degree, and medieval music bears direct witness to this fact. Church music and folk songs are the two forms which have survived, and all genuine early plays come under one or the other of these headings.

Plainsong first and then Gregorian Chant, for all Religious Drama, is obtainable both in written music and in gramophone records. Folk songs can be had, both in English and in other European languages, on gramophone records. Many of these foreign melodies have a dramatic quality that is startling. The way to use them for an English play is to allow the cast to listen carefully to the tune. When it is learned it can either be whistled (an

FIG. 8. Man Playing Pipe and Tabor

obvious way of providing music that is often forgotten) or sung with words improvised to fit the situation (a custom that occurs in every century) or played on the suitable instruments of the time. There is a far wider choice of instruments than most people imagine. The pipe and tabor were the most popular early ones. The tabor, a deep drum, was slung around the player's shoulder and rested on his right hip. He played it with his right hand while he played the pipe with his left hand. (*See* Fig. 8.) The pipe was held either straight or sideways. It is unlikely that anyone can do this nowadays, but it should be possible for the player to provide the steady beat on the tabor that is essential for this type of music.

If he is placed at an angle to the audience, and a record. played off-stage, the illusion can be created that all the sound is coming from him. Although dancers are supposed to provide their own music by singing (all the early dances are called Caroles for this reason), they do not usually make enough noise to drown their thudding steps, so records may be used as long as they are not orchestral.

The harp used was a small one balanced on the knee, the strings were plucked with the right hand.

The trumpet was used for flourishes, for announcing important people or visitors, and saying that dinner was ready. (*See* Fig. 9.)

The horn was used for hunting first, and not as a musical instrument in an ensemble until a later date.

Bagpipes, the modern ones will do for the stage, were used to entertain guests at meals and as an accompaniment to song.

Lutes came from Persia in the twelfth century and were the favourite instrument of the troubadours. (*See* Fig. 10.) Actors playing the part of these romantic men should at least be able to strike a few notes on their lute and know how to walk without letting the lute bump to and fro behind them. They should bring it into playing position

FIG. 9. Man Playing Trumpet on Cleft Stick

FIG. 10. Lady Playing Lute

with a flourish, dispose of the ribbons with which it is hung without getting entangled in them, and strike a romantic attitude while they tune up.

A small hurdy-gurdy, played by turning the handle and held on the lap, is one of the more amusing instruments of the thirteenth century. A portative organ, looking like a vastly enlarged pipes of Pan, is a great help if organ music is needed and difficult to justify, as the records for organ music are plentiful. (*See* Fig. 11.)

The travelling minstrels specialised in songs about wars, heroes, news and gossip. The troubadours dealt in love songs, and some of the loveliest melodies have been recorded.

The tumblers and acrobats, although they were not musicians, belong in this chapter as they travelled the country with the minstrels. By the sixteenth century England was known as a musical nation, polyphony was established, new instruments and musical forms were emerging. From now on the producer has a rich choice of all types of composers, instead of searching desperately for something that modern ears will recognise as music.

List of Instruments and Composers

11*th Century*. Folk-songs. Plainsong. Gregorian Chant. Pipes. Pipe and Tabor. Bagpipes.

12*th Century*. Celtic Harp. Lute. Trumpet. Horn.
Bernard de Ventadour, *c*. 1130. Walter von der Vogelweide, *c*. 1170.

13*th Century*. Hurdy-gurdy. Hand organs. Harps, and all the earlier instruments.
Adam de la Halle, *c*. 1240. Guillaume de Machaut, *c*. 1295. John of Dunstable, *c*. 1380.

14*th Century*. All the preceding instruments.
John of Dunstable, *c*. 1380.

FIG. 11. Man Playing Hand-organ

15th Century. Recorder, Shawm.
Malatesta Hammond, 1400. Guillaume Dufay, 1440. J. des Prés, *c.* 1445. L. Power. H. Finch, 1445. W. Cornish, 1465. John Taverner, *c.* 1495. Christopher Tye, *c.* 1497.

16th Century. Recorder, Shawm and Dulcimer (*See* Fig. 12) Arcadelt, *c.* 1510. Thomas Tallis, 1505. Zialen, 1517, Richard Edwards, *c.* 1523. Palestrina, 1526. Robert White, *c.* 1535. Vittoria, *c.* 1535.

This is not a complete list of composers of this time; it is meant to give a representative choice of easily obtainable music.

Modern Equivalents of the Sound made by Period Instruments

Pipe and Tabor. Pipe and modern Tabor.
Bagpipes. Bagpipes.
Harp. Harp.
Lute. Cello plucked, or Guitar or Mandoline (these are for stage purposes, not for concert performances).
Hurdy-Gurdy. This is a challenge to the producer's ingenuity!
Hand-Organ. Harmonium.
Dulcimer. The same as for lute.
Trumpet and Horn. The modern Trumpet and Horn.

Gramophone Records
Authentic Period Music

		Century
Two Thousand Years of Music:		
The Gregorian Chant and Early	O.OL 50209*	
Polyphonic music	Parlo. R1017	12th
The Minnesingers and the Troubadours	Parlo. R1018	12th

FIG. 12. Lady Playing Dulcimer

Columbia History of Music by Eye and Ear:		
Vol. I. Plainsong with organum and with counterpoint	Col. 5710	12th
"Christe Redemptor", "Conditor Alme Siderum"	Col. 5711	
"Nunc Dimittis", "Sanctus" "Hosanna"	Col. 5712	
History of Music in Sound:		
Vol. 2. Early Medieval Music to A.D. 1300	H.M.V. HLP3*	
Vol. 3. Ars Nova and the Renaissance	H.M.V. HLP5*	
"Gloria", boys' choir and trumpet. Dufay	Parlo. 1019	15th
Josquin des Prés	H.M.V. HLP6*	15th
German Choral Music	Parlo. 1020	16th
Polyphony in 16th Century	Parlo. 1021	16th
"O Come ye Servants of the Lord." Tye	R.G. 8	16th

Traditional Music

"Sumer is icumen in"	H.M.V. HLP4*
Carols	H.M.V. G3806–3807
Songs. Gaelic	H.M.V. B9799–9800 *and* H.M.V. F3367
English	H.M.V. B9775
Greek	Col. DC392

The Catalogue of Educational Recordings issued by H.M.V., Columbia and Parlophone should also be consulted.

Records for Period Atmosphere

Bamboo pipes.	DB2282–2278—Col. 2280–2279
Pipe and Tabor	H.M.V. B9577

Concertina	H.M.V. B9579–B9669–B9670
Melodeon	H.M.V. B9539–B9672
Bacca pipes	H.M.V. 9672
Fanfares	H.M.V. B9616
"Capriol Suite". Warlock	H.M.V. C2904
	Decca LW5149*
"Pavane in F Minor". Fauré	H.M.V. 7ep 7001†
	Decca RD27156*
	Decca SB5054*
with song	Decca AK1643
"Pavane d'une Infante defunte" Ravel	Col. DB2343–44
arr. Bream	Decca RB16560*
"Suite for Pipes." Vaughan Williams	Col. DX1345

Some of these records have three or four short pieces on them representing different periods, so the producer is advised to look up the composers if he wants to be strictly accurate and certain of music of the right date.

* Long playing record
† Extended play record

Useful Books

The Use of Music in Religious Drama	C. Le Fleming	(S.P.C.K.)
Music and Society	Wilfred Mellers	(Dobson)

A survey of the development of music and society showing the link between conditions and the effect they have on the music of their time. Intriguing illustrations of early medieval instruments.

The Rural Music Schools Association have offices all over this country and give advice on period music to their members, lend gramophone records and can recommend teachers, choirmasters and singers, and performers on most musical instruments. The Secretary's address is: Little Benslow Hills, Hitchin Herts., SG4 9RB.

The English Folk Dance and Song Society, 2 Regents Park Road, London NW1 7AY, has photographs of period instruments.

CHAPTER VI

PRACTICE SCENES

Suggested scenes from plays for practice in period movement—Mime scenes for each century with suggestions for gramophone records as music

SCENES for practice in period movement with suggestions for using the costume to point the dialogue.

Scenes from Shakespeare have been chosen as the average cast have copies of the plays.

Henry V. Act 3 Scene 4

An embroidress has samples of decorated gloves for the Princess to choose from. The references to "nail", "elbow" must be timed with fitting on the gloves. The curtsy of the sewing woman must differ from that of the lady in waiting who might be sent to fetch a purse in order to pay.

Much Ado About Nothing. Act 3 Scene 1

Productions of this play are dressed in whatever period the producer wishes, so in this scene the actresses could practise dressing Hero in clothes, jewels, and accessories; each century would thus have a different series of actions, as in the eleventh century the hair would be brushed loosely, while in the fifteenth, it would be pulled back and the eyebrows plucked.

Othello. Act 4 Scene 3

This series of actions would be exactly the reverse of the above scene, as Desdemona is undressing before going to bed. Here the moves could vary from taking off the correct period jewellery, shoes, slippers, replacing shoes, etc., and replacing the heavy dress with a loose robe. This scene could also be done in a different century, according to the period in which the actresses most needed help.

Romeo and Juliet. Act 1 *Scene* 5

As the dialogue here is in a definite rhythm this scene could be practised while doing a dance. It is in fact a good plan to improvise words in keeping with the character while doing the Pavane, which is a slow dance, as in this way the actors get used to the feel of dancing for fun. The steps will sink below the surface of the mind, which will be concerned with the conversation, and the freedom and grace of the movements will improve.

Measure for Measure. Act 3 *Scene* 2

The effect of flippant gossip can be emphasised if Lucio can practise his dance steps (if suitable for the production, Coranto), in any case a dance that has a showy little step rather than one that depends on the figures done.

Comedy of Errors. Act 2 *Scene* 1

If the actresses assume that they are dressed in sixteenth-century costumes, they can be making scent. Adriane can be so distraught that she waters the mixture with her tears, while Luciane can be pounding the petals in a bowl and then stirring them vigorously. These actions will help her to punctuate her more pungent observations with descriptive movements.

St. George's Play

Open the scene with an improvisation of a fifteenth-century banquet, using all the cast. After the diners have finished, let there be a procession of the mummers and minstrels. The play can start then, with a reading cast at the side and the actors doing all the movements without having to hold their books.

Everyman

Read out the first name on the cast list and ask every member to cross the stage in character and finish in a characteristic pose. Continue reading down the cast list until everyone has had the opportunity to move and act every character in the play.

Mime Scene for the Twelfth Century

Scene is a wood with a stream running parallel with the footlights. Girls and men enter dancing a Farandole, the girls with their dresses tucked up into their girdles to allow freedom of movement as this is the gay, rather wild way of dancing it. They are all singing as they dance, "Summer is a'cuming in." After the dance is over, they sit by the stream, breathlessly dabbling their hands in the water, the men cupping the water in their palms, splashing it on their faces and sprinkling it over the girls. Servants enter with pasties and jars of ale and serve the company. A minstrel has entered too and as the food is served he plays his pipe, moving to and fro among the eaters. The company, having eaten, get up and wander off-stage in couples. The servants sit and eat and a peasant with a child comes in. They are invited to join the meal, and the child runs backwards and forwards as first one and then the other offer him titbits. A hunting horn sounds and the company rush in and point off-stage right where someone important is approaching. A nobleman and his page enter, and bows and curtsies are exchanged. He is offered a drink and the piper plays a tune for him and gets a coin flung to him. The piper now plays a dance tune. The nobleman leads off with the lady of his choice and they all dance off with a Farandole. The servants watch them go and then lie down for a good sleep. The peasant shoulders his axe and goes off, but the child remains sitting on the bank of the stream and dabbling his feet in the brook. On the last note of the music a butterfly settles on his (or her) hand, and the child watches it.

Music. The Farandole is sung by the dancers. The entry of the servants and the serving of the food is done to H.M.V. 9577. The piper's tune is Columbia 2282, first tune.

The servants' meal and the peasant and the child's entry is done to 2282, second tune.

The nobleman's entrance and reception is done to 2282, third tune. The servants' settling down, the peasants' exit and the child's actions are done to 2280.

These records have short pieces on them with a slight gap between one piece and the next. The record plays straight through and actors freeze in a picture in the silence. If it is intended to perform in front of an audience, then warning must be given of these silences, so that applause is not given too soon and then withheld at the end.

Mime Scene for the 14th Century

Four ladies are sitting in a turret room with a window stage left and a door stage right. One is sewing a large silk handkerchief, one is reading a letter, one is sorting the balls of wool for the tapestry that the fourth is sewing on to a small square frame. A whistle is heard outside the window and the reader runs to it. She looks out and waves, turns and calls to the sewer, who drops the handkerchief and goes to the window. They both clearly cannot quite hear what is being called up to them from below, shrug their shoulders, cup their ears and finally understand. They come back and tell the others that the men are coming up to see them and want help with putting on their armour. They then hastily tidy the room while the first lady stands by the door to see when the visitors arrive. They take it in turn to look in the mirror and have their costumes arranged to the best advantage, then group themselves to welcome the knights. The watcher now warns that these are coming up the stairs and they enter and make their bows, just inside the door. Each knight then goes to his lady carrying a small piece of his armour that is obviously only an excuse to have a private talk. The ladies receive their tasks with slight mockery and proceed to fulfil them and then to see that all other buckles, etc., are well adjusted. The knights now ask for their tournament favours, each in an entirely individual way; matter of factly, imploringly, shyly or teasingly. The ladies respond also in an individual manner. One probably refuses, the knight shows temper and starts to go and lady relents. The handkerchief is shown, approved of and tied round the arm, the helmet or across the chest. One lady gives a rose which her lover kisses, tucks into a link of his armour, and then kisses the lady. One lady has nothing to give so she puts both hands to her lips and presents the kiss to her knight. He takes her hands and pulls her into his arms and kisses her lips as his favour. The fourth lady takes an embroidered fringed scarf and gives it to her knight, who receives it kneeling in front of her. She lays her hands on his shoulders as a sort of blessing. The knights all exit, the ladies watch them go, then run to the window and wave them good-bye.

The music for this is not strictly authentic in period; it has been chosen because it expresses the mood of the scene. It is Sicillienne (a sixteenth-century dance form), Columbia 2492. The first part is slow and the second part quick and excited. The knights enter at the beginning of the quick part and the ladies wave to them out of the window on the last note of the record.

Mime Scene for the Fifteenth Century

This is a scene to the ballad "Bring us Good Ale" by an anonymous author of this century. It is printed in *The Christmas Companion* (pub. Dent). The music is record Columbia 2278.

The scene is more precisely timed than the preceding ones and combines choral speech with the mime, although the speech must be robust rather than poetic.

The action is arranged for two sets of players, one set move to the music and do not speak, the other set speak but do not move. The speakers are the family and guests at a feast. They can be men and women, and are seated at a long table placed right across the stage, upstage, if possible on a dais.

The movers are the servants bringing in the various dishes, none of which find favour in the eyes of the diners who want "GOOD ALE". There is a steward who gets more and more flurried as the dishes are sent back, and a fool (professional) who tries to divert the diners from their grievances and fails dismally.

The scene opens with the first verse of the ballad declaimed by the master of the house, in a pleasant frame of mind. The guests nod agreement and look towards the door eagerly awaiting their ale. The music starts and the servants enter from stage right and carry their dishes up to the table for the approval of the guests, waved on by the steward. The guests signify their disapproval of the fare. The servants exeunt stage left in disgrace, the last one leaving on the last note of the first section of the music, e.g., where the first band comes on the record.

The second verse is now declaimed by the men at the table and all look again towards the door where the steward is getting ready to bring on the next set of dishes. (The dishes are carried in mime only, there are no properties needed unless the producer wants to work it up into a small item in an entertainment.)

The music starts again and exactly the same movements are repeated by the servants with increasing fear and haste. The guests again express disapproval and the servants stumble discomfited on the last note. The third verse uses high-pitched women's voices in a complaining whine, the atmosphere at the table is now definitely nasty. The fool tries to distract them, a plate is thrown at him which hits him on the side of his head and he sits down and rubs himself sadly. Music strikes up and the servants sidle on with cringing apology, make a pretence at offering to the now infuriated guests their dishes and go off at a run. (They have, of course, to run round the back of the stage to be ready for their next entrance.)

The last verse is spoken by all the diners. It starts on a low ominous note and rises, line by line, to a crescendo on the last line. There is a loud drum beat, the music starts and the servants strut in, ushered by the beaming steward; all carrying trays with mugs or beakers of ale. They circulate, giving a mug to each guest and one to the fool, and go off stage left. The music still continues as healths are drunk and the company congratulate themselves on at last having what they asked for. Then the master leads the lady on his right away from the table and all the company follow. They bow and curtsy and dance a Branle as the curtain falls. The music for the Branles is the record. During the Branles there can be a great deal of individual acting and not everyone need dance. One lady can console the fool, one man can prefer to continue drinking, but at least six should do the dance.

Twelfth Night was a tremendous celebration in the reign of Henry VIII, and there were many picturesque customs that are good mime material as well as some that are better left to the imagination.

The habit of wearing masks gave the courtiers greater freedom of speech and more chance to philander with a greater choice of ladies. There were candlelight processions, kissing rings hung up, and the costumes were decorated with extra knots of ribbons. Blind Man's Buff was a favoured game and eating and dancing alternated continuously for the days between Christmas and Twelfth Night. If the Capriole Suite by Peter Warlock is played through from beginning to end, with the exception of the Pavane, the various parts of the revelry will suggest themselves to the producer and the actors.

This is an opportunity to see how far they have all progressed in feeling for the Period Play, as they should now be able to throw themselves into a bygone age and improvise successfully enough to need no further instructions. If this does not seem at first possible it will be found that if the record is played over again, ideas begin to come and some sort of action is done by some of the players. If a short conference is held to pool the ideas, a scene will begin to shape itself, and the differing sections of the music will allow a variety of moods to be shown. There can be narrative using all the players or each dance form can have a different set of characters who come together for the finale. The scene can be the Great Hall or the Servants' Hall or a passage with windows in embrasures where dancers can sit out.

PART TWO

ELIZABETHAN, JACOBEAN AND STUART PERIODS

CHAPTER VII

THE SPIRIT OF THE PLAYS

Spirit of the periods—Development of plays and place of performance—Progression from Elizabethan to Jacobean and Stuart playing—List of reference books, period authors, and genuine period plays and modern period plays, both three-act and one-act

THE Elizabethan Play throws a vivid light on an age of rampant action and violent contrasts; the Jacobean Masque shows the way of escape from that world which was exhausting itself. This volume is intended for anyone embarking on such plays who, for various reasons, cannot do the necessary research for the purpose. It is only concerned with the theatrical possibilities of the plays and with what is practicable to present to an audience. These plays were entertainment of the most complete order for their intended audiences; the plays satisfied the extremes which composed the Elizabethan crowd and the masques excited the courtiers, for whom they were written, to great enthusiasm.

The Elizabethan period is sufficiently well known, in the popular sense, to make it difficult sometimes for the producer to galvanise his doubleted actors into the lusty life the plays present. Textual study at school has sickened many people of Shakespeare, and discouraged them entirely from attempting to read any other Elizabethans.

"If", they feel, "Shakespeare is the best, what must the others be like", and they reach thankfully for a thriller. They wallow shudderingly in sadistic violence, improbable blondes, crude humour and heroic rescues; exactly the same ingredients that the Elizabethans wanted and got from their plays. High tragedy, low comedy, brutal jests, cruel revenge and doomed love all exist in these plays side by side with spadelike prose and magnificent poetry. The audience is bludgeoned into attention by the violent happenings, transported by the splendid ringing sounds of the words and (which is also the main function of the thriller) carried away from suburban trivialities to another, larger world.

Elizabethan plays were written specially for actors and theatres known to the authors. The playwright was treated as a skilled employee. He was supposed to know the exact amount of stage room that was available, plus the acting capabilities of the cast, and he was expected to deliver goods which made the most of these assets.

The playgoing public was comparatively small and predominately townspeople, whether tradesmen or noblemen. The playwright knew what they wanted and blended it skilfully with what he wanted to write. In an age where new worlds were being discovered spiritually, mentally and physically, excitement of a violent kind was needed to attract people to the playhouse. The English language was growing richer and a feeling for fine words, led and encouraged by the Queen, gave the dramatists an advantage they used to the full.

The audience brought their own preoccupations and edible refreshments with them to the playhouse and the actors had to compete with these for their attention in a much more direct manner than the modern actor.

The Playhouse was built in a circle with the audience around three sides of the stage. There was no roof and no reason to suppose that the weather was any more equable than it is nowadays. In any theatre where the actor had to challenge Nature in direct competition (whether the theatre was Greek, Elizabethan, or Regent's Park) the acting had perforce to enlarge its scale. When the audience could look up at the vagaries of the weather and note blue skies or thunder clouds it affected the performances of the actors, who had to work hard to compete with the elements.

The plays were written in verse for a purpose, the length of the line carried the voice, the beat and the rhythm helped to establish the domination of the actor. The prose often used for the comedians presupposed slapstick business during which the words could be drowned in the laughter of the groundlings. It is also reasonable, remembering Hamlet's caustic comment on the temptation of the comics to gag, to think that the author did not intend to take too much trouble over lines which might not be heard. Printing was still a very costly business and the plays were written to be performed, not to be sold as textbooks for schools.

Actors were only classed as Rogues and Vagabonds if they were not attached to a special company; so, although certain changes in the cast were bound to take place in the course of time, the playwright knew which actors would be likely to play which parts at any given moment. He could also reckon on a large portion of the audience understanding references to matters of Court gossip, and an even larger portion relishing quips about local scandals. He knew that all the women's parts would be played by boys, who had a scarcity value and were temperamental to a degree. He knew, finally and absolutely, that there was no public conscience about the respect to the author due from the audience. If the play did not satisfy the audience, no power on earth would stop them from expressing their unexpurgated opinion at every pause in the action. The swiftness of the presentation with no waits for scene changes, bar orders, or curtain drops imposed a discipline on author and actor alike.

The actor needed a voice capable of tremendous range of tone and volume, and a body controlled to express every variety of emotion while encased, not to say hampered, by the rigid Elizabethan costume. He had to be able to convey an intensity of passion that would impress the groundlings, and to assume a nobility of manner that would convince the courtiers. The audience was so close that, were the actor to portray a simple tradesman, the courtiers had only to glance round to see if the acting matched the original model.

Equally, the apprentices sat cheek by jowl with the nobles, and could at once jeer if the portrayal was not true.

The modern actor is so unused to letting his voice rip, that he is apt to become fascinated by its full volume and forget the importance of pitch, pace and consonants. This will not do when playing any plays of this period. However golden the voice is, sheer sound is not enough, the sense of the words must come across. "Here cometh a foul murderer" must be what the audience hears and not "Eee-aww-eow-ererere" on a pealing wail. The style of acting throughout must be in key with the language; the comedians should not have the same vocal delivery that they would have if they were playing the poetic hero or the rhetorical Zeus. The modern producer of these plays starts with a number of text-books on the subject and a cast which is either apprehensive or over-confident. The modern audience has been cowed into knowing that if it does not enjoy the play, it has no one to blame but itself.

The successful producer of Elizabethan plays is the one who cares passionately for the fascinatingly complex characters who exist in such rich profusion in the plays. Even the tiny parts are rewarding; even the "walk-ons" need never find rehearsals boring with such words to hear. The producer must encourage his cast to leap over the hurdle of learning words as soon as possible, so that the urgency of sense and feeling can burst through. While some of the plots are involved and some of the language may cause difficulties, the dramatic force of the situations and characters is so strong that cast and producer can be carried over the problems in a wave of exhilaration.

The Elizabethans, of course, had no stage sets; any description of the scene that was necessary was put into the mouth of one of the characters. The shape of the stage of the period helped the actors; there were pillars for the "Here I will hide" speeches, and a balcony for the inner chamber so often used. Shakespeare never had to contend with the dismal square box of the Parish Hall stage. Therefore the modern producer must do something in the way of presenting his play in a manner which is acceptable to the audience. The really vital point is to have a variety of levels, so that the "See where he comes" speeches are not said by the actor face to face with the character to whom he refers. Lighting, while never used in the original presentations, is the most immense help in the modern theatre. The producer must remember that he is not presenting the play to an Elizabethan audience. Although he is dealing with the world's greatest dramatist, he must harness his imagination to recreate, with integrity, the basic quality that has made the play survive through the centuries.

The other dramatists of this period, both Elizabethan and Jacobean, need taking with a pinch of salt, but do not need salt thrown all over them. There is much that can be cut at the producer's discretion. What remains will still be exciting and dramatic; parts that demand virile acting and scenes that will grip the audience. The Elizabethan dramatists worked hard to create a form of play which the Jacobeans developed still further, but the reflection of contemporary life was markedly lacking in the Jacobean plays. They preferred to take themes and stories from the past, full of horrors, bloodshed and revenge. All these qualities were certainly present in Jacobean life, but not in the barbaric terms of the plays.

There is at the end of this chapter a list of these playwrights, all of whose plays are, of course, free from royalties.

The Masques are a totally different proposition. Although they were written mainly for amateurs, they hold some magnificent acting opportunities and are enormous fun for the producer. They are agonising for the person who enjoys using an acting edition with all stage directions clearly marked. It would be impossible to follow the stage directions of any masque literally unless the company had a bank balance of roughly £22,000. If, on the other hand, the producer has a taste for the fantastic and a cast of widely differing talents and experience, the masque is the medium which will give all the scope that both need. Ben Jonson's *Masque of Queens* has a cast which includes 24 ladies, 12 beauties who do not speak and 12 hags with juicy speaking parts. If a smaller cast is wanted, six witches could be exorcised and the rest snatch their lines. All the masques are capable of being suitable for any amateur who has the courage to adapt them to local conditions. The masques were the logical development of the pageant or entertainment put on for visiting royalty. They grew from the loyal address, spoken by the most notable person to welcome royalty, into short speeches from other locals and finally included songs, dances and stage effects. They became an entertainment of the Court because the emphasis was laid more and more on the gorgeous costumes and the actual masks which were used very coyly indeed. The Masquers were all courtiers, amateurs who were masked until the finale. Unlike the pageants which had dealt with historical characters, they portrayed gods and goddesses and mythical characters. Queen Elizabeth, in spite of a definite bias towards hearing herself described as a goddess, never took part in a masque, but Anne of Denmark and Henrietta Maria enjoyed acting in them. The masques were an important landmark in theatrical history, as they were a blend of verse, song, dance and comedy embellished with magnificent costumes, scenery, lighting, and stage machinery; they led the way to opera, ballet and stage presentation as it is now. They even had revolving stages, and so many cunning stage devices that for a long time England led the way in stage tricks and illusions. The script was not literary; it was meant to be used for a revel, and finally set in the form that survives. The distinguished people had all the speaking parts. The dances were done by the masquers (other courtiers) and the comedy was usually done by professional actors and tumblers. Wiser than many amateurs, they had an appreciation of just how difficult it is to be genuinely funny.

Ben Jonson wrote many masques, and Inigo Jones designed such lovely and ingenious settings that he stole all the thunder. Jonson's remark that "painting and carpentry are the soul of masque" must be put down to sour grapes.

The downfall of the masque was due to two things. Firstly, the ridiculous sums of money they cost, as competition between the City companies reared its ugly head. The Inns of Court, for instance, spent £21,000 on one performance of James Shirley's *Triumph of Peace*, and other companies surpassed this figure.

Secondly, with the coming of the Puritans, all such frivolity ceased and all the theatres were closed.

The theatres were to reopen during the Restoration of King Charles II, but the masques were not performed in theatres. They were played at Court, and in the City halls such as Merchant Taylors and the Guildhall. This was because part of the charm of the masque was that the actors descended at intervals and invited the onlookers to come and dance with them on the floor or on the stage. It was Audience Participation and Arena Production, Theatre in the Round and the Old World Music Hall all rolled into one.

In case all this sounds too intimidating, it might be of interest to mention a few modern productions of masques, performed by very differing groups which only have one thing in common: no money to spend on stage presentation.

A Women's Training College's students wrote their own masque from the classical model of Jonson, built their own open-air theatre and delighted a rural and urban audience. The students of the Summer School of the British Drama League put on Jonson's *Masque of Queens* one year, and another year did Neville Coghill's *Masque of Hope*, written for the present Queen when she was Princess Elizabeth. They had two weeks' rehearsals and the budget for each production worked out at roughly £2. 10s. Costumes and settings have to be fantastic so that anything and everything can be pressed into service. To quote an example, Neptune, in the *Masque of Hope*, wore a gilded arrangement of tennis netting, gilded seaweed and gilded shells. It was an English summer, so he rehearsed all through in a raincoat.

The masques can be done indoors or outdoors. The Anti Masque is the part which debunks the glorious Gods and Goddesses and gives great scope to comedians.

There was a brief revival of interest in masques around 1908, but the surviving scripts tend to be rather pale and sentimental and the producer is advised to go back to the period when they flourished and were successful.

The actors and actresses in a masque have to adopt a heroic attack for the verse, using a full voice and broad gestures. No lines are thrown away and there are no asides. Each character makes a definite theatrical entrance, advancing to the front of the stage and addressing the audience as he introduces himself. He should make a special bow to any notables in the audience before starting to speak. The technique is very similar to that of the modern pantomime and should be carried through with style and panache.

The masques all finish with a set piece of triumphant grouping or with a variant of the familiar walk down that takes place at the Palace steps at the end of the pantomime. The bows at the finale are in triplicate, to the left, to the right and to the centre starting by looking up at the gallery and finishing graciously at the stalls. This is because in the original Court productions the servants were allowed to watch from the gallery if they finished their work in time, so naturally vociferous applause had to be acknowledged when it came from above; but the actors' final smile had to be at the high-born people in the seats of honour below.

One stage direction may cause bewilderment as the word is not modern English. When the violins are asked to "frumple", it means they have to play a little mocking tune. It seems a pity that this word is used no longer as it is so expressive.

All the masques are neatly divided into sections, each quite distinct from each other, so the cast can also be divided, which simplifies rehearsal considerably. There can be actors, dancers, comedians, and if wanted or politic, a group of singers. There need only be two rehearsals when the entire cast is present; the first one and the dress rehearsal. There can also be one producer for the whole thing and three assistants, each responsible for the technical side of singing, dancing and the comedy.

The Jacobean playwrights mostly revelled in stark tragedy and showed a childlike pleasure in planning horrid revenges. The modern actor must stretch his imagination at every rehearsal until it breaks, if he is to retain and project his initial shock or horror to the audience. Improvisation at every third rehearsal is an immense help and will save time in the end. The time-pushed producer may find this hard to believe but it is a fact. If the situation is lifted out of the play and put into a modern setting, different facets of the characters are revealed. It is not denied that it is difficult to think of the modern equivalent for some of the situations. If a dinner guest instead of putting out his own hand to greet his hostess, suddenly produced a dead one from his pocket, explaining that it belonged to her brother, it would cause comment. In a Jacobean play it merely shows a habit of the character.

The masques have these attractions to offer:

Cynthia's Revels, by Ben Jonson, was written for boys. It starts with a scene to charm any boy, a struggle which developes into a running battle, as to which shall speak the very showy introduction.

The Masque of Queens, by Ben Jonson. This was the masque written for Queen Anne of Denmark. It starts with an exciting scene of witches trying to raise a storm with awful spells. The scene then changes completely and there is a procession of beautiful Queens and some entrancing songs and dances.

The Triumph of Peace, by James Shirley. This gorgeous spectacle cost the Inns of Court £21,000 to present to their Majesties, King James I and Queen Anne in 1624. It is most amusing in its dialogue between fictitious characters such as Confidence and Opinion and has a very funny scene when the wives of the property makers and stage hands break in because they have not been given the seats promised to them.

The Vision of the Twelve Goddesses, by Samuel Daniel, is ideal for an all-woman cast of actresses and also for an all-woman choir. It can be produced on a fairly small stage which can be built up with different levels and many of the entrances can be made through the auditorium. It is decorative rather than dramatic.

These are roughly the three differing types of masque the producer is likely to meet; the first has violent contrasts in cast and scene, the second and third have a consistant cast and scene and a great deal of humour, and the fourth concentrates more on setting, costumes, song and dance. The one thing that they have in common is that they were written for amateurs and therefore they demand the qualities that amateurs still can bring to them.

To sum up, the Elizabethan plays beat and throb like a drum, the Jacobean plays alternate the clash of cymbals with the tolling bell and the masques sing with the frumple of the violins.

List of Useful Books

An Introduction to Tudor Drama	Frederick S. Boas	(O.U.P.)
Stuart Masques and the Renaissance Stage	Allardyce Nicoll	(Harrap)
Scenes and Machines on the English Stage during the Renaissance	L. B. Campbell	(C.U.P.)
The Court Masque	Enid Welsford	(C.U.P.)
**Introduction to Stuart Drama*	Frederick S. Boas	(O.U.P.)
The English Masque	H. E. Evans	(Black

*This is an interesting analysis of fifteen dramatists with a chapter on Masques and Drolls.

The British Theatre Association, 9 Fitzroy Square, London W1P 6AE, has a play library, and gives advice and information to all its members; books can be borrowed singly as well as in sets for play-reading .

RaDiuS, St. Paul's Church, Covent Garden, Bedford Street, London WC2E 9ED, specialises in advice and help on religious drama to all its members.

List of Playwrights

Sir Thomas Wyatt	1503 (?)–1542
Edmund Spencer	1552 (?)–1599
Sir Philip Sidney	1554–1586
John Lyly	1554 (?)–1606
Robert Greene	1560–1592
George Chapman	1559–1634
Daniel Samuel	1562–1619
Christopher Marlowe	1564–1593
William Shakespeare	1564–1616
J. Day	1574–1640
John Fletcher	1574–1625
Philip Massinger	1583–1640
Francis Beaumont	1584–1616
Richard Broome	1585–1652
Nathaniel Field	1587–1633
James Shirley	1596–1666
Thomas Kyd	1558–1595
H. Porter	1597–1640

Some Genuine Plays of these Periods
are contained in:

Great English Plays	ed. Harold F. Rubinstein	(Gollancz)
Bell's Plays Vols. I, II and III		(Bell)
Representative English Comedies Vols. I, II and III	ed. Charles Mills Gayley	(Macmillan, N.Y.)

Some Modern Plays about these Two Periods

Three-Act

Elizabeth the Queen	Maxwell Anderson		(French, N.Y.)
Mary of Scotland	Gordon Daviot		(French, N.Y.)
Queen of Scots	Gordon Daviot		(French)
Spring 1600	Emlyn Williams		(Heinemann)
Mary Stuart	Friederich Schiller		
	trs. by J. Mellish		(Bell)
	trs. by S. Spender		(Faber)
Will Shakespeare	Clemence Dane		(French)
Charles the King	Maurice Colbourne		(French)
King's Way	Joan Brampton		(Deane)
Oliver Cromwell	John Drinkwater		(Sidgwick & Jackson)
Gallant Cassian	Arthur Schnitzler	17th Century	(Gowans & Gray)
	trs. by Adam L. Gowans		

Cyrano de Bergerac	Edmond Rostand trs. by Henderson D. Norman and Brian Hooker		(Heinemann) (Allen & Unwin)
Elga	Gerhardt Hauptmann trs. by Ludwig Lewisohn	17th Century	(Secker & Warburg)
The White Saviour	Gerhardt Hauptmann trs. by Willa and Edwin Muir	16th Century	(Secker & Warburg)

One-Act

**Recruit for Drake* (in *Plays for the Family Goodman*, 1485-1666)	L. du Garde Peach	1595	(Pitman)
**Strolling Players* (in *Practical Plays for Stage and Classroom, Series* 1)	L. du Garde Peach	Late 16th or early 17th Century	(U.L.P.)
**The Victim*	Evan John	Early 17th Century	(French)
The Dark Lady of the Sonnets	G. Bernard Shaw	16th Century	(Constable)
**The King's Servant*	Mary Pakington	1639	(French)
**Women at War*	Edward Percy	1645	(French)
Allison's Lad	Beulah Marie Dix	1648	(Nelson)
**Blind Milton*	Edna Mary Howe	1667	(French)
**Battle in the Kitchen*	Mary Biscombe	1653	(Queckett, Evans)

* Suitable for Youth Clubs.

CHAPTER VIII

MOVEMENT IN COSTUME

Outline of costume from 1558 *to* 1630*—Movement in costume—List of costume accessories for movement for each period—List of costume books—List of artists for each period, who sum up the visual aspect of the times*

IN a battle between the players and the Elizabethan costume, the costume often seems to win, and succeeds in suppressing the personality of the players. The doublets and farthingales appear capable of walking by themselves from the costumiers to the dress rehearsal, through the performances and on to the next company, with a lofty disregard for the transitory bodies that briefly inhabit them. As the real Elizabethans were all strongly, not to say peculiarly, individualistic, this is the worst thing that could happen. It is refreshingly evident when the wardrobe is *not* hired, and the clothes express the character's choice; the play gains at once in reality. Some companies fear that if a set of such clothes is made it will tie up a good deal of money; or they will be put in the position of having to use exactly the same costumes for parts as different as Benedict and Osric because the initial outlay must be justified. This need not be the case if the company is prepared to have an adaptable wardrobe, with interchangeable garments, as suggested in costume books. It is worthwhile to strain every nerve, and everyone's purse to achieve this kind of wardrobe, as every penny spent is an asset, instead of a sad memory of the costumier's bill in the accounts.

The change in outline from the Elizabethan to the Jacobean and then to the Cavalier is like the gradual deflation of a balloon. The breeches sank from the balloon shape to the melon in James I's time and drooped into a loose soft knickerbocker in Charles I's reign. The stiff padding of the Elizabethan breeches provided built-in cushions when men sat on the hard oak stools, and many bitter complaints were voiced when, in Charles I's time, the cavaliers had the same furniture but only soft satin.

The outline of the upper part of the figure changed from the doublet with its curving stomacher and melon-shaped sleeves to the longer doublet with stiff sleeves and finally to a loose jacket worn over a loose shirt with lace ruffles at throat and wrist.

To put it briefly, the Elizabethan clothes could stand up by themselves, the Jacobean could lean against a wall, while the Cavalier clothes could have taken off from the ground in a strong breeze.

Where Drake would straddle, Guy Fawkes would stalk and Lovelace would flap. *His* hat had a floppy brim and a streaming feather, his boots had a flap turned over at the top or his shoes had rosettes or tongues that flipped. Even the hair descends from the crisp shagginess of 1558 to the long soft curls of the Cavaliers.

The outline of the Elizabethan man is typical of the age. It is assertive, glittering, stiff with an arrogance that displayed itself in ruffs and farthingales regardless of cost or comfort. It is one of the most difficult costumes to wear convincingly. The whole pose of the body is totally alien to every attitude that the modern uses easily and yet all the Elizabethans were such individualists that they cannot be presented as walking waxworks.

The doublet fitted tightly to the body, the ruff fitted stiffly round the neck, stockings reached to above the knee and were fastened up to the waistline by points or laces—these are the three main strangenesses for the modern actor. He should rehearse with a token ruff, a doublet and hose as soon as possible, in order to discover where the pinch comes. Even if he only tries it in his bedroom, he will be startled at the way his movement is hampered. There might be a scene where he throws himself angrily into a chair, drums with his fingers on the arm of it and then springs furiously to his feet. By the time he has done all this in his improvised garments so much will have come apart and down, that he will be only too thankful he is rehearsing in private.

A similar downward droop had occurred in women's clothes. The wide farthingale gave way to the stiffened Jacobean skirt, and finally to the graceful flowing line of Queen Henrietta's dresses. Padding and stiff embroidery had gone, the bodice was laced across the front and deep lace collar and cuffs were worn instead of the high ruff.

The hair, taken up on top and frizzed in Elizabeth's time, dressed high but more smoothly for James, was by 1630 a charming sight. It was either brushed back from the face or there was a row of little curls across the forehead and the back hair was dressed high on the back of the head in a knot. The side hair was braided, curled or hung loosely at the side of the face and was tied back with ribbons. No lady went out in public without a mask. This was a small affair tied on with ribbon, or rectangular, and mounted on a holder like a lorgnette.

Movement became more graceful as the artificial stiffening went out of fashion, and the body could dominate the clothes instead of vice versa. It was not only possible to run in a Charles I gown, but it even paid ladies to do so. The skirt billowed and followed the movement charmingly. Shoes had a medium heel and now, at last, there was nothing to upset the balance. No heavy headdress, no drumlike farthingale, no rigid ruff; this meant a freedom that had been denied to women since the early medieval period.

It is essential for the actor to discover at the first

possible moment what he is going to wear and whether there are any hand props or accessories. There may be no hand props relevant to his scene in the play but he might ask himself if any normal person exists without any accessories, except patients in hospitals. A young man may not call them accessories, he may think of them as necessities, but handkerchiefs, keys, purses or notecases, letters, combs are the things that make the difference between a suit of clothes in the shop and a suit with an owner in it.

The Elizabethan had his own habits of hoarding, and the items chosen by the actor must be in keeping with the character. It helps if they can be used dramatically. If a love letter is referred to but never seen, it still helps to have it in the pocket, but generally speaking things which can be used dramatically should be chosen. There is a list at the end of this chapter to help the choice, but it is no use just carrying something as an extra. Personal property must be personal; the actor or actress must know why they chose it and how they want to use it. A fan, for instance, is often carried by an actress who does not fan herself and clearly finds it rather in the way. A fan carried by another actress is waved the whole time as if it worked by electricity, even during dialogue, in which she complains of the cold. Yet a third actress will hang the fan from her girdle, then remember it suddenly and begin to fan herself in a conscience-stricken way as if it were a forgotten duty. Fans are dramatically very useful for pointing lines and to fill in silences, but their full importance will not be discovered quickly; they must be taken to rehearsal early on.

The main difficulty for the actress is the immense amount of room that the farthingale takes up. It is often necessary to approach a door sideways and gently edge the leading shoulder and hip through it before allowing the rest of the body to follow, so that although the legs are walking forwards, the body is turned. This slight twist of the waist is better than a crablike sidle.

When approaching a chair from the right side, room must be allowed to sweep the farthingale forward from the right hip past the chair before taking a small step backwards to sit down in it. It is not easy to find any substitute for the farthingale in which to rehearse as no lampshade is large enough, but a child's hoop, fastened with strings to the belt helps the actress to gauge roughly the amount of space she is likely to need. Shoes had a medium heel for indoors and a wedgelike shape for outdoor wear in muddy weather; neither of these are difficult to manage. The long, tight bodice and rigid stomacher are essential for the right outline and entirely strange to the modern girl. If a couple of rulers are wedged down the front of the body, held in place by the waistband of dress and skirt, it will immediately convey to the actress the way she must move. The body can turn from the waist but it cannot give or sag. The arms cannot hang at the sides because of the line of the skirt, so that there are three alternative resting positions. The hands can rest lightly on the edge of the farthingale, they can be placed on top of each other, palms up, at the waist, or they can be clasped together at the waist with the thumbs on top and knuckles pointing down. There was a stiff roll at the top of the sleeve so that the under arm was held away from the body. The ruff, like a piefrill, was most attractive and, although scratchy, is easy to wear. The ruff, wired and boned and standing up at the back of the head, needs careful attention to head angles if the audience is to get the full benefit of the actress's facial expression. It is not possible for the actress to judge for herself; the producer should watch and see that the ruff does not hide her face. The actor has the advantage here, that as his ruff is the flat type, so it focusses attention on his face. The men's ruffs became bigger and bigger as time went on until absurd proportions were reached. A dandy would choose an enormous ruff where an ordinary gentleman would wear a medium-size one. As these ruffs are quite easy to make, it should be possible to get an interesting contrast in such a way without relying on the costumier, who cannot be expected to cater for such individuality. Henry VIII had made an edict that handkerchiefs must be square, but they could be of plain linen or lace trimmed or spangled. Gloves were richly decorated and fringed and sometimes even poisoned; these can be most effective for characteristic gesture. Combs and mirrors were carried by gallants, and dandies used to comb their beards, wax their moustaches, use perfume and curl their hair.

The movement for the actor must be swaggering and virile. The men still had plenty of physical activity in their lives, even if not as much as in medieval times, and this must show. All men could fight, ride and walk miles if they needs must, and physical prowess was important and admired. The hat was swept off with a brave flourish, the cloak swung gaily and the flat square shoes were planted firmly on the ground. There was so much padding, stiffening and trussing up, that balance had not the unconscious ease it has nowadays. A man had to make an allowance for the extra room he took up and the extra weight he carried and for the fact that in the narrow streets everyone jostled.

Fans were carried in all three periods. In 1558 the fans were the folding type made of chicken skin painted with portraits or scenes of dalliance or gilded flowers. Feathers, either spiky or fluffy, were favoured. The Queen herself liked peacock feathers particularly. Some ladies had hard fans shaped like a pingpong bat, and many of these had a little mirror in the centre. When the sleeves fitted tightly with a roll of stuffing under the arms, the fan movement was more from the shoulder, but when the sleeves were soft or short, the fan movement came from the wrist. The Elizabethans and the Jacobeans therefore used the shoulder movement, and the Cavalier ladies used the wrist to wave their fans. They now had a most attractive shape for their fans. These were square, mounted on a stick, and had lace eyeholes through which the ladies could peer without looking inquisitive. The lace frill at the cuff added grace to the sway of the fan. There is a very complicated language of the fan which must have been invaluable for intrigue and flirtation. It is useless for theatrical purposes as the audience would not know the code.

The country ladies of any of the periods under consideration did not wear such rich materials as the court beauties, and were often several years behind with the fashions. News travelled slowly, dresses were made of material that lasted for years and were handed down from mother to daughter. In a stage presentation these things must all be taken into consideration, and a scene set in Devonshire should not look the same as one set in St. James's Palace.

Serving maids all wore plain, one-colour dresses with an apron and bonnet-shaped cap of linen and a plain kerchief around the neck. Men servants wore breeches, plain doublets of leather or cloth and low round shoes with a plain tab. For holidays the colours were gayer and the jerkin often had pewter buttons down the front.

The producer can help the actors to bring the characters to life if he suggests suitable accessories and hand props. He can also help the audience to recognise the status of people in the crowd. Trades and professions had their distinctive dresses but, as nowadays the audience would not know many of these uniforms, only those useful for stage purposes have been given.

Apothecaries, lawyers and doctors wore dark brown, grey or black with plain linen ruffles and cuff bands.

The protestant clergy wore a long cassock, white tunic with long full sleeves and a sleeveless gown of black or any other sombre shade. The full white sleeves of the under tunic emerged from the sleeveless gown. The hat was either a four-pointed cap or a flat one with ear flaps.

Merchants, who became very important at this time, wore plain clothes made of good material; their cloaks were hooded or furred, and their hats were of beaver. The older men would stick to the older fashions.

It was laid down by the law, in a number of cases, exactly what might and what might not be worn by various sections of the populace, so that it was much easier than it is now for a shopkeeper to tell to what section of society his customer belonged.

Lower servants wore blue coats, and so did the apprentices, similar to the uniform of the modern schoolboys of Christ's Hospital.

Monks' habits have not changed through the centuries, but after the dissolution of the monasteries by Henry VIII the friars were not the familiar figures that they were in the medieval period.

Pedlars, such as Autolycus, would choose brightly coloured clothes such as russet breeches and jerkin, white kersey stockings and perhaps yellow buckles to their shoes (*see* Fig. 13).

Countrymen wore sheepskin doublets, felt hats, kersey stockings and thick shoes for work. For a feast day they wore, according to their taste, grey, white or green kersey stockings, russet, blue or red doublet faced with another colour, pewter or painted wooden buttons down the front and a green or red hat to match the kerchief round their neck. Each tradesman had a different kind of apron but for stage purposes it is sufficient if each has either a different coloured apron or ties it differently, without bothering which apron belongs to which trade.

Masque costumes were a wonderful mixture of fact and

FIG. 13. Ballad Sheet Pedlar

fantasy, and the designs of Inigo Jones are some of the most beautiful in theatrical history. The courtiers who wore them were, from the neck to the waist, gods and goddesses, decked with gold and jewels representing corn or flowers. From waist to foot they were equally clearly Jacobean with the usual skirt or breeches. Their hair-dressing was Jacobean with a Masque headdress perched on top (*see* Figs. 14 and 15).

No lady would have dreamt of appearing as Venus without heeled shoes, corsets and a small farthingale under her draperies.

Women, it must be remembered, were still banned from the professional stage, had indeed never appeared on it. The medieval actresses of early times had been nuns and when the plays moved out of the church no woman took part. So the ladies in the masques had the added charm of complete novelty. As they were also Court ladies, they were in a very strong position to make their own conditions as to what they wore and how they wore it. The modern actress owes them a debt of gratitude, as they were the thin end of the wedge which was to open the door to the notorious and lovely Restoration actresses on the professional stage.

Although few people now understand the symbolism of the use of colour at this period, it may help the producer if a brief mention is made of it.

It is an interesting experiment to dress a character in his appropriate colour at rehearsal and see what difference it might make to his interpretation or to the scene generally. It can even affect the stage position of the character. If the producer had intended to dress the character in crimson, whose traditional colour is willow green, it could well be that in the green colour the actor would have to be brought further forward in order to stand out in the same way as the crimson had made him dominate when he stood further back.

FIG. 14. Jacobean Masque. Man

FIG. 15. Jacobean Masque. Lady

Willow green stood for despair. If an actor had gone off in blue, to do some desperate act and returned in a later scene in willow green, he had only to hold his entrance position for the audience to realise with sympathetic horror that he had failed and doom was upon him.

Carnation and flame colours were reserved for lovers, happy and successful, passionate and desperate or merely mildly united; but this tradition did not apply to married people. Only while the pursuit was still on, did they flaunt these shades.

Yellow was worn by Fools, but a Court Fool did not dress like a stage fool; he had more liberty and could wear blue, red or green trimmed with other colours.

Mulberry was popular everywhere and could be worn in the town, the country or even as a livery by servants.

Sky blue was entirely a colour for servants in the sixteenth century. The blue worn by apprentices was darker as they had paid for their training and were in the process of becoming recognised as skilled workers.

Orange and tawny colours were reserved for courtiers; although other colours could be chosen, these two marked the courtier and were not worn by the workpeople.

Straw colour meant abundance, which could be interpreted as honours, money, wealth of land, or even charm.

At one period Queen Elizabeth insisted on all her ladies-in-waiting dressing alike in white and silver only. Brides did not wear white unless they particularly wanted to; there was no feeling about it being appropriate and as far as the Court ladies went, it was probably not.

Popinjay blue was a most beautiful vivid blue-green and was supposed to be the mark of a flirt. It was exceedingly popular among the Court ladies, used for part of the dress, not for the whole dress. The modern idea of "separates" as a useful way of stretching a small wardrobe was fully anticipated by the Court ladies. Popinjay sleeves could be tied in with "points" to a dove-grey dress as a lure, and when the mood changed and the suitor had to be kept at bay, dove-grey sleeves and a pure expression showed him how mistaken he was in his original opinion of the lady. For those damsels with a taste for dramatising themselves, a straw-coloured dress could have carnation sleeves when love was successful, yellow ones when she wanted to explain it had all been in fun, and willow-green sleeves, underskirt, and fan when her lover had been unfaithful or had jilted her. The possibilities were endless and fully exploited in the theatre of the time.

Widows were always supposed to wear black. They had to cover their hair completely with whatever head-dress was in fashion, made in black with a black veil. When she began to wear a couple of ornaments and pushed her cap back to show her hair, it was a sign that a widow was ready to accept a new offer of marriage.

Servants, clad in black, showed that an important member of the household had recently died. Of course the Court went into black whenever Royal Mourning was decreed.

People usually wore black or white for their execution, but Mary Queen of Scots, dramatic to the last, chose scarlet.

Rulers

England		*France*		*Spain*	
Queen Elizabeth	1558–1603	Francis II	1559–60	Philip II	1556–98
		Charles IX	1560–74		
		Henry III	1574–89		
James I	1603–25	Henry IV	1589–1610	Philip III	1598–1621
Charles I	1625–49	Louis XIII	1610–43	Philip IV	1621–65
Oliver Cromwell	1649–60	Louis XIV	1643–1715		

James I had Anne of Denmark as Queen.
Charles I had Henrietta Maria of France as Queen.

Accessories for Movement

Costume accessories for women to help with hand movements

1558 *onwards*

A train can be worn for festive occasions and looped up with hooks, ribbons or buttons for dancing.

With the velvet bonnet worn for outdoors can be added a plume, or a buckle or a jewelled brooch can be pinned on it.

Pearls can be worn looped across the stomacher, around the neck, in the hair across the forehead, as earrings or as bracelets.

Other jewels can be worn in shoe buckles, lockets and garter clasps.

Small hand mirrors can hang from ribbons at the waist.

A triangular small bag can hang from the waist and can hold scent bottle, coins, penknife, scissors and a handkerchief.

Muffs can be carried, and scented and embroidered or spangled gloves.

Courtesans wore a deathhead ring. Married women wore their wedding ring on the first finger of the left hand, but this is not advisable on the stage as it would muddle the audience.

Gowns to be laced up the back.

Sleeves may be tied on with points.

Bands of linen, lace or cambric to be adjusted at wrists.

Belts and girdles of gold, silver cord or twisted silk cord may carry gloves, mirrors or fans, or masks, pomanders or eggwatches.

Shoes to put on for outdoor wear have high cork soles like "wedges". For indoor wear shoes have high heels and can be of leather, silk or velvet and can be laced up.

Ruffs to put on may be pie frill or catherine-wheel shaped, and starched blue, white, pink or yellow.

1590 *onwards*

The wide upstanding lace collar to the dress may be tied with a bow above the sides.
A ruff may be put on underneath to hold it up.
Hair may be dressed more smoothly without jewellery on the forehead, but lace ruffs, feathers and jewels may be used to ornament the hair.
Maids may do their hair plainly with a knot on the neck.
They may wear a shawl, put on with a wide linen collar, linen cuffs and linen cap.
(Naturally these clothes did not go immediately out of fashion; the dates show the trends of fashion.)

1620 *onwards*

The bodice can be fastened in the front with a series of bows or jewelled buttons, a deep lace collar can be put on and deep lace cuffs, and tied with a soft bow or fastened with a brooch.
The hair can be curled with a row of little curls across the forehead, or cut in a light fringe.
In the first part of Charles I's reign the hair may be curled to fall each side of the face or it may have a knot at the back of the head with side curls, or brushed straight back.
Hair can be trimmed with pearls or feathers.
Country women can wear homespun blue, black, red, green or grey with a square handkerchief round the neck and a broad brimmed beaver hat.
Shoes may be ornamented with shoe-roses made of ribbons and jewels.
Sleeves of the overgown may be tied with a knot of ribbon, so may a sash, and the overshirt may be caught up with knots of ribbon.
Veils can be worn for outdoors, or hooded cloaks and a small mask.
Pendant earrings, gold and silver bodkins, rings, necklaces and all sorts of jewelled buttons can be worn.

The handkerchief can be buttoned to the dress.
Feather fans, round and oval, can be used, but the folding fan of ivory, satin or leather, either shell-shaped or oval, was more fashionable, and Italian paper fans were becoming the mode.

In all these periods the face can be painted, the eyebrows pencilled, rouge and powder used. Hot irons can be used to curl the hair, and dye for the hair was used. After 1630 patches were used cut in crescents, triangles and stars of black silk or velvet and placed on the cheek or neck.

Men's accessories to help in hand positions

1558 *onwards*

The purse hangs on one side with a slit behind to hold the dagger.
Gloves have cut knuckles to show the rings.
Men can wear a pointed beard or moustache, or be clean-shaven.
Hair can be curled or frizzed with or without the beard or moustache.
Sleeves can be slit and clasped with gold clasps, and have buttons as ornaments or can button closely.
Shoes can be tied with a cord which comes from the back of the heel, not the instep; can be of material or leather with a buckle to fasten, or a rosette for ornament. Men wear coloured leather boots for riding.
Stockings of wool or silk embroidery may be pulled up over the edge of the breeches or gartered by the knee.
The wide breeches must be stuffed with material (so that they can be shown as work done by tailors). Those that are cut in the tight French way can be pushed up in puffs. The slashed breeches are Venetian and the puffs need pulling out between the latice-shaped braiding.
Short cloaks or a longer Venetian cloak can be worn slung over the right shoulder.

The doublet can have sleeves tied into it by ribbons or laces with tags, which are called "points".

Hats to wear or hold or adjust the trimmings—a change of trimmings for a festive occasion.

Hat shapes—steeple crowned, narrow brimmed or flat crowns and broad brims.

Trimmings to hat bands are of ribbon, lace, silk cord or gold chain, with or without plumes.

1590 *onwards*

Tobacco pouch may be carried at belt, and tobacco chewed.

Tobacco boxes with mirrored lids may be used.

Clay pipes may be used and lit by tinder boxes.

Tooth picks, ornamented and gilded, may be used.

Gloves are scented, hair is frizzed, curled with tongs and dyed.

Hair may be worn rather longer than the Elizabethan—moustaches and beard still fashionable.

Pocket watches are fashionable.

The melon-shaped breeches may be buttoned at the knee or tied.

Tall boots may be used instead of shoes.

The hat brim may be worn wider and a square ruff may be tied round the neck.

Apprentices can wear flat caps, doublets and breeches.

1620 *onwards*

Swords can be worn on the left side and a circular cloak can be draped over the left shoulder.

Cloaks can be fastened with straps to hang from the shoulders, or draped over the arm.

A muff can be carried.

Waist-high canes, with carved heads or bunches of ribbons on them may be used.

Black patches of various shapes may be used on the face.

Men wear (and can finger) lockets, rings, jewelled points,

jewelled daggers, earrings, lace collars, lace cuffs and a wide sash about the shoulders or waist.

The lace cuffs may be turned down or up.

Shirts can be open at the neck.

The Vandyke collar of wide-pointed lace may be tied with ribbons or fastened with a brilliantly jewelled brooch, or the strings passed through a jewelled ring.

Elaborate garters can be worn and lace edges turned back over the boot tops.

The boots (high heeled and square toed) can have replaceable linings to the turn-over of satin, silk or velvet.

Spurs are nearly always worn and a titled man may wear red heels.

Knots of ribbons may be fastened almost anywhere—the gallant would have more than the student.

Breeches may be untied at the knee, but should have a row of bows at the waist.

The waist of the doublet can be pulled in with a lacing tied in bows, and breeches can be buttoned over a lining which shows by a row of buttons and loops.

The doublet may be tied with a broad or narrow sash round the waist.

Hair can be tied with a ribbon; a fringe may be worn.

Lovelocks are the two locks at each side of the face and these may be curled, braided or tied with ribbons; the moustache may be waxed, turned up at the ends or sharply pointed.

Hats can be worn with a broad brim turned up at back, side or front and ornamented with flowing plumes.

List of Useful Reference Books

For help in Costume, Setting and Properties of the Period

A History of Everyday Things in England, Vol. II, 1500–1799 — M. & C.H.B. Quennel (Batsford)

English Homelife, 1500 to 1800 — Christina Hole (Batsford)

Interesting and practical background for any producer, these books are not concerned with the theatrical side.

Dressing the Play Norah Lambourne (Studio)
This gives materials, details of patterns in vogue for stencilling dresses, ways of dyeing materials for dresses, tapestries, banners, stained-glass windows, etc. How to make jewellery, armour, weapons, and how to plan an adaptable wardrobe. Also how to design and plan the costumes for an entire production for each period.

Dressing the Part Fairfax P. Walkup (Harrap)
Survey of costume from the Roman times to present day, with small drawings showing details of shoes, head-dresses, hair-dressing, under garments, etc. No actual patterns of how to make them, although some details drawn showing cut of coats, etc.

English Costume in the Age of Elizabeth Iris Brooke (Black)
Very good coloured plates.

Adaptable Stage Costume for Women Elizabeth Russell (Garnet Miller)
Basic bodice and skirt with additions and accessories for each period from Saxon to Victorian. Detailed patterns and sewing instructions.

List of Artists of the Period

16th Century

Michelangelo	Raphael	Andrea del Sarto
Giorgione	Titian	Tintoretto
Veronese	Luini	El Greco
Albrecht Dürer	Pieter & Jan Breughel	Antonio Moro

17th Century

Claude Lorrain	Pierre Mignard	Frans Hals
Rembrandt	Jan Steen	Pieter de Hoogh
Vermeer	Rubens	Van Dyck

Architect: Sir Christopher Wren.

Sculptor and Designer: Inigo Jones.

CHAPTER IX

OCCUPATIONS

Occupations and games and amusements of the periods for stage, arena or pageant production—Classified list for each period: servants, tradesmen, ladies, etc.—Useful book

THE ordinary business of living became progressively easier from the Tudor reign of the sixteenth century to the Commonwealth of the seventeenth century. Houses were built on the same plans as nowadays with an entrance hall, small and large rooms, kitchen and stables.

The outside appearance changed considerably between the reigns of Elizabeth and Charles I. The Tudor houses of the sixteenth century were mostly of pale cream plaster and black beams, but new houses were being built in the shape of the letter "E" of warm rose-coloured brick. The roofs were gabled and pointed, also of rose-coloured tiles, and the chimneys were ornamented by the way of bricks laid in different patterns. The windows were long, low casements with small diamond-shaped panes.

The Charles I houses were square and taller than before, with tall sashed windows. Pillars were built to support the porches and to embellish each side of the windows. In all these periods there was a place outside the front door to tie up a horse.

Although a family might live in the same house for generations, this can be ignored for stage purposes. It is baffling for the audience to see a Stuart family in a Tudor house. Unless the play stresses the fact that the house is an heirloom, it is better to show a Stuart family in a Stuart house.

Tudor gardens had walls to them with trees trained flat against them. Herb gardens had lavender, rosemary and other herbs planted in beds shaped like knots, which were edged with box hedges.

The Elizabethans introduced wooden staircases with beautifully carved newel posts and bannisters, and the long picture gallery, where the ladies of the house could walk in rainy weather, the children play, and the young people practise their dance steps.

In Stuart houses the globe had its place in the study or the schoolroom, it was not merely an ornament.

There were plenty of servants and, although the strict division of duties of the Middle Ages had lapsed, there was plenty of work for them to do. Pages still existed, but it was more of an honorary title than a complete job. Pages always had a part to play in official ceremonies and their duties were confined mainly to these occasions.

On the stage ladies of the period usually sit doing nothing for hours, but this is not an accurate picture of their lives, and in many cases their occupations could add interest and reality to the scene.

They were trained and expected to cope with all household emergencies. Even Lady Macbeth had to give orders to prepare for the visit of the King, before she presumably looked in her address book for the names of useful cheap murderers. All bed linen and personal linen had to be made, food prepared, preserved and inspected, wines and possets brewed, ointments, potions (pure and poisoned) and lotions made, before the ladies started on the frills of life such as lace making and embroidery. (*See* Fig. 16.) Printing was expensive, so the children had hornbooks. These were oblong, shaped like a slate, mounted on a handle which had a hole with a cord to hang it by. (*See* Fig. 17.) The wood was covered with a sheet of horn, under which was a piece of paper with the letters of the alphabet on it, either in print or writing, and with numbers and a prayer. The children learned from these, and when they had finished one lesson another

Fig. 16. Lady Making Beauty Potion

Fig. 17. Boy (Jacobean) with Hornbook

sheet of paper could be inserted under the transparent horn.

All recipes had to be copied out by hand and ladies bound their own books of these with silk or velvet and an embroidered bookmark. Wax candles were used and made by the stillroom servants.

When the stage direction says "A room in the manor", the producer has a chance to make an unusual choice, and need not subject the audience to yet another panelled square with a mullioned window centre back. Rooms and houses reflected their owner's taste, and there would be some men who would only feel at home in their own stables.

In many plays a scene begins with the servants preparing for a visitor, and these actions can tell a great deal to the audience, both about the household and the visitor. If there is only a perfunctory straightening of a few things and one servant roughly combs his hair with his fingers, it shows a casual staff and an unimportant guest. If every possible surface is being polished feverishly while an under-servant is cuffed because of his wrinkled stockings, the audience is prepared for what is to follow. As houses and their furnishings changed during the three periods so the duties of the household altered. These actions help to draw attention to any special detail that the producer has chosen to convey the period of the play. They set the period in the mind of the audience, and they feed the imaginations of the actors.

The games and amusements, with their alternating spasms of action and pause, are most useful in pointing dialogue. They should be played in a characteristic manner by each actor, and with mannerisms and individuality. The vigorous games were played by the men and the quieter ones by the women, or older men. Some were clearly of the people and some belonged to the Court. Reading was still an accomplishment, not an everyday amusement of the working man, although he could read a playbill or an edict.

English children have always had a wide choice of games and toys, and these can add a welcome touch of gaiety to a pageant. The children used in pageants often seem to hang about until the maypole comes and they can do their dances. In Tudor and in Stuart times they would all have had their own little ploys.

All occupations and amusements, it cannot be too often stressed, must be treated from a production point-of-view, with attention to character and atmosphere, not merely used as trimmings in a play. In a pageant, where the intention is usually to include as many people as possible, they can be used as pattern and decoration. The producer should keep this distinction of function clearly in his mind.

Either work or play can give great variety in a static group, can give a rational reason for a change of grouping, and is invaluable in an arena production where the angles from which the cast must be viewed are so wide. A game of kayles or ninepins gives a chance for one or more actors to run forward to set up the fallen pins, for a concerted move for them all to see a lucky hit, or a group exit to bring back a stick that has been hurled too far. A game of dice can make an admirable excuse for eavesdroppers, who can appear absorbed in the game but are able to lean backwards and listen to a plot.

The great advantage of games on the stage is that they make the actor himself use so many different levels in his own body. Where a producer is working on a small stage and cannot have steps and dais, a game will often solve these problems. An actor will naturally have to stoop to roll his ball at bowls, he will kneel to see if his ball has touched the other and he will want to stretch after crouching to set the jack. These attitudes will spring naturally from the game and give variety to the group, whereas he could not possibly stoop, kneel, stretch and crouch merely because the producer wanted a change of position.

Character shows up disconcertingly in games. One man will seize every opportunity to practise, even when alone; while another must have an admiring spectator to feed him with praise. The card cheater carries his own marked pack; the born gambler will try his luck with anyone. Individual characterisation is the important point, it must not be lost in period movement but heightened by it.

There are points that are better treated theatrically than truthfully. While table manners were rough according to modern standards they *were* manners and there were many hints on etiquette. Bones were chewed, but politely. Fingers were dipped in the offered bowl of water and dried on a napkin and the mouth was wiped before drinking. For stage performances it is usually assumed that the manners shown are the best of the time for the simple reason that if the worst were shown the audience would be so enthralled that no attention would be paid to the dialogue.

The audience for the masques consisted of guests, the Court and the Court servants who were used to ceremony and to formal manners. So the manners of the Gods and Goddesses were the same as those of Dukes and Duchesses, while the comedians had the manners of the workers as they were professionals. Their comedy could include practical jokes such as setting a chair and withdrawing it just as the person sat, and custard throwing.

In the time of Charles I lace-making was becoming universal. Peasant women made the coarser kind and ladies and young girls had their little pillows and bobbins always at hand. Needlework of all kinds was taught to little girls, and the ladies of the house revelled in decorating their rooms with hanging tapestries, pretty cushions, chair seats, curtains and tablecloths trimmed with lace or embroidered by themselves. They would never have tolerated the bedraggled nondescript pieces of cloth that the average actress uses as a hand prop. Embroidery frames can be large enough for four girls to work at, if the completed panel is to be hung on the wall, or they can be a tiny square if one girl is putting her crest on a handkerchief.

Yellow tallow candles and rush dips were made and used by the working classes. Wax candles were made and used in fine houses. Pewter, brass and silver candlesticks were used and had to be polished. Candles had to be snuffed with snuffers made like scissors with a small box at the side which caught the wick as it fell.

A tinder box was used for lighting anything. This was a box with steel and flint on top and a little heap of rag underneath inside it. The steel and flint were rubbed together until a spark fell on to the tinder. The spark was blown until it glowed, when a stick dipped in melted brimstone was laid across it. When the flame flared the candles and the rush lights were lit from it. The tinder had to be sorted and dried in the oven and the rushes for dips had to be gathered from the river; while the wax had to be taken from the hives, so that even this primitive form of lighting involved many women in varied work.

Laundries were special rooms with stone floors and boilers for heating water. There were wooden tubs with bats to beat the clothes. A washing tally like a hornbook checked the list of clothes.

Dry clothes were sprinkled with rosemary or lavender. Starch was ground at home and during Elizabeth's time it was the fashion to have coloured starch—white, blue, pink or yellow for ruffs. Ironing was done with heavy box irons or with lighter ones the same shape as modern irons. The ruffs, cuffs and lace frills were fluted with goffering irons, shaped like glove stretchers. The clothes were often washed out of doors in the river, which could be mimed in a pageant. The ironing, goffering or tallying could be done in another room than the laundry, if these occupations are needed in a play. Soap was made at home in the shape of a ball.

Spinning wheels were invented in the sixteenth century. Up to then the spindle had been used. If there is a scene where the country cousin comes in, she could bring her own spindle and admire the modern inventions she saw in towns. A house-proud Stuart lady would have three or four spinning wheels so that no one need waste a moment.

Stuart ladies read in three or four languages; kept personal and household and also estate accounts; and wrote up their diaries and letters with ease and fluency.

The pages were expected to clean their own silver coat buttons, shoe-buckles and sword. In a large or noble household the kitchen servants, including the cook, would be men, but this might lead to casting difficulties with an amateur group.

Sea coal or logs were put in an iron basket which stood in the fireplace and would be moved by two men servants into the room where the fire was needed. The logs or coal were stored in a basket beside the fire and it was an underservant's job to see that the fire was kept up.

Servants would eat at a bare table with wooden or pewter plates and mugs. Wooden plates were round, but pewter plates were square and had a hollow on both sides so that they could be turned over for the next course. Horn mugs and spoons were often used. Naturally the servants of a fine house had more amenities than those of a poor one, and countrymen had simpler utensils than townsmen.

As meals were both an occupation and an amusement, a brief summary of the food eaten at each meal is given here:

Breakfast was bread and ale sometimes with cold meat, fish or cheese.

Dinner was eaten around noon, and consisted of fowl, roast meat, such as sucking pig, ribs of beef, large cheshire cheeses, with canary, sherry, claret, white wine, cider, ale, beer or punch (which was served from a bowl); there were also various tarts, pies and crystallised fruits.

Supper was small; the same food as breakfast, only more of it, and was usually served between six and nine o'clock.

In case some producer should wish to put on *Streetcar named Desire* in Stuart dress, water closets had been invented and bathrooms also existed, although they were more for show than use.

All the information in this chapter is taken from authentic sources, but nothing is included that is impractical for presentation. For instance, although many different games of dice were played, they have not been specified as the differences are too small to be effective. On the other hand the game of Kayles has been listed as it could be used in a pageant.

Occupations for Elizabethan Plays

Household Servants. Sweeping the floor with a bristle broom (servants of an inn would use a withy broom).
Cleaning the convex mirrors.
Polishing the walls of linenfold panelling.
Polishing the stairs and newel posts of the new lovely wooden stairs.
Pewter mugs, plates and basins to be polished.
Silver candlesticks, bowls, spoons to be polished.
Wax candles to be made, involving dipping and redipping the wick in melted wax which first had to be heated and strained through a cloth so that it burned clearly.
Tinder box cleaned and made ready for use; little pieces of rag torn up and placed in the bottom part of it, after having been first dried; the steel and the flint tested to see that they would work; a new stick laid ready and one

or two spare sticks dipped in the melted brimstone and put on one side.

Checking the laundry with a washing tally shaped like a hornbook (this could be used in the *Merry Wives of Windsor*).

Spinning, weaving and mending the linen for the house.

Sprinkling the linen with lavender or rosemary, folding it up or tearing up old sheets for bandages. This should all be done with two or three servants working at the same time.

Making soap and rolling it into balls.

Personal Servants. Cleaning and polishing small trinkets, box jewellery, using a small saucer of spirits or cleaning liquid and a tiny brush like a tooth brush and a small cloth. (Each household had its own recipe.)

Polishing silver buttons, sword and dagger hilts, tobacco boxes, and dressing-table sets.

Embroidering dresses, slippers, bedspreads and cushions.

Turning down the beds, putting away jewellery, dressing and undressing their employers, brushing, curling, cutting and dyeing their hair.

A manservant was also expected to brush, comb and curl his master's hair, beard and moustache, but a barber would be more likely to be called in to cut and dye it. Some men would have a barber to call each morning to shave them and see to their hair, but others would expect their personal servant to be able to do all but the highly skilled work, such as cutting and dyeing.

Starching the ruffs with white, blue, pink or yellow starch.

Ironing with light irons shaped like modern ones.

Ironing with heavy irons shaped like boxes.

Fluting the ruffs with goffering irons shaped like glove stretchers.

Ironing and fluting cuffs and frills of night robes and pillow cases.

Making spills for lighting paper.
Filling and cleaning tobacco boxes and pipes.

16th Century Games

Kayles, which were ninepins played with a stick thrown at cone-shaped pins set in threes on a diamond-shaped board. Bowls, bullbaiting (obviously with the bull placed off-stage), cock fighting (the actors could hold property cocks which had their legs tied together); tilting with staves, fireworks (very suitable to provide an exciting finale to a pageant), singing rounds or madrigals, all dicing games, chess and card games.

Children's toys. These are useful for stage setting, or for market or fair scenes where they would be sold, or for pageants where the producer has to use up schoolchildren who have not learnt folk dancing.

Dolls, trumpets made of cow's horns, drums, popguns, hobbyhorses (these can be just a wooden horse's head mounted on a stick, or they can have an elaborate spotted canopy on the stick like the horses had in the old tournaments), rattles shaped like a starfish with a bell on each point, toy lambs (with a collar of rose ribbon, and a fleecy white wool coat spattered with gold).

17th Century Games and Amusements

All those of the preceding century.

Processions with mock dragons, sea serpents and other monsters.

Fire-eaters, plaiting mats and baskets, plaiting strips of vividly coloured paper to make hats and baskets to sell at fairs with confits in.

Occupations for All Three Periods

Men

Clerks. Making inventories on long scrolls, writing and sealing letters with large seals of red or orange wax.

Paper, of a rough kind, with uncut edges, may be used, if it is not snow white but parchment colour.

Clerks often had wooden boxes with a lock and key for cash or important or private letters.

Gardeners had spades, forks, rakes, shallow garden baskets like trugs. They were also responsible for seeing that the fountain worked. Some of these fountains were practical jokes, so that as a certain flagstone was trodden on, the walker was deluged in spray. This could be used in a comedy scene with satisfaction, at least to the producer if not to the actor.

Flowers grown were roses, lilies, iris, marigolds, violets, pansies, small pink daisies, lavender, rosemary.

Barbers. Visiting barbers carried towels, a wooden soap bowl, razors in a wooden case.

Poultry men carried the birds strung at both ends of a stick carried across the shoulders. They plied their trade in the streets and called at houses for customers.

Dentists carried towels, bowls for blood, and forceps.

Watermen carried a large butt of water between two men with a small can hung on the side to dip into the water for customers who only wanted a drink. Sometimes they had a pitch and sometimes they went through the streets and served the poorer houses.

Surgeons had all kinds of fearsome instruments, bandages and poultices (*See* Fig. 18).

Ladies

Knitting with bone needles using either wool or silk or cotton yarn to make stockings, caps, purses or scarves.

Writing poetry or household lists on small ivory tablets.

Writing on pieces of paper lessons to be put in the children's hornbooks. This should of course be done on paper cut to fit the hornbook.

Painting hoops in stripes for children's toys.

Painting lambs with gold spots either for toys or wedding parties.

Painting battledores and shuttlecocks with flowers and stippling the feathers with silver paint.

Making pillow lace on a small cushion.

Embroidering handkerchiefs, cushion covers, reticules, in wool or silk.

Copying out recipes into books which they had made themselves and covered with velvet, silk or linen.

Making potions, lotions, ointments, with small pestle and mortar (*See* Fig. 16).

Drying oranges, rose leaves, rosemary, and lavender to put in bowls.

When the lady of the house does these things the paraphenalia is more personal than when the stillroom maid does them. In one case there would be a small pestle, etc., and a silver or pewter bowl, in the other wooden bowls and kitchen implements. The maid would have a stouter apron than her mistress, who might have ribbons to tie it with and a frill round the edge.

In a country house the mistress would probably have her own special recipe for confits, making them out of marzipan or crushed almonds, rolling them into fantastic shapes in her fingers and colouring with vegetable colouring poured out of little bottles. These could also be passed round to visitors, either packed into confit boxes or heaped up in small bowls.

Servants

Stuart. Laying the table with a white cloth, spoons, forks and knives, goblets and silver spice boxes.

Carrying round a ewer of water and napkin for the guests to wipe their fingers and mouth with after the meal.

Carrying round the food to the carver, such as roast and boiled fowls, roast ribs of beef, roast leg of pork, boar's head (this for special banquet), whole dressed pike or other fish (always fish on Friday), enormous Cheshire cheeses and loaves of bread.

FIG. 18. Stuart Gentleman Consulting Surgeon

FIG. 19. Stuart Servant Arranging Wall Hangings

Serving canary, sherry, claret, white wine, cider, ale, beer or hot-spiced possets. Possets should be served like hot punch from a bowl with a ladle into each goblet.

House servants had the tasks of the previous period plus a few new ones:
Plaster mouldings had come into fashion and had to be dusted with feather dusters.
Walls were hung with the new hand-printed cottons brought from the East, and these had to be laced with cords on to long rods, hung on hooks on the wall and shaken when they were dusty. (*See* Fig. 19).

Amusement for Outdoor Scenes for Men of all Three Periods

Hunting, hawking, bowls, golf, hockey and football, netting fish, quarter staff fighting, wrestling, cock-fighting.
Golf and hockey sticks were practically the same size, rather smaller than modern hockey sticks, rather larger than modern golf clubs. The ball was made of dark leather.
The fish nets were small and used with both hands.
The quarter staff and bowls were the same as nowadays.
The football was melon shaped of dark leather.
Quarter staff fighting and wrestling was done with two men at a time and the crowd laid bets.
Races with hurdles to be jumped were popular with the crowd on Feast days.

Indoor Games

Quoits, chess, backgammon, cards, bobbing for apples, dicing, battledore and shuttle-cock, indoor tennis.
Real or indoor tennis was played in shirt and breeches with a pear-shaped racket and small ball. It was a very vigorous game and while not suitable to show on the

stage (it is too fast a game), costume and kit could be used in a scene taking place apparently directly after a game, to show the characters were athletically inclined.

Some Feasts and Ceremonies for Use in Pageants

May Birchers went round with branches of trees on wedding eves if the bride or groom were popular; if they were not popular the custom was to put chaff outside the house. The modern custom of giving the bride a guard of honour, when she walks under an arch of swords, was interpreted in many different ways in older times, and each trade had its own custom. If the groom was a cobbler, coloured leather shavings were strewed in front of the pair; if a carpenter, shavings were used; a butcher had sheepskins, and two or more decorated lambs were borne in triumph. A farmer had grass or flowers, or garlands were twined round ropes and swung as the couple passed. Riders carrying a cake on the point of their swords had a race, when the prize was the bride's ribbon garters to be worn in the winner's hat. The nobler ladies had knots of various coloured ribbons as bridal favours, lightly attached so that the visitors could snatch them off for good luck and wear them in their hats.

Useful Book

Life and Work of the People of England — D. Hartley and L. Allen (Batsford)

CHAPTER X

MANNERS AND DANCES

Manners and customs—Bows and curtsys—Dances for each period, Galliard, Coranto Canaries, La Volta—List of reference books on dances

THE criticism often made of descriptions of period movement is that not enough detail is included. The producer and actor must realise that if a detail is not mentioned, it is either because it is not important or it is unknown. Descriptions of period movement are based on the study of contemporary pictures and sculpture and, after the sixteenth century, books of manners together with a certain amount of guesswork based on this knowledge. If a picture exists of a lady making a deep curtsy and another of a lady making a slight curtsy, then the intermediate stages are fitted in according to the movement that she is likely to have made wearing the clothes of the period. Stage movement only has to give an impression of the period, so if the basic lines are right the details are not vital. Basic lines of movement should follow and show off the lines of the costume. To give an example, the famous portrait of Madame Recamier reclining on a sofa in an Empire dress, high waisted with a soft clinging skirt, would have been impossible had she been wearing an Elizabethan farthingale and stomacher. The actor, therefore, selects the expressive movement without fussing about too many details or overweighting his acting with totally unnatural gestures. He must, in his movement, be characterised, occasionally decorative and at home in his clothes. The Georgian bow, with its neat footwork, does not fit the square-toed shoes of Henry VIII, while the hand flourish which shows off the

Georgian lace frills is wasted in a period when a stiff linen cuff is worn. Stage movement has always to convey something to the audience; period movement has to convey that something plus a sense of period.

Manners in the Elizabethan Age were a blend of the ceremonious and the boisterous. They appeared ceremonious because the clothes were stiffened and padded so that the movement of the body was very restricted. They were boisterous because the spirit of the age was lusty and all-conquering. The courtiers of Elizabeth were all men who led an active life; sailors, adventurers, explorers and all came to court between their expeditions. These were the men that the Queen liked and encouraged. There were, of course, the diplomats and statesmen of an older generation, but these did not influence the manners or set the fashions. This was done by Raleigh, Drake, Leicester and such men.

The ladies-in-waiting to the Queen had to keep well in the background, their courtships had to be conducted in secrecy, for fear of the Queen's displeasure, and woe betide any hapless damsel who dared to cast an eye publicly on an attractive man. That would be usurping the privilege of the Queen. This meant that one could tell at a glance whether the Queen was present or not. If she were, a prim mien and downcast eyes were the order of the day, otherwise Her Majesty was quite capable of dealing out a heavy box on the ears. Her hard hand, laden with heavy rings, could make this a really painful punishment, and as she also disliked crying women, tears had to be suppressed.

Although the Church had lost a great deal of its power, Church dignitaries were treated respectfully; people crossed themselves before the altar, at the news of death and at the mention of witchcraft, but the simple overwhelming faith of the Middle Ages had gone for ever.

The nobles had also lost their power, but there was an

increasingly powerful body of middle-class tradesmen growing up in the towns. The trade guilds, with the intricate system of apprenticeship, now provided the bulk of the population in place of the peasants under their feudal lord. This led to the increase of respectful but markedly independent manners.

Children ran wild in private, but were well mannered in public. The difference between manners at court and in the country was very noticeable. There were even books published telling a young man how to behave when he came to London and moved in polite society.

The country manners were friendly and straighforward; each person was well known to the others and had a definite place in the community.

The Elizabethan curtsy was a stiff affair. The arms were stretched out to the side with the hands resting on the edge of the farthingale. The skirt was not lifted. Both knees were bent slightly and the head was inclined towards the person to whom the curtsy was directed. The knee bend was naturally lower when the curtsy was to the Queen as she entered and, until she gave permission, no one rose. If it is in a play where the actress has to enter to give the Queen a message, the curtsy is made and the actress stands for her speech. A curtsy was always made before leaving the Queen.

The Jacobean lady did the same curtsy with a slight bend from the waist to either side, but with no sagging in the middle. The Cavalier lady had a variation of this curtsy which shows off the dress well. The skirt was lifted slightly at the sides, a step back was taken on either foot and the weight was transferred smoothly to the back foot while bending the back knee. This gives the skirt a sweep back in a graceful, flowing movement. (*See* Fig. 20.)

The Elizabethan bow: Stand with legs straddled, weight on both feet but one foot forward; bend both knees while taking off hat, straighten knees while putting on hat.

Stuart bow: Take off hat, step back on either foot, bend back knee while sweeping hat across chest, straighten knee, put on hat.

The actress who is going to sit down in a farthingale must approach the chair warily. Her hands must guide the width of the skirt past the chair and lift the back

FIG. 20. Stuart Curtsy

breadth slightly so that it bags up at the back and she is actually sitting on the part that falls behind her knees. When she gets up she must rise on to whichever foot is forward so that the skirt falls clear of the chair and the material hangs in straight folds behind her. The actor has an easier time; as he has built-in cushions in his breeches and only has to consider an effective position.

Manners at table varied considerably in Elizabeth's time, but by the end of Charles I's reign, etiquette at meals was much more civilised. An Elizabethan Englishmen happily picked up the juiciest pieces of meat on his plate with his fingers and cheerfully licked his spoon clean of gravy before plunging it into the communal custard.

The Italians were considered fussy to the point of affectation because they cut the food on their plates with a knife and fork and even had one spoon for the first course and another for the second. The thin edge of this wedge was inserted in English manners when the servants were ordered to bring round a jug of water into which each diner plunged his spoon or fork for a hasty swirl. Things then went rapidly down hill until the Stuart period, when forks appeared on every table of any standing and spoons were set for each course. Probably the grandfathers sat and sucked their spoons defiantly, but they would be frowned upon by their daughters-in-law.

The food was put on dishes and decorated in order to be shown, first to the master of the house and the important guests and then to the lesser fry before it was served. Cups and glasses stood on a side table and were brought to the drinkers when they called. It can be well imagined that there was no new-fangled nonsense about cleanliness among the servers, and dregs of ale would be tipped into a bowl, if a particular mug had to be filled with canary and no clean one was ready. Venetian glasses were coming into fashion. This made the matter more difficult than when pewter was used and no dregs could be detected, just one more point in favour of former customs.

Important people had a ewer of water and a towel placed on a cloth in front of them to wash their hands; the whole thing was then lifted off bodily by the cloth. This action should either be carefully rehearsed for neatness or carefully considered for a comedy sequence. A flashlight is thrown on the social rating of the times by the contemporary order that silver vessels should be used for barons, bishops and upwards.

Dessert was lavish and there seems to have been no niggling niceties as to where the stones were spat. Dates, apricots, peaches, quinces, figs, oranges, lemons, plums, cherries, pears, apples, mulberries, walnuts and almonds were all eaten with abandon.

Bins or "voiders" were provided for scraping the plates into, but a rich harvest would clearly have been gathered by sweeping the floor as well.

The fires were built up with large logs in the sitting room; the kitchen fires had the voiders emptied into them. (Stench never really worried the Elizabethans; their noses seemed to match the lustiness of their times.)

Elizabethan men kept their hats on at table after removing them for grace. At the end of the meal, they felt in their hat bands where they kept little mirrors and looked to see that no food hung about in their beards or moustaches. If it did, it was dabbed away with a table napkin by the dandies and just sucked off by the rank and file.

The extreme gallant would also whip out a small comb and tidy his beard into a spade shape, a fish shape or a small point.

The lady's make-up was so elaborate that it was all

done in her bedchamber; there seems to have been no re-touching in public.

One action was never done in any of the three periods by ladies, only by wenches, and that was to sit with one leg crossed over the other. This is really because the corsets worn by gentlewomen made this action most uncomfortable, if not actually painful. Wenches did not wear corsets for the obvious reasons that they had a great deal of physical work to do and needed freedom in which to stretch or stoop.

Movements are direct and decisive; rarely does an actor have to do the fidgeting and fiddling with furniture that in modern plays conveys that he is facing a psychological dilemma.

The movement for Shakespeare's Fools, such as Fabian, and Feste and Touchwood, should be trained and smooth in the same way that waiters have a professional bearing and deftness. It is not at all necessary to make them into pseudo ballet dancers, or give them gestures with wagging fingers as if they were embryo Pierrots.

They should, however, be sharply differentiated from the rustic clowns such as William and Clotin, who are slow, clumsy countrymen. Ladies-in-waiting were often of good family, but poor relations taken into the grander household in order to give them a chance to make a good match; therfore their behaviour is on the same lines as that of the lady of the house. Waiting maids would have two different sets of manners, one for their social superiors and one for their equals.

In the Stuart households there was a friendly and family relationship between the staff and the household, and servants brought their troubles to be solved by the master and mistress of the house.

The tradesmen of all these periods were often craftsmen as well, so they took pride in their work and had a certain independence of bearing and address. They would do simple bows alike to their fellows or to their employers and their wives would do a simple curtsy, not a low one except to Royalty.

The Elizabethan men were known everywhere for the excellence of their dancing, and spared no pains to keep that reputation. English dancing schools flourished and many hours a day were spent there by gallants determined to master the energetic steps and the expert arrangements of the dances. The steps in themselves were tricky, but the real skill lay in adapting them to the music. The Galliarde had certain set steps, but the order in which they were danced was decided by the man while he was actually dancing it. On him rested the responsibility for planning the steps so that they made an attractive pattern, making a pleasing alternation of high and low jumping steps and an extra flourish for the finish. It was a superb chance for men to show off and they seized it with both feet. They were used to an active life and London did not offer many opportunities to let off steam. The Galliarde with its leaping and prancing steps was designed for young men who could vault on to a horse easily and they all enjoyed it enormously. It was simultaneously a test of brain and brawn; quick decisions had to be taken at a moment of great physical activity, very much as they would have been taken while hunting. There were also many sailors at court, and sailors have always had a good sense of balance developed during storms at sea. Only very vigorous young men would have thought of bounding up and down for three quarters of an hour at a time in Elizabethan dress. The lady's role was more decorous, but absolutely essential. She was the admiring audience who was allowed to dance a few modest steps, while the gentleman drew breath for his next caper. If the man was an expert dancer (or if he held such an opinion of himself), he danced with a lady on each side of him to applaud his ballon.

The dance music sometimes includes bars for the bow and curtsy; where it does not the producer is advised to have it played, as it helps to start the dance off tidily. A curious deafness seems to fall upon anyone learning a period dance; they can neither hear the time nor the melody nor the music. So, if the producer is to retain his reason, he is wise to allow three times the number of rehearsals he had imagined necessary. The steps in themselves, with the exception of the Galliarde, are not difficult, neither are the figures; but the style is important and the rhythm must be clear. Dancing was such a favourite way of passing an evening, that it can be utilised as an effective curtain raiser if desired. A whole suite of dances can follow each other in a masque, but the fashion of inviting the onlookers to join in may not be feasible. On the other hand, if a rowdy finish is needed because the masque is played during a social occasion, then the Coranto would provide an ideal finale. The Coranto would be an excellent choice for this kind of romp, as the initiated can yank the visitors into the hopping steps without too much effort.

In Elizabeth's time, Balls were only opened by dancing the Pavane. The dances after this could be Galliardes, Corantos, La Voltas, and Country Dances, as well as Almains. The Pavane ended with a kiss (*See* Fig. 21).

The Pavane was a slow and stately dance; the Galliarde was a quick and vigorous one. The Coranto, which gained in popularity in the seventeenth century, was a delightful and varied dance, and La Volta was a gay dance, in which the lady was lifted high in the air and swung round her partner.

The Country dances were extremely popular both in town and country, although some changes were made when they were danced at Court.

In the sixteenth century the English were known far and wide for the excellence of their dancing, and dancing

FIG. 21. Elizabethan Pavane (End)

schools flourished, in which young men bounded and leapt as they practised the Galliarde.

In the seventeenth century the French Branles came into fashion, probably introduced by Queen Henrietta Maria, wife of Charles I. The Galliarde had disappeared by this time and the Courante had become very different from the Coranto, although the couples still used miming passages. The country dances still continue to be danced as before.

These dances were done with a light and graceful style at Court and were never romped through except at harvesting time by the villagers. Greensleeves, All Flowers of the Broom, Turkeyloney, Peppers Black and Roger are all dances of this period.

In all the dances there is a difference of opinion about which foot to begin with so it is only necessary to consider the stage position. The gentleman always gives his right hand to the lady.

There are many different Galliardes and none of them are easy, but they express so perfectly the robust exuberance of the Elizabethan Age that it is worth making a special effort to include them, particularly in a pageant. If young boys who are good boxers can be chosen, the footwork will not present many difficulties and they will show the bouncing leap off to its greatest advantage. The music is in triple time and there are five steps (the steps are practically the same as the Tordion, but the springs are much higher in the Galliarde). (*See* Fig. 22.)

For stage purposes the dance can be arranged by the producer to be long enough to make an effect without entirely exhausting the dancers. If a genuine Galliarde is needed then a qualified dancing teacher should be engaged.

The dance can either be danced straight forward and back, or it can be taken in a circle if space is limited. The dancer can repeat the first step or he can do a different

FIG. 22. Elizabethan Galliarde

step if he first reverses the five steps with which he began. In each count of six beats there are one rest and one pause by the dancer in a special position.

The Galliarde starts with a Reverence and this can be the same as the one that is given in Part I, p. 57 for the Pavane, or on p. 132.

Pieds Croisés: Here the man lifts his right foot in front of his left knee and hops on the left. He repeats this jump changing on to his right foot with his left foot now opposite his right knee. Once again he jumps on his left and then right (four jumps in all). Then the same jump on his left foot, but this time taking the right foot behind the knee and another little jump bringing the right leg out in front, stretching it and patting it on the ground.

The last three counts are called a Cadence and the whole series of six steps take two bars of music.

In the next step the leg is swung like a pendulum with the arms swinging to balance, so that if the hop is on the left leg, the right leg is raised in front with the left arm forward. If the leg is swung at the back, the same arm as the raised leg swings forward (*See* Fig. 22).

The Five Step consists of five of these swinging springs, the right leg swinging forward and then back, then the left swinging forward, then the right swinging forward and back and finally the forward point on the ground as in the Cadence.

The raised leg movement is like a strong kick in the above step, but there are also steps where the raised leg is cut across the supporting leg as in the Scottish dances, first in front, then behind, with a spring to each cut. Sometimes the springs are all done on the one leg while the other cuts in front, behind, in front, behind, and the step finishes with the cadence. This cadence is very helpful to inexperienced dancers, as it helps them both to get their breath and to know how far they have got in the dance, the producer can always rehearse them from the last cadence, instead of counting bars anxiously. There were quite strict rules as to when it should be done originally, but for theatrical purposes these can be ignored, unless it takes place in a documentary.

Even contemporary performers found this dance took it out of them. Arbeau warns them not to spit too often or constantly, to blow the nose and strongly recommends that they provide themselves with a handsome handkerchief.

The Volta is a dance which is even showier, as the lady is lifted bodily in the air and swung round the gentleman. A doubt was expressed at this date as to whether it was proper, honourable or healthy to have such a movement executed by lusty gallants, and it seems unnecessary to say that this put the seal on its popularity.

The Double of the Pavane can be done both in the Galliarde and the Volta if the first step is taken on the jump, so that the sequence is spring, walk, walk, close, and as it has to fit into triple time the counts of two and six are held as pauses.

In the La Volta the lady moves round the outside of a circle round her man. She has to make her steps rather larger and the man has to keep his steps fairly small, if they are to keep in touch with each other.

Start the Volta by making the usual Reverence, finish by holding hands, standing side by side, and then do the sprung doubles alternately to the right and the left as many times as wished and finishing at the end of a phrase of the music.

The same doubles can be done turning on the same spot, letting go of each other's hands, sometimes both turning the same way and sometimes the lady turning to the left and the man to the right.

The lift must be approached with gusto and properly rehearsed. The man releases the hand of the lady, catches her round the waist with his left hand, poises her on his left hip, steadying her with his right hand on her waist at the right side, and swings her round in the air as many times as he likes or can manage. The lady helps by putting her right hand on the man's shoulder to get a good take off for her spring. Her left hand is supposed to hold her skirt down and it is probably because this was rather casually performed that the moralists made their nasty comments on this step. If the hold is firm and the lady times her jump as the man is ready to lift her, the step is easily done and excitingly effective.

The Canaries can be recommended if there is very little time to rehearse, as each step is repeated, going first forward then back again, first by the man and then by the lady. This takes up a lot of time in performance considering that the dancers have only had to learn one step. A simple version of a Canaries step is as follows:

Point the right foot in front and raise it in the air with a hop.
Put it down in front on the heel.
Tap it on the ground in front on the toe.
Spring on to the right foot, and tap the left on the ground.
Tap the left heel on the ground.
Tap the left toe on the ground.

The hops travel forward and backward as the gentleman dances toward the lady and away again followed by the lady dancing toward the gentleman and away again. The steps can be made more lively by substituting the kicking movements of the Galliarde for the taps, but this must only be done by the gentleman, the lady must continue to do the subdued tap.

The Coranto is perhaps the first dance which mentions the modern custom of "cutting in", and this could be used with dramatic effect in a scene of rivalry. The steps are Simples and Doubles danced in every possible direction, to either side, forwards, backwards, and turning. The partners start by holding hands, but let go whenever it is more convenient. When the lady's hand is released, it gives a chance to the stag line to cut in, and a man can finish his turn with a flourish and find to his chagrin that his partner is coying up at another partner. The Simples and the Doubles are done with the hop on the first step, as in the Galliarde and the Volta, but in 2/4 time, as in the Pavane.

As these dances were often in a sequence, one dance followed another without a pause to change partners. Doubtless the cutting in was in response to agonised glances from some man who was landed with a bad dancer for half an hour at a time, and the cutter-in was prompted by male friendship rather than by love for the lady. A Basse dance would be followed by a Retour, then by a Tordion, and the whole thing could go on for three quarters of an hour. This is a good way of presenting dances in a Pageant or in an Arena production: it can begin with a long procession of dancers on to the dance space. It is not effective on a small stage where the actors are crammed into a small space and the figures can not be seen clearly.

It should now be clear that there are only a certain number of steps used in these period dances; the differences are made by the rhythm of the steps and whether they are walked or hopped or sprung (a hop means hopping on the same foot and a spring means the foot is changed with a jump). If a company plans to do several period plays, it is well worth while calling a special session to learn the basic steps. e.g., Simples and Doubles, and showing the actors how they may be varied. Human nature being what it is, the producer is advised to call this session as an ordinary rehearsal, and not until every-one has arrived should he break it to his appalled cast what is in store for them. In some cases, it is better to lock the door before this announcement. In case this advice seems unnecessarily brutal, it must be said that the cast always enjoys the dances in the end, but men especially are apt to be pigheaded and prejudiced about dancing at all; if only they can be induced to try they invariably turn out to be good performers and can peacock it most successfully. This is an important point since, as it has already been stated, Englishmen were renowned for their dancing and these dances must be done with the proper male complement. Men's bodies have not changed and it is utter nonsense, coupled with sheer laziness, for a modern man to say that he cannot do these dances.

Some definitions of the meanings of the dance names which should help give an idea of the type of movement at which the dancers should aim:

Pavane: after the peacock's pride of bearing.

Galliarde: lively or nimble, which refers not only to the movement, but to the variety of ways in which the steps may be arranged.

Alman or Allemande: German or heavy type of movement with the feet, although the hands are held high.

Basse dance: low, in other words without jumping steps.

La Volta: to turn round, as the main step is the turning spring accented by the lifted lady.

Coranto: swift or gay—this dance developed in seventeenth century into the

Courante: stream or brook, as it advances or retreats and the knees bend slightly and repeatedly as a fish flicks its fins, which described how the movement changed.

Canaries: there are two explanations of this name; one that it derives from the Canary Islands, the other that it was originally danced in a costume with waving plumes.

These dances came from France, Italy, Spain or Germany according to the nationality of the reigning Queen, or to what particular influences were fashionable. Therefore a certain amount of historical checking up on these points is sensible before deciding on the dance to be chosen.

Torch dances and Sword dances were performed at fairs and fêtes, and Morris dances would also be seen. These were done by the comics mentioned in the masques and would have grotesque or acrobatic variations, if enough ale had been taken beforehand.

The Courtiers had a totally different style of dancing called the Noble style, which the ordinary actors never used. The ladies still left all the showy steps to the gentlemen and contented themselves with small foot movements and a graceful carriage of the head and arms. These, enhanced by expert management of their skirts, just left them enough time to gaze constantly and admiringly at their partners.

The long gallery in the country houses had an influence on the type of country dances that became popular with the country gentry. They preferred dances in which long lines were formed rather than those in a circle. Sometimes the top couple started and by the end of the first figure were at the bottom. They then worked their way up the line until they came to the top again and then the dance finished.

Sometimes the top couple went down one place at the end of the first figure, then the dance finished when they had worked down to the end of the line. When arranging the dance for the stage, either of these alternatives will take too long and hold up the drama. For a pageant or a masque, however, they are ideal because in this case the dance is part of the entertainment and not just an extra trimming.

Stage dances should rely on style and figures rather

than on steps, but pageant or arena dances, which last longer, need the added interest of a variety of steps.

Simples and Doubles occur in every century in every European country. Simple: one step forwards, sideways or backwards, and close. Double: three steps forwards, sideways or backwards, and close. Italian, Spanish and French variations of these steps are easy and effective. They can be justified if a foreign Queen is on the English throne and if she is not, doubtless some character has brought them home from a trip abroad. They differ from the English steps generally; having more sophisticated head and shoulder movements and, more rarely, in the actual footwork.

The Courante was a charming and light-hearted dance. It is a useful one for stage purposes as the basic steps can be danced in such different styles. It can be done for a country revel with high skips and free movements, or it can be danced at a Court ball with grace and polish. The time of music is easier for modern players than most period dances and there are some pretty figures to arrange if it is needed for arena or pageant work. The basic movement is a step, a hop and a pause, and it is the way the hop is done that governs the whole look of the dance. It can be a jump, a bounce or a rise on the ball of the foot only just off the ground. The dancers should practise walking and jumping with the music.

The difference between the Coranto and the Courante is mainly that of style. The Coranto was danced in a springy manner and the Courante used the same steps but in a more gliding manner. The following is a stage version of the Courante (*See* Fig. 23).

Three couples stand side by side with the ladies on the right of the gentlemen. The hands are held about waist level so that the jump does not drag them apart. They all dance up the room with the basic step, then the gentlemen dance back again, leaving the ladies behind. The

FIG. 23. Courante, Stuart Period

first gentleman dances up to his partner, who scorns him. He dances back to his place, miming how he takes his rejection. The second gentleman then does the same steps and sequence, although he can alter the mime as he pleases. If the first man has been carefree about his repulse, the second can be furious and the third can be heartbroken. . . . After all three men have been refused, the ladies become panic stricken that they have been taken too seriously, so they in turn dance up to the men and ask them to dance. The men accept and they all dance together. Arbeau, the great dancing master of the period, waxed very sarcastic about all the liberties which were taken with this dance in the way of altering steps and sequences. Since, even in its own time, there was so much latitude, the modern producer need not fear unalterable rules. The men were apparently most ingenious in the miming; one even did a strip tease act to induce his lady to accept him.

Dances of the 16th and 17th Century

Formal	*Country Dances*
Siciliana	Greensleeves
Chaconne	Turkeyloney
La Volta	All Flowers of the Broom
Passe pied	Peggy Ramsey
Galliarde	Peppers Black
Pavane	Basilena
Courante	Mill Field
Coranto	Almains
Mattachins	
Bourree	
Rigaudon	

The music for these formal dances may all be found in the work of the composers listed in Chapter V, and if gramophone records are used they will probably have two, three or even four dances on one record. The country dances are also recorded, but with the introduction of long-playing records it is useless to give numbers as they will be out of date by the time this book is published; the written music may be found in Playfair's *Dancing Master* or in Melusine Wood's book recommended in this chapter.

Useful Reference Books

Historical Dances from the 12th to the 19th century Melusine Wood (C. W. Beaumont)

This gives historical background and reasons for the development of the Dance, descriptions of the steps and dances taken from manuscripts of the period, but is not concerned with stage arrangement. It is scrupulously accurate if a documentary programme is needed or if the dances are to be done purely for the dancers' own amusement, but the dances are not very easy to work out in a hurry without tuition.
Music is included.

Manners and Movements in Costume Plays I. Chisman and H. E. Raven-Hart (Deane)

Excellent legal, military and religious ceremonial section and a special chapter on duelling, fighting and wrestling.

Orchesography Arbeau (C. W. Beaumont)

One of the most famous books on dance written by a seventeenth-century dancing master. This should be read not only for knowledge but also for amusement.

Modes and Manners Max van Boehn (Harrap)
trs. by Joan Joshua

Volume II covers the period of the sixteenth century and is a mine of information about social customs and conditions at Court in various European countries, with comments on the legal system of punishments, imprisonment, torture, also contemporary accounts of dress and extravagances of revelry that are not for the squeamish.
Volume III covers the period of the seventeenth century in the same way.
Most of the information is for the historian and cannot be adapted for the stage, but the book is most fascinating and gives the producer a clear picture of the period which throws

a light on many of the unexpected reactions of Jacobean characters to what appear to modern eyes unusual incidents.

The English Dancing Master	John Playford 1651
Apologie de la Danse	F. de Lauze 1623 Trans. Joan Wildeblood (Muller)
The Dancing Master	Trans. C. W. Beaumont from P. Rameau (Beaumont)
The Book of the Courtier	B. Castiglione (Dent) Trans. Sir Thomas Hoby (Tudor Translations XXIII, Everyman's Library)
History of the Masque at the English Court	Lacroix (Didot)
Social Life in Stuart England	Mary Coate (Methuen)

The Imperial Society of Teachers of Dancing, Historical Dance Branch, Euston Hall, Birkenhead Street, London WC1H 4AJ, will supply a list of teachers qualified in this subject.

CHAPTER XI

MUSIC

Musical forms of the periods—Instruments used and their modern stage equivalents—List for each period of composers, instruments and suggested gramophone records

THE music covered in the three periods of this book starts with secular music sweeping all over England, rising to its height with the Madrigal. This period ends in the seventeenth century about 1630 with a second period until 1660, when the solo song and catch were coming into their own. The dramatic music of the masques was an innovation which eventually led to opera. The modern producer should be sensitive to the atmosphere in the music. He should not become so besotted with unusual period instruments that he subjects the audience to weird noises that convey shunting trains in agony rather than melancholy over four corpses. He must also remember the difference between the Court music and the music of the countryside. Rural people changed very, very slowly. Sometimes they did not change at all, just went on in the same way for a couple of hundred years. Communications were not easy, and this, plus the English character, meant that the country tunes were not dropped when new ones arrived, but merely added to the repertoire.

Music making was so much a part of Elizabethan life that it was taken for granted. Everyone sang both solo and part songs and most people played at least one instrument. It was the recognised amusement at parties and each guest was expected to take his share in entertaining the others. Countrymen, townsmen, nobility and commoners were all united in the active pleasure of singing and dancing. Court ladies and gallants were expected to have a high standard of accomplishment and Queen Elizabeth was a notable performer on the virginals.

It is obvious that in the time of Shakespeare any actor might be called upon to sing a song in his part and this did not raise the same casting difficulty that it does nowadays. Any actor wishing to play in Elizabethan, Jacobean, or Stuart drama should be able to give the impression of singing and playing an instrument capably.

Madrigals, songs written in up to seven parts, were the most popular music in Elizabeth's time, and the loveliest ones were written then. Plenty of modern choirs have recorded them, so the producer has a wide choice. It seems a pity not to give the actors the pleasure of learning and singing a madrigal together if the script calls for one. This was so usual a pastime in the sixteenth century, that if a member of the household had to be called away during the singing, any servant could step forward and sing the missing part until his master returned.

Drinking songs with rousing choruses and solo love songs come into many plays and the actor is advised to try to sing them, not only because they belong to the part, but because the singing of them is bound to improve his breath control and the pitch of his voice.

Most of Shakespeare's songs have to be sung to modern settings as the original melodies are not known. Some folk-dance tunes fit his country songs and the producer is advised to experiment on these lines. Shakespeare asks for music if he considers it necessary for the play; music, songs, flourishes or drums are definitely stated in the directions. The modern producer is often impelled to include additional music if the action of the play is to be continuous. Successive short scenes may need a slight change of minor items such as stools, benches or even a blackout, and the producer may feel that music is essential to tie up the loose ends. For this purpose it is more important that the music should be in key with the mood of the scene than that it should be strictly in period.

At the end of the chapter there is a list of composers of the period who have written music in many different veins.

The main instruments played were the virginals, the lute, the viol da gamba, the viol d'amour and the recorder.

The virginal was an early keyboard instrument, and there are a reasonable number of short pieces recorded on it.

The recorder is the same instrument that has now come into fashion again; so there should be no difficulty in obtaining a performer. There are also gramophone records if they are needed. Four to six recorders can be used at the same time; one by itself is apt to sound thin, which perhaps accounts for the prejudice against them held by people who have only heard one at a time.

The lute is a stringed instrument with a gourd-shaped bowl. It is slung across the shoulders with gay ribbons and the strings are plucked. It is used for love songs, sung by men or women and also oddly enough, for laments. If the actor holds it on his knee and plucks the strings to synchronise with a gramophone record, it is easy to give the impression that he can really play. If it is easier to obtain, a guitar can be played off-stage, and it will give a good effect.

The viol da gamba is a stringed instrument between a violin and a 'cello in size. It is held, as the name suggests, between the knees and played with a bow drawn across the strings. An actor with a feeling for comedy could make excellent use of this instrument.

The instruments were usually considered suitable for separate types of music: the viols (viol da gamba, viol d'amour, etc.) for chamber music and the lutes for songs, dances and laments.

The Hautboy band of Shakespeare's time would have one instrument for each of six parts, consisting of parts for two oboes, two cor anglais and two bassoons which gave a rich depth of sound. These were more the instruments played by the professionals.

Side drums, kettle drums and big drums were used a great deal in stage productions.

Trumpets, normally tuned in D in the sixteenth and seventeenth centuries, were sometimes in C for contrast. They were sounded three times before the opening of the play.

The cittern, another instrument with strings and frets, was sometimes played, and if the producer wants to convey an out-of-date household, he can choose this. No one in the audience will realise the point, but producers must occasionally have a little fun. The actor can hold the cittern (any book of ancient music will have a picture of it) and the musicians in the wings can either play two violins or one mandoline, *pizzicato*.

For country fairs, the pipe and tabor were still popular and dancing bears would have a leader who played the pipe. The country gentry who sent their sons and daughters to Court for visits would be more up-to-date and play the latest instrument.

The pipe was a very old instrument and was a simple pipe like a three-holed flute which could be played straight or sideways with one hand.

The tabor was a deep drum and could be slung from the shoulders and rested either on the right or the left hip, or it could be poised straight in front of the drummer. If the pipe and tabor are played by the same person, as was customary in the medieval period, then the pipe is played with the left hand, and the tabor with the right hand. (*See* Fig. 8 in Part I.) If possible, the tabor should be played during the Pavane as the deep beat adds immensely to the dignity and ceremonial effect of the dance.

The musette was a small bagpipe used in the country.

The spinet was a development of the virginals; from a stage point of view they sound the same, rather thin and tinkling. The virginal is supposed to have been named thus as it was invariably played by ladies, and unmarried girls were supposed to learn to play it. The spinet was also played mainly by spinsters; the lute was the instrument that was the men's favourite.

The pentagonal spinet dates from roughly 1552, so only the most up-to-date families would posses one at this time; it would be more usual to see the virginals.

In the seventeenth century the spinet became a popular instrument and the shape changed to an upright spinet. They all sounded very much alike, so that if one shape cannot be easily obtained, another can be substituted without anyone objecting except the pedants.

The volume of sound from all these instruments is apt to fight a losing battle against coughs from the audience. The producer is strongly advised to use a record on a really good amplifying machine, and to try it out in sufficient time to substitute something else if it is not satisfactory.

Certain composers specialise in certain types of music, so, as well as the list of composers' dates, here are some descriptions to help classify the choice.

Giles Farnaby wrote mainly pieces for the virginals and one or two madrigals.

Thomas Morley wrote mostly gay madrigals with fascinating counterpoint (he also wrote a delightful book *Plaine and Easy Introduction to Practical Musicke*, 1598).

Palestrina is noted mainly for Church music, specially for his Masses.

Thomas Weelkes wrote songs and madrigals of a particularly tuneful nature. His Ayres are much easier for modern ears than those by many composers of this period.

Thomas Campion wrote mainly songs for the lute.

The French dance-songs seem to have influenced Dowland's songs and tunes, although his greatest work is considered to be "The Pilgrime's Solace".

John Bull is a most useful composer to consult. He is a composer of keyboard and vocal music. He was himself a brilliant organist and his greatest works are considered to be *In Nomine* in A minor, and the *Walsingham Variations*, as well as Pavanes and Galliardes.

The organ had been popular from the fifteenth century when a small portative one was played, and it held its place for Church music until 1650, when Cromwell ordered all organs to be destroyed as heathen instruments.

List of Composers of These Periods

Palestrina	*c.* 1525–94
William Byrd	1543–1623
Cavalieri	1550–1602
Maranzici	1553–
G. Gabrieli	1557–1612
Thomas Morley	1557–1603
Richard Carlton	1558–1638
Vulpuin	1560–1613
Anerio	1560–1614
Giles Farnaby	*c.* 1560–*c.* 1600
Gesualdo	1560–1615
Peri	1561–1633
Thomas Campion	1562–1620
Sweelinck	1562–1611
Dowland	1563–1626
John Bull	1563–1628
Alchezi	1564–1628
John Daniel	1565–1630
Anthony Holborne	(?) –1602
Michael Cavendish	*c.* 1565–1628

Nathaniel Pott	1567– (?)
Monteverdi	1567–1643
Thomas Bateson	1570–1630
John Bennet	*c.* 1570 (?)
John Wilbye	1574–1638
Thomas Weelkes	(?) –1623
Orlando Gibbons	1583–1625
Frescobaldi	1583–1643
John Jenkyns	1592–1678
Henry Lawes	1596–1662
William Lawes	1602–1645
William Young	(?) –1671
Rinki	1623– (?)
Le Begue	1630–1702
Lully	1632–87
Buxtehude	1637–1707
Corelli	1653–

Modern Equivalents of the Sound made by Period Instruments

Gittern, Cittern or Rebec: Two mandolines or two violins played pizzicato.

Lute: Piano chords played arpeggiondo
or guitar plucked
or lute key on harpsichord.

Trumpets: Modern trumpets, but tuned in D; if available, cornets would be better.

Viola da Gamba: Modern double bass.

Kettle Drums: Modern one tuned to key of other instruments.

Tabor: Large modern Tabor struck with padded stick or back of knuckles.

Some gramophone records are given, although at the

moment there is a difficulty as so many are being re-recorded as long-playing records.

Some Charming Madrigals

Though Amaryllis dance in green	Byrd	5 voices
The Sweet and Merry Month	Byrd	6 voices
Oyey has anyone found a lad	Tomkins	4 voices
Cupid in a Bed of Roses	Bateson	6 voices
On the Plains Fairy Plains	Weelkes	5 voices
Say Love if ever thou didst find	Dowland	4 voices

All these are recorded, if a record is needed.

Some Useful Incidental Music

Ave Maria	Arcadelt (*c.*1510–*c.*1567).
Fantasia op de Maneer van en Echo	Sweelinck (1562–1611).
Passomezyo de Doulce Pavane Lecquemade Galliarde lo Fanfare	Loejwen *c.* 1570.
Sonata in E Minor	Rosenmuller (1619–84).

Useful Books

Shakespeare's Music E. W. Naylor (Curwen)

This gives actual music for the period, including the drum march for *Hamlet*, a Coranto, a Gigue and a Pavane, and is most helpful in the modern substitutes for period instruments.

Music and Society Wilfred Mellers (Dobson)

This gives a survey of the link between music and society with some helpful remarks on the period.

Historical Anthology of Music Davison and Apel (C.U.P.)

Volume I: Up to 1600
Volume II: Baroque

Actual music of the periods—short pieces ranging from Church music to secular dance tunes, including Pavanes, Salterello, Amalos, etc.

The Fitzwilliam Virginal Book	Fuller Maitland	
Muzich der Alte Zeit	Litolff	
Old Keyboard Music Two volumes	Oesterle	(Schirmer)
The Use of Music in Religious Drama	C. Le Fleming	(S.P.C.K.)

The Rural Music Schools Association have offices all over this country and give advice on period music to their members, lend gramophone records and can recommend teachers, choirmasters and singers, and performers on most musical instruments. The Secretary's address is: Little Benslow Hills, Hitchin Herts., SG4 9RB.

The English Folk Dance and Song Society, 2 Regents Park Road, London NW1 7AY, has photographs of period instruments.

CHAPTER XII

PRACTICE SCENES

Practice scenes from plays suggested—Mime scenes

Scenes for the 16th Century

Elizabethan Scenes:

THESE are some poems that could be a basis for a scene of mimed poems, e.g., one or more speakers for the poems while the actors mimed the content:

These four could be grouped in a Pastoral scene.

The Passionate Shepherd to his Love	Christopher Marlowe
The Maid's Reply to Her Love	Sir Walter Raleigh
Coridon's Song	John Chalkhill
The Merry Month of May	Thomas Dekker
Agincourt	Michael Drayton
Hymn in Praise of Neptune	Thomas Campion
To his Mistress, Queen of Bohemia	Thomas Wooten

These three are of rather a later period and show three different moods of praise, one to triumph in battle, one to a mythical god and one to a very real woman. They are excellent practice in the style of speech needed for this period, and need clarity of consonants, breath control and, above all, a feeling for poetry as a living thing, not a meaningless ringing sound. As the poems are so different, they could be spoken by three statues on pedestals widely spaced, either on the stage or in the arena. This would be ideal for avenue arena, one at each end and one in the middle, especially if spotlights can be used.

The scene could begin or end with a group of madrigals

which set the period in the most perfect way. If a madrigal is needed to finish the scene *Though Amaryllis Dance in Green*, by Byrd, finishes with the word "adieu" repeated several times, which could be used for the exit of all the players.

These scenes and the following mime scenes are included in order to give the cast a chance to do concentrated work in period movement, to music of the period while acting in the style of the period as a preparation to using the script of the period. The producer is strongly advised to use this method of training his cast; and to encourage them to experiment in acting historical incidents, or miming folk songs, if they are to bring out the true flavour of the period play. The cast will find it exceedingly difficult to catch the spirit of the period if rehearsals are confined to the script.

Mimes for the 17th Century

Jacobean Mime.
"The Wedding Day"

The scene is the village green.

The characters are: James, a butcher
William, a cobbler
Dorcas, a village maid
Phoebe and John, bride and groom (a butcher)
Audrey and Richard, bride and groom (a cobbler)
Jane, mother of Dorcas
Robert, father of Dorcas
Celia, sister of Dorcas
Charles, a farmer
Villagers.

The village green with a trestle table and benches stage right. The Lych gate is upstage left, or, if no scenery is going to be used, the gate to the church must be clearly indicated by the direction of the final procession.

All the villagers would wear their best clothes. If wished, the Lord of the Manor, with wife and daughter, could come to the wedding and take their place at the head of the procession to give a formal air to the move towards the church. All the characters wear knots of ribbon to show that they are going to a wedding. The brides do not wear white but have a best dress of a light colour and carry a small bunch, not a bouquet, of flowers in their hands, and they wear gloves with tassels at the wrist. The bridegrooms have nothing to differentiate them from the other young men, who also wear their best clothes. (*See* page 102.)

The villagers, with the exception of the brides and bridegrooms, are getting ready for the wedding. They are setting up trestle tables and benches, bringing out flat loaves of bread on trenchers, ribs of beef, pasties, pies, tarts, cakes, and pewter and horn mugs.

Each villager proudly displays a contribution which is presented to the brides' mothers and which is admired by everyone before it is placed on the table.

Dorcas flounces on, pursued by James, the butcher, offering her a ham. When it is put on the table, he offers her his heart. She wavers and he attempts to clinch it by giving her a knot of blue ribbon. She takes this and pins it on her left sleeve, but will not give him a definite answer. He moons off into a corner downstage right and she runs off left. One of the women condoles with him but he still sulks. Dorcas comes on again carrying a pie which she puts on the table and turns round to find William behind her. He presents her with a pair of green shoes which she tries on with much delight. They fit her and she dances round in them. William then makes it clear that he is in love with her and asks for a kiss. She hesitates and he gives her a knot of pink ribbon which she pins on her right shoulder. She then blows him a kiss and backs off right, while he goes down stage left and falls into a pleasant daydream.

John strides on with his friends who bring with them the gilded sheepskins that are to be spread in front of the bride and groom as they leave the church. They practise spreading them to make this ceremony clear to the audience. The groom is shy but one of the friends prances round imitating a proud bridegroom and calling to Dorcas to act the bride. This she does with many glances towards James. She is obviously summing up the advantages of being a butcher's bride. Father now appears with a snow white lamb, spangled with gold, which he leads with a pink ribbon rein. Dorcas wavers visibly and James springs up full of hope.

The crowd gathers round and admires the lamb and moves off to the table for a quick one. Richard marches on with his friends, men and girls, all waving strips of brightly coloured leather and plaits of the same material. They show how the strips are to be laid down as a carpet and the plaits form a guard of honour like swords over the heads of the happy pair. A friend plays the part of this groom in a contrasting manner from the last. Dorcas still plays the bride, but now she is looking at William, wondering whether she will choose to be a cobbler's bride. William comes forward with a hopeful air.

The two real brides, Phoebe and Audrey, now appear, are met and kissed by their grooms and mingle with the crowd.

The stage now has the cobbler, Richard, his friends, family and Audrey, his bride, on one side and the butcher, John, his friend's family and Phoebe, his bride, on the other. James is downstage right; William downstage left and Dorcas is in the centre. There is general jollity.

Now Charles enters with Celia and Dorcas at once realises that she could have an even more glamorous guard of honour if she marries him. She advances on him invitingly.

James and William are infuriated and rush forward and stand between her and the interloper. They take it in turns to plead with her, pushing each other out of the way; but she edges away from them and beckons Charles to come to her. The two rejected suitors, united in their fury, stride to the tables to drown their sorrows.

Dorcas and Charles now have a coy little chat downstage right. The others all crowd round the happy pairs teasing them, and the bridesmaids bring in little bunches of broom, which are tied to the sleeves of the bridesmaids and the ushers. The two processions form up and are ready to go to the church.

Dorcas runs across the stage, looking back at Charles, but he is waving offstage at Celia, who comes to him, and they exchange loving, very loving, kisses. There is general but kindly laughter at Dorcas's dilemma, and an older woman comforts her. Dorcas looks at her two ex-suitors, but they will not see her and she follows the procession disconsolately, first throwing the pink and blue knots of ribbon on the table in front of the men. They look at them in a surprised way, then fill their mugs again and toast each other and walk off in the opposite direction.

Dorcas turns just in time to see them go, gets ready to cry, but suddenly catches sight of her green shoes and is slightly consoled. She picks up a twig of broom for her sleeve and goes off to the wedding.

PART THREE

RESTORATION, GEORGIAN AND REGENCY PERIOD

CHAPTER XIII

THE SPIRIT OF THE PLAYS

Spirit of the Restoration plays—Development of plays and place of performance—Style of acting—The Georgian theatre and its setting—Regency audience and plays—The modern producer's problems—List of reference books, genuine period playwrights and modern period plays, both one-act and three-act

THE Restoration Comedy is, perhaps, the *enfant terrible* of the period plays. The speeches are shockingly funny, no character hesitates to say aloud things which in a later period are only implied. The situations in themselves might be construed in an innocent manner were it not for the shattering frankness of the speeches. A timid member of the audience might well be unable to believe his own ears but they were not written for timid audiences. They were written for a comparatively small section of society, the sophisticates of London, who were revelling in enjoying themselves after the end of the reign of the Puritans. Charles II was on the throne, the exiles had returned to England and their possessions; and the theatres, which had been closed for twenty years, hastened to please their patrons. The plays, therefore, were written for a specialised public and must be judged accordingly. They come into the same category as the modern Intimate Revue which assumes a certain knowledge of the world and a blushproof audience.

The fact that actresses were now playing the female parts, instead of the boys who up to now had always taken the female parts, encouraged the authors to introduce many more scenes of seduction and pursuit than had hitherto been seen. The plots became far less concerned with who killed who than with who paired off with whom; the swords and daggers of the earlier period gave way almost entirely to the barbed darts of Cupid. Love was a highly involved game, and the more complications there were the better. This was due to the French influence of the Comedy of Manners. Where the Jacobeans wallowed in a blood-bath, the Restoration playwrights pranced among the roses.

The playhouses were small and intimate. The theatres were roofed in, the stage had retreated from the audience and now had a proscenium arch and a drop curtain. There was still an apron stage on which short scenes could be played but the picture-frame stage was beginning to show itself. The Masques had shown what could be done in the way of scenery and scenic effects, but it is well to remember that these effects had not been seen in the theatre. The Masques had been played in large halls such as the Inns of Court. The Theatre was now embarking on a new phase of its existence; new authors, new techniques of acting and a new way of presenting the plays. It also had a new type of audience and, although this has given us an enchanting series of comedies, it was in many ways unfortunate. The Theatre up to this date had been of the People; after this date it became the toy of Society, and remained so for far too long.

There were only two theatres which had the King's Patent to perform drama alone, the others had to put on a mixed bill which could include anything from acrobats to wrestling matches. The ordinary member of the public rather naturally felt that he got more for his money if he went to the mixed bill than if he only saw a play. Charles himself set a very good example by going regularly to the theatre. Unhappily it was about the only way in which he did set a good example and there was a general feeling among the reputable members of the community that if the King went there it was no place for a solid citizen to frequent. The fact that the King chose some of his mistresses from among the actresses went far to confirm this attitude. The point could be made that he chose far more mistresses from among the Court ladies; the solid citizen probably felt that what the eye did not see, the heart could not grieve at.

The Puritan view took a long time to disappear among the working people (if it ever did) and actresses were considered little better than prostitutes. The Court were not concerned generally (only personally) with the morals of the actresses; so they were free to enjoy the charming new spectacle of a talented group of players performing a glittering set of plays. The intrigues that they saw on the stage were fully appreciated by a Court that practised the sport nightly, and the epigrams delighted a King who was himself extremely witty. This type of audience put the actors on their mettle. They were playing Court ladies and gentlemen and being judged by the real thing, so that the manners and style had to be beyond reproach. The fops, who so often appear in these plays, had to have the right mannerisms to arouse an audience, who saw them in their own circle, to instant knowledgeable laughter. There had to be the right touch of satire, too, as there is a limit to the extent to which people will laugh at themselves.

The spirit of the period was an exuberant one, with gaudy flourishes and a gay abandon. Life was exciting and full of promise and success was in the air, not only for the highly born but for the artisans, the merchants, the apprentices and the whole country. This phase lasted from 1660 to about 1710.

The accession of Queen Anne who did not care for plays was followed by the reign of George who did not understand English, so the theatre attracted a different type of public. The tradesmen and the growing middle-classes were sound in their morals and unsound in their taste. They asked for pathos rather than tragedy and sentimentality rather than passion. The emphasis was now more on the heroine than on the hero and platitudes took the place of wit.

The shape of the theatres was changing and this influenced the style of acting. There was still an apron stage but it jutted out in front of the proscenium arch. The theatres were larger and the feeling of intimacy between audience and players was getting lost. The grand style of acting was settling down into a special technique. From 1705 to 1780 is an age of actors and actresses with little or no respect for playwrights. There is an unbroken record of talent from Nell Gwynne onwards, including Betterton, Mrs. Oldfield, Wilkes, Booth, Quin, Garrick, Peg Woffington, Macklin and Mrs. Siddons. What they wanted was vehicles for virtuosity and what they wanted was what they got. They did not have it all their own way, however, as the public also had to be given what it wanted, which was variety and light relief. This meant dances (particularly the Hornpipe, which they welcomed in any pause of the proceedings), songs and pantomimes. Even Garrick had to give in and act as Harlequin in his own pantomime production in 1727. The eighteenth century public was a demanding one and the actors were its servants.

The Georgian Theatre, practically bereft of good playwrights, concentrated on acting and mechanics. This makes it comparatively easy for a modern producer, if he wishes, to reproduce a Georgian play in its original setting without all the problems that an Elizabethan play poses. In the last half of the eighteenth century the stage had wing flats and used side wings and back shutters. These were moved and rearranged in full view of the audience. There were often practical doors and windows, built-up effects of cliffs or rocks and cut-outs of trees and bushes.

The stage was lit by hoops of candles hanging from the ceiling or candles in wall-brackets and "floats" or footlights of candles set in a trough in front of the apron stage. Garrick altered this to lighting placed at the side of the stage with reflectors. This is a significant change, as it meant that the apron stage was left in shadow, and this in turn meant that the actor retreated from the front of the stage to where he could be seen. The apron stage had to wither away and leave the actor with the awful problem of the Aside. The Restoration aside was simple. The actor only had to go to the edge of the apron stage and he was in the heart of the pit, which was delighted to be told of his fell designs on any lady's virtue. He could wink at them and they could wink back. He could then swagger upstage carrying the good wishes of every man in the pit.

In the Georgian theatre the actor could come to the front of the stage but it would be too much in shadow for a wink to be seen. So the aside had to be taken upwards while standing on the lighted part of the stage and the extra emphasis must be done with the voice and eyes while something had to be done with the rest of the cast so that they could pretend they had not heard. The aside had to be thrown into the air, like a child who, knowing that he is saying a forbidden swearword, will practice it when he is by himself. Deaf people can cause some dismay by unconsciously speaking aloud, and this tone is the one to be aimed at by the modern actor for such an aside.

The long list of authors at the end of this chapter seems to contradict the fact that there were no playwrights, but in this period there were many more plays published than were performed. Plays did not run very long—eleven days was a spectacular run—and authors could make more money from the book than from the production.

Towards the end of the eighteenth century there was a reaction from sentimentality and Goldsmith and Sheridan were the chief exponents of this trend. There is a glittering rocket of comedies to light the close of the century. These were played with polish and extreme elegance both of diction and movement and tax the modern actor in all that these imply. These plays need authority in acting sustained throughout without hesitation or faltering: words and actions timed and executed as in an intricate dance, coupled with an airy, crisp attack. The sense of fun and debunking positively crackles from the dialogue and the unforgivable sin is to take life heavily.

It requires a genuine imaginative effort for moderns to play Georgian comedy effectively. The diction has to be precise but not affected (except in the case of fops) and the integration of speech and movement exceedingly accurately timed. This cannot be achieved mechanically; it must spring imaginatively from understanding how the people behaved and why. Players must have a clear picture of the ideas they are presenting and the characters they are meant to be. White wigs are like a uniform, they tend to destroy the individuality of the players and make it tricky for the audience to recognise different characters. Throughout the play strong characterisation is needed if this is not to happen. Luckily the plays all provide this in speeches which show marked personal idiosyncracies. In spite of this, the actors often get bogged down in their trappings. They represent paper dolls instead of the Georgians who flourished at a time when eccentricity was encouraged and admired.

The British talent for doggedly ploughing on in the face of defeat is seen at its best, or worst, in many productions of costume plays. High-pitched trilling laughs ring out falsely between pompous speeches as the cast proceed to tramp heavily on any sparks of comedy. The actual physical control of speech and movement needs to be of a high standard, but it is the imagination which must be first kindled to give the flicker and sparkle that will fire the audience to applause. The actor need not aim at authenticity but at the *effect* of authenticity to recreate the play for the present-day audience. The idiom is strange for many rural audiences, so points must be clearly brought out. The actor as well as the producer must be able to invent business for any jokes that may take a little time to travel across the footlights.

The actor playing period tragedy sometimes fails to strike the happy medium between being dull and being "ham". He should learn the words even sooner than usual so that he is entirely at home in the idiom and has no fear of running out of breath at the crucial moment. The moderns can take in the fact of thousands being killed by an atom bomb with nonchalance but are apt to giggle if they see six men killed one after the other and their corpses left about the stage. This is partly the producer's problem; he must cultivate a pretty talent for disposing of corpses. The actors will get plenty of practice in killing and getting killed, so they must work out a variety of positions for dying.

There is a vast amount of real and passionate emotion in these plays which, in their original productions, swept the audience off their feet. The freshness that the average amateur can bring to these emotions should enable the plays to have a similar success with present audiences. It is all too rare to see chances given to a player to tear a passion to pieces without an immediate anti-climax, but here all the scenes can be played up to the hilt, or rather up to the opportune fall of the curtain.

Melodrama originally meant that a serious play had

music to enhance the drama: soft trills were for the heroine, sinister notes for the villain and throbbing chords for love-scenes. The Melodramas held sway from 1770 onwards and were very much stronger meat than the more familiar Victorian melodramas that are often burlesqued. Terrible things happened alike to the guilty and the innocent. They sometimes give the impression that the playwright thought of something dreadful and then put it into instant action with whoever was the next character to enter regardless as to their suitability. There is always a confidant who has a succession of dreary one-line speeches such as, "And then?" or "Pray continue, Sir Philip", and Sir Philip always does. These parts have to be played up with intense concentration if the scene is to come across and the actor must never relax during the long listening periods. A typical example of such a scene contains a description of a man who discovered his betrothed in the arms of his brother and saw red. He snatched the girl away with one hand while with the other he buried his dagger (which he had handy) in the heart of his brother. "What followed?" queried the confidant. What indeed! It will at once be realised that an actor in melodrama will have to be ambidextrous as well as talented to sustain such roles. Plays such as *Castle Spectre* (Matthew Lewis, 1797) etc., also revelled in stage effects and trap-doors through which the horrid apparitions could appear and disappear to cause the maximum amount of dismay. Stage effects were of a very high standard at this time and were the talk of theatrical Europe. England had bigger and better ones than any other country. This trend is most amusingly summed up in *The Drama at Home*, where a manager has written a play with only a detonating bomb in each act, so that there is no necessity for actors at all.

To sum up, the Restoration Comedy burns like a Guy Fawkes bonfire, the Georgian Comedy sparkles like a catherine-wheel and the Regency Tragedy glows like a murky lantern. Each must have its qualities and style appreciated, presented and communicated to the audience.

LIST OF REFERENCE BOOKS

The Playgoer's Handbook to Restoration Drama 1660–1710	M. Elwin	(Cape)
English Restoration Drama—its relation to past English and past and contemporary French drama from Johson via Molière to Congreve	M. Ellerhauge	(Levin & Munksgaard, Copenhagen
Plays about the Theatre in England from 'The Rehearsal' in 1671 *to the Licensing Act in* 1737*—or, The Self-Conscious Stage and its Burlesque and Satirical Reflections in the Age of Criticism*	D. F. Smith	(O.U.P.)
English Comic Drama 1700–50	F. W. Bateson	(O.U.P.)
English Pastoral Drama, from the Restoration to the date of publication of the 'Lyrical Ballads' 1660–1798	J. Marks	(Methuen)

An 18*th Century Playhouse, Theatre Royal, Bristol*	James Ross	(O.U.P.)
In the Transactions of the Royal Society of Literature, Vol. xxii, 1945.		
The Georgian Playhouse	Richard Southern	(Pleiades Books 1948)
The 18*th Century Theatre at Richmond, Yorkshire*	S. Rosenfield	(York Georgian Soc. 1947)

These three books are concerned with the actual theatres, not plays, and give a clear description of the settings and use of the stage of the period.

An Introduction to 18*th Century Drama* 1700–1800	Frederick S. Boas	(Clarendon Press, Oxford)

This is a survey of playwrights and an analysis of their plots and style in writing.

Best 18th Century Comedies
Edited by John E. Uhler (Knopf, N.Y.)

The title explains itself.

Restoration Comedy 1660–1720 Bonamy Dobrée (O.U.P.)

A History of Restoration Drama 1660–1700 Allardyce Nicoll (C.U.P.)

The Drama of Sensibility—A Sketch of the History of English Sentimental Comedy and Domestic Tragedy 1696–1780 Ernest Bernbaum (O.U.P.)

This book is included because, while not giving direct practical help, it throws an intriguing light on the drama of the period.

The British Theatre Association, 9 Fitzroy Square, London W1P 6AE, has a play library, and gives advice and information to all its members; books can be borrowed singly as well as in sets for play-reading.

Some Playwrights of the Period

John Dryden	1631–1700
Sir George Etheridge	1634–91
William Wycherley	1640–1715
John Dennis	1657–1734
William Congreve	1670–1729
Colley Cibber	1671–1757
Ambrose Philips	*c.* 1671–1749
Joseph Addison	1672–1719
Richard Steele	1672–1729
Nicholas Rowe	1674–1718
George Farquhar	1677–1707
John Gay	1685–1732
George Lillo	1693–1739
James Thomson	1700–48
Edward Moore	1712–57
David Garrick	1717–79
John Home	1722–1808

Isaac Bickerstaffe	1724–1812
Arthur Murphy	1727–1805
Oliver Goldsmith	1730–74
Richard Cumberland	1732–1811
George Coleman	1732–94
Hugh Kelly	1739–1817
Richard Brinsley Sheridan	1751–1817
Elsie Inchbald	1753–1821
Thomas Morton	1764–1830

Two useful Collections of Plays are:

Types of English Drama 1660–1780. Ed. D. H. Stevens (Gunn)
This includes 22 plays of this period.

18*th Century Plays* Ed. J. Hampden (Dent)
This includes 8 plays of this period of very varied types.

Some Plays by Modern Authors about these Periods

Full Length

1680	*In Good King Charles' Golden Days*	G. B. Shaw	(Constable)
1669	*And So to Bed*	J. B. Fagan	(French)
1710	*Viceroy Sarah*	N. Ginsbury	(French)
1716	*The Immortal Lady*	C. Bax	(French)
1735–88	*The Man with the Book* (Dr. Johnson) (Contained in *Columbia University, Copy*, 1928)	A. Porter	(Appleton, N.Y.)
1748–73	*Clive of India*	W. P. Lipscombe and R. J. Mimey	(French)
1760	*The Mask of Virtue*	C. Sternheim	(Gollancz)
1784	*Berkeley Square*	J. L. Balderston and J. C. Squire	(French)
18th Cent.	*The Marquise*	N. Coward	(Benn)
18th Cent.	*The Man with a Load of Mischief*	A. Dukes	(French)
1810	*Penny for a Song*	J. Whiting	(Heinemann)
1814–19	*The First Gentleman*	N. Ginsbury	(French)
1815	*He was Born Gay*	E. Williams	(Heinemann)

One-Act Plays

18th Cent.	*The King's Daughters*	J. Hayes	(Garnet Miller)
1766	*Count Albany*	D. Carswell	(Deane)
1776	*Great Catherine*	G. B. Shaw	(Constable)
1796	*Man of Destiny*	G. B. Shaw	(Constable)

CHAPTER XIV

MOVEMENT IN COSTUME

Outline of costume from 1668 to 1820—Movement in costume—List of costume accessories for movement and hair-styles for each period—List of costume books—List of artists who sum up the visual aspects of the periods

THE outline of costume from 1668 to 1820 covers almost every variation possible to shroud the human shape. In 1668 the man's face, hands and calves are the only recognisable features. He wears a large-brimmed plumed hat, heavy periwig with curls over his shoulders and forehead, squarecut coat and waistcoat hanging to his knees, wide stiff cuffs and ruffles reaching to his knuckles, and knots of ribbon wherever a clear surface threatens to emerge. The lady covers herself with bell-shaped skirt and sleeves and obscures the shape of her head with a high fontage like a mantilla and veil. She is allowed to show her face, her hands, neck and bosom when she is indoors but when she goes out she must wear a small mask and a large hooded cloak (*see* Fig. 24).

From 1690 the man's figure starts to emerge until by 1810 he is clad in such skin-tight garments that almost every play of muscles can be clearly seen. The lady of 1810, not to be outdone, wears a dampened muslin dress clinging closely to her figure; but no one is likely to bother about watching anything except the very intriguing decolletage. This is just (and only just) decent and even this is a concession to modern squeamishness, as contemporary accounts make it abundantly clear that nothing was really concealed.

The Georgian costumes are exactly in the middle of these two extremes. Both sexes have corsets, high-heeled

FIG. 24. Restoration Lady

shoes, white wigs and lace ruffles at neck and sleeves. The men have beautiful brocades and satins for their costumes and so do the ladies. Both dresses and coats have tightly-fitted waists and full skirts, stockings are of silk, jabots and cuffs of lace. The lady has a hoop and sometimes panniers or the skirt open over an elaborate petticoat and the length of the skirt varies from time to time. The variety of hats worn during this hundred years is bewildering, so a costume book must always be consulted. The man wears a sword from the Restoration to the Regency when it was forbidden by Beau Brummel.

Perhaps it might be summed up that the Restoration man is like a gaudy parrot, the Georgian man like a white peacock and the Regency man like a sleek swallow. These clothes all impel certain movements, if only the actor will allow them to and not try to behave as if he were in his usual clothes.

Stage movement from 1668 to 1820 abounds in flourishes. The Restoration play demands a flourish like a dashing signature written in scarlet ink with an ultra-broad nib. The curlecues of the Georgian plays are more like an exquisitely graceful letter inscribed with the finest of pens. The most common mistake of actors is to confuse these two periods which differ in essentials of spirit and style.

The Restoration man has to carry off heavy over-trimmed garments and needs a swaggering movement of the whole body. He has to remove a broad-brimmed plumed hat with a sweep, if it is not to give the effect of falling off through topheaviness. The actor must stand no nonsense from his costume; he must dominate it with delight.

The best walk is with a fair stride and a firm standing position to finish in, not just a cessation of the walk. If the weight rests on the back foot and the other is placed forward and to the side, with at least the length of the foot between the back and the front foot, the actor will be in a good position to address any part of the stage. His arms should be held slightly away from his body so that he is ready to make the broad gestures that his wide cuffs emphasise. Delicate finger-work is rather lost in this period but it comes into its own in the Georgian costume. Here the actor can have a cane to wave or a muff or a handkerchief, if he finds difficulty in hand gestures. Other movement accessories are suggested in the list at the end of this chapter. These extra details are meant to help in characterisation, which is vital in all plays of any period. They are not intended to be added as an indiscriminate extra touch. They were used just as cigarettes nowadays, to point epigrams, and must not be made fidgety.

The position of the arms must be carefully studied in front of a mirror, as the costume tends to make the actor look like a box with a head coming out of one end and legs emerging from the other. He should sit squarely on his chair; lounging upsets the set of the coat. He can use a turn from the waist with great effect and can bend sideways, but to bend forward the back must be kept erect and the diaphragm held in.

There is a relish about the movement of this broad type; it should show swagger and a pleasing feeling of superiority. The control should not be careful but zestful.

The extreme fops exaggerated their movements in a staccato way, they minced rather than strode. They had a quick turn of the head to flick their curls, they would clutch their muffs and peep over them and toy elaborately with their canes. They could make great play with waving handkerchiefs or a flower and their mannerisms were often ludicrous. The actor can also use a mannerism of voice, either deeply drawled or a very high-pitched and an affected delivery. It should always have a clear diction, as many of the fops are given the most gorgeous comedy lines. (*See* Fig. 25.)

FIG. 25. Restoration Man

The lady's movement, while it should be graceful, has a vitality and attractive bounce that epitomises the spirit of the age. The waist must be flexible but firmly controlled and there must never be the suggestion of a sag in the middle. The ladies preened and pranced like pigeons, drew their heads in and fluttered their eyelashes as they melted into the gentlemen's arms, and altogether showed the complete knowledge of their charms that is apparent in the newly-curled poodle. All this needs practice, preferably in front of the glass. The actress must be aware of the picture she presents; the head poised proudly, the body with a trim waistline, and the hands arranged in an attractive position suitable to the character she is playing.

Movement was an art that every girl learned as part of her education, and it is useless to try to present it in a modern, realistic way unless the play is presented in modern clothes. While the inner characterisation must have clarity and reality, the outer shell must have a decorative quality. The dress often has to be lifted and set down again; it must happen in a graceful sweeping curve, not merely be picked up and then dropped. The fan can almost be classed as a weapon; it was used for skirmishes, pitched battles and absolute surrender. It had as much life as a tame bird; it was never the metronome, beating relentlessly, that is seen in modern actresses' hands.

The confidential ladies' maids who figure in many plays aped the manners of their mistresses and had a pseudo polish. They fancied themselves and their mistresses were fancied; the difference must be clear.

High heels are a menace for men who will not use commonsense and moderate their stride. Wide skirts are tiresome for girls who always choose pencil-slim models; the actress must use trial and error before she can feel comfortable in her walk. It is impossible to say in a book how each of the many hundreds of movements used in a play should be done. The study of pictures, together with an understanding of the character, are the best help to players.

All period movement is partly guesswork based on pictures and the fact that the human body has not altered basically. The only real difference lies in the fact that the clothes restricted the movements. No Georgian lady could hope to smash a volley through at tennis in the same way that a girl in shirt and shorts can do now. The effort would result in a split bodice and sleeves, painfully jabbed ribs from sharp corset-bones, a skirt torn by the raised foot and an actress flat on her face as she trod on the hem and fell headlong. It is the air of elegance that is important and this is attained by the carriage of the head and shoulders and the delicate hand and wrist gestures of one who has never had to use force for anything.

Modern men often fling themselves into a chair and the modern chair bounces them right back. A Georgian man proceeded circumspectly. Grasping the chair-back with his right hand he would lower himself slowly on to the edge of the chair. Then sliding his left leg out in front of him, he would cautiously bend the right so as to ease the strain on his breeches. Once sitting, he could afford to draw in the left leg until he could rest part of his weight on his left foot and place his left hand on his sword hilt. When he wanted to get up, he again grasped the chair-back and pushed his weight forward, gradually transferring it from his right foot to his left until he was standing upright. This is worth practising, as it is the only way to be sure that the costume will be returned to the hiring firm in the condition in which it arrived and not split in several places. These places, it may be worth mentioning, are just those which would be most embarrassing for the actor who has to stay on the stage for the next scene.

When the lady sits she has to see that her skirt is

smoothed under her and that she does not sag at the waist or cross her legs.

All servants have much freer movements, as obviously their clothes were cut so that they could do their work properly. All country clothes, too, were cut with more room to move, as the countrymen and women, whether villagers or rich people, led more active lives. They had to ride or walk through fields or over very bad roads if they wanted to exercise.

The Georgian dress, both for man and woman, needs an erect carriage of the head and shoulders and a taut waist if it is to give the correct effect of elegance. Full frills of lace fall from the elbows of the ladies' dresses and from the wrists of the mens' shirts, so the elbow movements of the one sex and the wrist movements of the other should make use of these assets, with a circular twist to throw the lace back. The wigs must be securely fitted so that the head can be tossed or sharply turned without discomfort or uncertainty. Cloaks were worn by both sexes and can add immensely to the emphasis of a turn or an exit. The full hooped skirts take up a good deal of room and must be manoeuvred through doors; they will not sweep obligingly past obstacles, as the Restoration skirts do, but will hitch up and show the awkwardness of the actress. They need care when sitting down and it is easier for the actress to use her hands to take each side of the skirt, spread it out and rearrange it as she sits. At one period, the skirts were reasonably short and cleared the ankles, but they were always stiff and cumbersome.

The men's coats had stiffened skirts and should be lifted aside as the actor sits down. The sword also needs careful handling if it is not to give its owner some nasty moments. The left hand can rest gracefully on its hilt for most of the time until the actor has become accustomed to allowing for the extra room the sheath needs. Other actors in the scene will soon learn to give a wide berth to the clumsy wearer and this means that the scene will lack the right grouping. When the sword is drawn, it must be done quickly and confidently: no one of that period would have taken out his weapon in a fumbling manner. When it is replaced, the actor must readjust his coat so that it sits well over the sheath. All swordplay should be done extremely well in a straight play: there is endless opportunity for comedy in bad swordplay. (*See* Fig. 26.)

There is scope for a producer's sense of comedy in the fact that in the eighteenth century the actors and actresses all wore contemporary costume and wigs with only a top dressing of period detail to show that they were Ancient Gods or Egyptian Royalty. A tartan scarf draped round a complete Georgian suit would indicate Macbeth, and ropes of scallop shells festooning pink satin panniers, with a pearl wreath on a towering white wig, would tell the audience that Venus had just risen from the sea. There was no importance attached to dressing the character in period or to realistic details such as wearing dusty shoes if the character was supposed to have come in after a long walk.

A modern producer dealing with a modern play for a modern audience has to recreate many details that a period audience never bothered about at all. There are often objections to putting on a Georgian play, as the costumes are expensive to hire and if they are made by the company they may only be used for the one play. The programme for the season could be planned to include one serious Georgian play: then, later in the season, a producer with a sense of satire could be asked to produce one of the heroic Georgian plays in the Georgian manner, that is to say, using the costumes with the extra details as suggested above. The audience would thus have a new experience and would delight in the humour. *The Governor of Cyprus* by John Oldmixon, or Aaron Hill's *Aziera* would both lend themselves to this scheme as they include foreign costumes

FIG. 26. Georgian Man Fencing

that would be easy to convey in some telling detail. If this experiment is tried in a village, the audience should be given some warning of what to expect and it might be worth while to plant a knowledgeable person in the middle of the hall to lead the laughter. It would disconcert the cast if the entire play took place in respectful silence because the audience were not sure if the comedy was intentional.

From 1800 onwards a slightly different type of curtsy was used because of the high-waisted dress with the narrow skirt. The long line from waist to instep was broken ungracefully if the front knee was bent in the usual way. The curtsy was therefore taken stepping back and bending the back knee, which left the front leg extended to its full length with the toe pointed. The dress then clung to the thigh and kept its straight line. The hands could either be held out to the side, or the fan could be clasped to the bosom. If a small train was worn, it usually had a loop which fitted on to the little finger of the left hand while the right hand held the fan. If the dress had a reasonable amount of fullness, then it was picked up with both hands at the front and a curtsy was made as before. Sitting down presents no difficulty, but the back must be held upright and the legs must not be crossed. The walk should be a smooth glide with small steps, a straight back and a well-poised head. The little flat slippers seem to tempt the actress to trip to and fro on her toes but the sight of the whole cast trotting about for a long scene is unnerving—they look so like mechanical toys. The foot movement is exactly the same as in an ordinary walk. There is no constriction around the waist, so the ladies can turn and languish at their partners and bend sideways to look admiringly at any gentleman in sight.

The actor's walk is best done with one arm bent behind his back while the other hand rests on the lapel of his coat. This is also a good standing position, as the coat usually fitted very tightly across the shoulders. Fobs were worn hanging from the waistcoat pocket, and can be fingered, or a watch can be put in that pocket. A gentleman did not cross his legs in the presence of ladies but sat upright. Amongst his own sex he could lounge as much as his clothes permitted. He invariably used a walking-stick out of doors and if he had to raise his hat it was held on high until he had passed the person he greeted.

Accessories for Movement

These accessories are meant to be considered from the point of view of helping with "business", not as extra trimmings.

1668–1720

List of Kings and Queens of the Periods

Charles II	1668–85
James II and Anne	1685–9
William III and Mary	1689–1702
Queen Anne and Prince George	1702–14
George I	1714–27

As the French kings had such an influence on fashions in dress, manners and furnishings, they are included in this chapter.

Louis XIV	1643–1715

Men's Movement Assessories from 1668–1720

Watches, round and egg-shaped, were hung from the neck by ribbons or put in the waistcoat pocket.

Long canes with gold, amber or carved heads were carried: slits were made in the cane to take the loop, which was decorated with bows of ribbon and tassels.

Large flat, square or round muffs, with ribbon bows and frills of lace, were hung from the neck.

Full periwigs with long curls all round the sides and back were worn with a parting in the middle of the front which later became turned into a curled fringe and, slightly later, the fringe curled up into a pompadour or large quiff.

Tobacco may only be smoked at home.

Broad-brimmed beaver hats with plumes at the side fastened with a buckle were worn and at this time men started taking their hats off in the house.

The sword now had a knuckle bow hilt instead of a cross. Shoes had square toes, high red heels and the tongue came up over the instep; a wide bow of wired lace or a jewelled buckle.

Silk stockings for gentlemen, woollen for servants.

Ladies' Movement Accessories from 1668–1720

Ear-rings, rings on every finger, choker necklaces, bracelets, jewelled ribbon knots and bows on person or costume.

Muffs large, flat and long or square.

Fans of paper, gauze silk, satin or lace, all folding.

Ladies can wear triangular fichus or lace or muslin, or a long narrow strip of lace round the neck, tied in a bow or tucked into the bosom.

Silk, satin or lace aprons tied with ribbons.

Cloaks with hoods of any colour, but reaching to the hem of the dress.

High-heeled shoes, with a frill of lace round the ankle for "best".

Hair taken up in a knot on top of the head, curled on the forehead (but not at the sides) and a "Fontage", a head-dress of lace rather like a mantilla, with ribbons falling down at the back.

Reticules, pomanders, gold or silver-headed canes, small enamelled boxes for comfits, small watches, silk parasols —very tiny.

Black crêpe or muslin was worn for mourning and the wig had black powder.

1680–1800

Peasant women could wear a laced bodice, folded linen handkerchief round the neck, flat plain hat and a full-skirted dress with a large apron.

Peasant men could wear plain shirt and breeches of stout material, laced jerkin, heavy shoes and a wide-brimmed hat with a square crown. *Running footmen* carried sticks with hinged tops which held the message, and wore soft shoes.

Black pages wore a copy of the smart clothes, topped by a gay turban usually of silk and satin. They sometimes had a holder on their shoulder into which the handle of their mistress' parasol could be fitted if they had to hold it up for long periods.

Doctors may have a pomander on top of the cane, which can be tapped to release scent, tortoiseshell lorgnettes or quizzing-glass.

Fops may carry large combs of tortoiseshell and ivory which they may use in public and keep in their muffs on a long ribbon.

Soldiers may carry pikes or muskets: they may wear a moustache before 1680, and a small chin beard after 1680.

Officers may wear a dress sword on the left side and may finger a fringed sash and heavy gold epaulettes.

The sword hilt may go through a slit in the coat.

Snuff boxes may be gold, silver, jewelled or enamelled.

They may have seal-rings, watches and jewelled buckles.

1700–1770

Apple-green, sky-blue, shell-pink, turquoise, deep rose, primrose, daffodil-yellow, were all colours worn by fashionable people at the Court. White was exceedingly popular, both for men and women. Chinz was worn exclusively by women: vivdly striped silk was worn by both sexes. Towards the end of this period, the shades of mouse, puce and Vandyke-brown became the mode.

1730–1770

Lists of Rulers

George II and Caroline of Anspach	1727–60
Louis XV	1715–74

HAIR. *Men.* Powder used on wigs, curls were drawn back from the forehead and grouped at the side of the head and a black bow worn at the nape of the neck. Wig-bags of black taffeta sometimes held the back curls.

Ramillies wig had a short pigtail at the back, with a bow at both ends.

Rich dressing-gowns of figured brocade could be worn over the shirt and breeches. Turkish slippers with curled-up toes, and a draped small turban until the wig was put on—if the scene takes place in a bedroom.

Ladies. Hair simply dressed away from the forehead, curls at the side of the face and a knot at the back. A small cluster of flowers, circlet of pearls, knot of ribbon or one rose could be poised at the front of the head: long curls over the front of the shoulders for a ball.

Mobcap: a round cap pulled in with ribbons can be worn indoors and kept on under a wide-brimmed straw hat for walking, or a lace cap with lappets can be tied under the chin. Shepherdess hat, tilted at the back to hold artificial flowers, can be tied under the chin, and small ruffs of ribbon or lace worn high around the throat.

A hood, square or rectangular, with a turned-back fold of a contrasting colour, can be worn out of doors, or a Venetian hat of black velvet tricorne-shape, with a lace veil which fastened under the chin.

Black velvet ribbon tied round the throat or wrist, with a diamond or pearl brooch in the centre, or sky-blue taffeta creased in deep folds round the throat, with a double string of pearls over it.

Buckles of gold, silver, steel, or jewelled, may be used for the shoes, cloak and throat-ribbon.

Handkerchiefs can be trimmed with lace and be as large as bandanas.

Patches of all sizes can be worn on the face and shoulders.

All make-up, both for men and women wearing white wigs, needs to be more pink-and-white than usual, otherwise the wig makes the face look orange. Even character make-up must be adjusted if it is not to look ridiculous. Both men and women wore make-up from 1668 to 1800 or so: therefore, the complexion must give that appearance from the stage.

1770–1820

List of Rulers

George III and Charlotte of Mecklenburg-Stretlitz	1760–1820
Louis XVI	1774–93
First Republic	1795–99

1770–1800

Ladies' Movement Accessories

Patch-boxes, comfit-boxes, smelling-bottles.

Gloves and mittens in white, cream or pastel colours.

Bracelets, earrings (stud or pendant), rings worn on any or every finger, necklaces of gold, silver, pearls or ribbons with a drop-pendant: cameos in rings, earrings or brooches.

Flowered Indian or Chinese shawls.

Parasols with ruched edges.

Chatelaine, hung on a ribbon or a silver chain from the waist, holding smelling-bottle, thimble, scissors, etc.
Powder-boxes and puffs holding white powder for dress occasions and black powder for mourning. Powder was also kept in a container like a huge pepper-pot and shaken over the head or wig.

1800–1820

Men's Movement Accessories

Shoes plain and varnished with flat heels may be strapped or buttoned over the instep and long pale pantaloons may be strapped under the instep.
Boots may be pulled up to the calf higher in front than at the back.
White or pale stockings may be worn normally and Dandies may wear striped ones.
Hair may be brushed forward in a classical way for normal occasions and powdered for formal wear. An elderly or bald man may wear a wig.
Watches and fobs may be worn two at a time, one at each side.
Toothpicks may be used, signet rings worn, twisted canes or walking-sticks carried, short canes swung or tucked, and a quizzing-glass on a stick or ribbon used.
Men of this period can adjust their black silk stocks and add a lace frilled jabot or they can twist a fold of material round the stock and tie it loosely in front with short hanging ends.
Coats can be fastened with silver, brass or jewelled buttons.
They may comb the hair into curls on the forehead, leaving it shaggy at the back of the head, and wear a hat with a cockade of feathers.
They can wear plain or embroidered gaiters.

1800–1820

Ladies' Movement Accessories

Bodices to fasten high around the neck with a brooch.
Ruffles may be put on wrists to fall over the hands.
Shoes to be buckled high on the side and worn out of doors.
Hair may be knotted in Greek style with curls hanging on each side of the face. Feathers, pearls and/or roses may be poised on top.
A lace veil on the front of the bonnet may be drawn like a curtain across the face.
A married woman may wear a turban of brocade or gauze.
A widow must wear black—so must a widower!
Ladies of uncertain age must wear lace caps indoors.
These can be fastened under the chin or drawn with a ribbon into a frill round the head and may have ribbon or lace streamers hanging down at the back.
Immensely long stoles may be worn, made of lace gauze, satin or brocade.
Velvet riding-habit may be worn with tricorne hat, gauntlet gloves and riding-whip carried. A shako hat may be worn. The narrow dress may be buttoned up the back and a fichu may be crossed on the bosom.
For evening a train may be added and held up by a loop of ribbon on the little finger.
A wide-brimmed straw hat may be tied under the chin with ribbons or swung in the hand, which may also carry a reticule.
Locket-watches, cameo sets of bracelets, brooch, earrings and necklaces of garnets, emeralds, diamonds or pearls, may be worn.
Snake necklaces and bracelets were popular.
Muff and matching jacket or fur or swansdown may be worn.

Stockings may be trimmed with lace or embroidery. (Useful work for ladies' maids.) Garters may be put on.

List of Useful Reference Books

A Short History of Costume and Armour (1066–1800) (chiefly in England) F. M. Kelly (Batsford)

Costume Design and Making M. Fernald and E. Shenton (A. & C. Black)

This book gives actual patterns for costumes which can be cut to scale and made to fit the individual.

English Costume of the 18th Century J. Laver (A. & C. Black)

This has charming coloured plates of many costumes.

Dressing the Play Norah Lambourne (Studio)

This includes costume, property-making and suggestions for building up an adaptable wardrobe for impecunious amateurs.

A History of the Uniforms of the British Army C. C. P. Lawson (Peter Davies)

What They Wore: A History of Children's Dress M. Jackson (Allen & Unwin)

Adaptable Stage Costume for Women Elizabeth Russell (Garnet Miller)

Basic bodice and skirt with additions and accessories for each period from Saxon to Victorian. Detailed patterns and sewing instructions.

List of Artists of the Periods

These are in chronological order, which will help to sum up the visual aspect for clothes and decor.

Sir Peter Lely
Sir Godfrey Kneller
Wenceslaus Hollar
Inigo Jones
Anthony Van Dyke
Watteau
Lancret

Nattier
Boucher
Fragonard
Greuze
Vigée Lebrun
William Hogarth
Sir Joshua Reynolds
George Romney
Thomas Gainsborough
John Constable
Sir Thomas Lawrence
William Blake
Rowlandson

Inigo Jones was also a sculptor and a stage designer.

Another name worth noting is that of "Capability" Brown who designed the gardens at Versailles as well as many well-known English gardens and started a new fashion in garden landscapes.

CHAPTER XV

OCCUPATIONS

Occupations, sports and amusements of the periods for stage, arena and pageant production. Classified list for each period: ladies, gentlemen, outdoor servants, indoor servants, cottage-dwellers, tradesmen, etc.—List of useful reference books

CLOTHES and lovemaking seem to the actor to dominate all these plays and although both could be classified either as an occupation or an amusement, a background must be filled in. London social life was getting more complicated in its trimmings, housewives were doing less work and servants had different duties with each generation. Country life, even, was changing as the regular service of stage-coaches brought the new fashions sooner to avid young ladies; and at the end of the eighteenth century the rise in popularity of the Spas led to smart circles functioning at Bath and Harrogate.

Love scenes can be played as ardently as need be but they will be more intriguing if the lovers have been given a solid background. The other people in the play have to be given amusements (if the author has callously denied them lovemaking) or at least occupations. These should all be planned by the producer with an eye to the probability that the character would choose them, and this is much easier in the comedies than in the tragedies. There is Lady Teazle's own assurance that she did worsted work at a sewing-table, inspected the dairy, looked after the poultry, combed the dog and practised at the spinet. The tragic heroines needed all their stamina to support the dreadful things that happened to them; it is unlikely that they had any energy left over for embroidery.

The servants' duties changed as the way of life changed with succeeding generations. Valets, instead of polishing armour, powdered wigs (*see* Fig. 27), and ladies' maids tripped out to change romantic novels at the circulating library. When candles were the only illumination, candle-snuffers were always in view (*see* Fig. 28); and it is only by careful attention to such details that a picture of the life can be shown.

Outside the houses there were many individuals doing the work that is now done by civic authorities. Dustmen and watermen are two such examples. Each town had a Towncrier who called the news. There were also watchmen who kept order if appealed to but, if they thought things were going to be difficult, were quite capable of turning a deaf ear.

Crowd scenes for city or country fairs or markets would have pedlars, quack doctors selling pills and ointments, street dentists (complete with bowls for the blood), women selling gilded gingerbread men, fortune-tellers and gipsies.

In the market there would be stalls of fruit and vegetables, stalls selling home-made fruit cordials, cakes and biscuits, and cobblers and barbers touting for customers. Street sellers all had their own way of calling their wares, often to an haunting melody. These street cries are often used as songs at concerts now, but their effectiveness for stage and pageant work has been almost entirely overlooked.

Every village green had its stocks, a punishment for small crimes, where the prisoner had to sit with his arms, feet and head thrust through holes in wooden boards while the villagers could throw refuse at him. The Shrew's Bridle, for scolding, was still used in the country and some producers might like to suggest that a troublesome actress rehearsed with this as a prop. The shrew was unable to talk while wearing the bridle. Whipping-posts were to be seen in some streets and of course Tyburn had its public gallows.

Fig. 27. Valet Adjusting Wig on Stand

Fig. 28. Maid Snuffing Candles

The streets were so filthy that people went to any function in a sedan chair carried by four chairmen. These could be hired like taxis, but noblemen would have their own, with their crest or coat-of-arms on them. The chairmen would probably dice to pass the time while waiting for fares; they would be most unlikely to read, as a taxi-driver does.

As the eighteenth century advanced, the household had to have more and more servants, each doing his own special work and not deigning to do anything else. Servants were always tipped by the visitors who came to meals and would line up waiting for it, as they do sometimes in a modern hotel.

The producer who wants to show a wealthy household can use as many small part actors as he wants if he gives each one of them a specific job to do as a servant. They were all inspected by the major-domo each day to see that they were properly dressed and did credit to the establishment. Cleanliness did not matter so much as an appearance of neatness.

Architecture was now entering a long stretch of time when all the houses were pleasant in design and colour. Soft rosy bricks, well-proportioned rooms and doors and windows, polished floors and white paint, all added up to a gracious way of life. China ornaments and Chelsea figures on shelves, cushions and rugs in every room and chintz curtains for windows and beds made the interiors charming. William and Mary had brought in the Dutch habit of growing bulbs in bowls and the tulip had become so fashionable that it was seen in fabric and embroidery designs. Windows at the beginning of the seventeenth century were tall and sashed with square panes. They became taller as the century advanced but were usually flat. Towards the end of the eighteenth century the little square balcony outside the first floor windows became the fashion and sometimes the window was also a square bow and sometimes a bulging bow. Houses still had a place where a horse could be tied up outside the front door and often a mounting-block as well.

Gardens were changing in the most extraordinary way from the herb garden and clipped hedges of the Elizabethans. There was a growing cult for landscape gardens with water used as a decoration. Ponds, streams with stepping-stones, rustic seats and houses are all possible settings for romantic scenes. This fashion came from France, where Capability Brown was playing about with Versailles and making the eight *trompe l'œil* the aim of anyone with an avenue of trees. People trimmed their gardens with ruins; clean and tidy ones were preferred, which rather ruled out the real thing. Later still, the noblemen were to build their Follies (as well as commit them in private), tall towers serving no useful purpose except to show that the owner could afford to indulge his whims. They could be pressed into service on the stage for a specially coy game of hide-and-seek.

17th Century Occupations

For Ladies

(Ladies who lived in towns would not be likely to occupy themselves with household matters in the same way that their country cousins would, so the personal things such as sewing and knitting would be more suitable for a play that was set in a city.)

Sewing with thread wound on a bobbin, small scissors, square or heart-shaped pincushion, and a polished work-box probably inlaid with mother-of-pearl, or a wooden box painted with gay flowers.

Knitting with bone needles using wool, silk or cotton yarn to make caps, stockings, purses, gloves or scarves.

Writing letters or household lists, using quill pens of brilliant colours, and shaking sand from a holder like a large pepper-pot to dry the ink which was in a china, pottery, brass or silver pot.

Painting in water-colours either small landscapes, portraits or children's toys. Dolls' faces could be painted, or hoops in gay stripes, or battledores and shuttlecocks. The feathers of the shuttlecocks were often painted in bright colours.

Making lace on a small pillow.

Embroidering handkerchiefs, cushion-covers, chair seats, bell-pulls or reticules with birds and flowers in wool or silk.

Making up beauty potions and creams and lotions in small bowls with pestle and mortar. These should be tested during the scene to show the audience whether the mixture had to be taken internally or externally. Pink, yellow or green colouring was added and the mixtures put into little china or glass pots, jars or bottles.

Drying oranges to make pomanders stuck with cloves. This would be particularly likely to be done during a period of plague.

Drying flower petals and lavender to make scent or to put in spotted muslin bags for the linen cupboard.

Making sweets or almond biscuits that did not need cooking, only mixing, colouring and moulding into shapes of fruit or flowers.

All these occupations can be used in the eighteenth century in addition to those listed.

For Gentlemen

No work was done in these periods by gentlemen who lived in London, except writing letters or Parliamentary speeches; in this case they used the same equipment that is listed in the Ladies' section.

They could practise fencing or dancing, or choose material for new clothes, or be fitted for clothes, shoes or wigs. They could also sample several kinds of snuff before deciding on which to order.

Country gentlemen could check items in estate ledgers, which were long and narrow, bound in red or brown leather. They could also mend whips or clean pistols, although this was usually done by servants.

For Household Servants

Laying the table with a white cloth edged with lace or embroidery, spoons, forks, knives, goblets and wine-glasses and silver spice boxes.

Cleaning out the candlesticks and putting in fresh candles with wicks snipped neatly.

Brushing the cushions and rugs with soft brushes and hard whisk brushes.

Polishing shoes and shoe-buckles and scraping the filth off the pattens and clogs used for outdoor wear.

Polishing furniture, washing windows and paint, sweeping the hearth and bringing in baskets of small logs.

Ironing lace ruffles of shirts, using a flat iron for large surfaces and a small pointed iron for the gathers.

Cleaning and polishing the swords, sheaths and belts.

Gardeners. Growing and tending roses, lilies, iris, marigolds, violets, pansies, pink daisies, lavender, rosemary, tulips, forget-me-nots, daffodils, lilac, wallflowers and sweet williams.

Clipping the box hedges that rimmed the flower-beds.

Working with spades, forks, rakes, Dutch hoes, and carrying trug baskets for cuttings.

All these occupations continue through the centuries following.

18TH CENTURY OCCUPATIONS

For Ladies

Serving chocolate out of a pot with a long handle like a saucepan, or coffee out of a tall, thin coffeepot (*See* Fig.-29), into small cups sometimes without handles but with saucers and coffee-spoons.

Towards the end of the eighteenth century, serving tea out of silver teapots with silver milk jugs, teaspoons and sugar-bowl and tongs.

Serving small cakes and biscuits with tea or coffee: the cakes as small as *petit fours* and the biscuits finger-shaped, coloured pink, white or chocolate, and placed on flowered china plates or on silver salvers.

Playing and singing at the spinet or harpsichord (*See* Fig. 35).

Tying fresh ribbons to the chatelaine that hung at the waist, holding thimble, bodkin, tiny silver notecase and pencil, scissors and smelling-salts.

Filling small china, silver or enamel comfit boxes with sweets of marzipan or pink sugar from a large china bowl.

Embroidering chair seats, cushion-covers or firescreens either in wool or silk, in *petit* or *gros point* or other embroidery stitches. A small round frame could be used or a large standing one.

All the occupations of the preceding century can also be used.

For Household Servants

Dusting and fitting in fresh candles to candlesticks that stood on tables and to candelabras of carved and gilded wood or of glass or crystal, with five branches on each side, and to wall-brackets holding two to five candles.

Filling tinder-box with rag. Dusting small decorative bottles that stood on the mantelshelf. Putting foot-

FIG. 29. Lady Serving Chocolate

warmers into footstools—the footstools sometimes had a hinged lid and sometimes were made of fur and shaped like a tea-cosy lying on its side.

Watering potted plants and flowering plants that stood in china pots made like an openwork basket.

Polishing pewter and brass plates that were used as ornaments to hang on the walls and stand on shelves either in the dining-room in a town house or the parlour of an inn or country house.

Brushing the upholstered chairs and sofas that came into fashion in this century, and combing the tassels on the cushions.

Filling the wine-cooler in the dining-room and setting the wine glasses in openwork wicker baskets made with a separate compartment for each glass, and polishing the glasses with a linen glasscloth.

Cleaning the flowered wallpaper with a crust of bread, and brushing the silk wall panels with a long-handled soft brush.

Cleaning the ashes out of the fireplace (usually an iron basket set in an ordinary fireplace), filling a large log basket and setting the tongs, poker and hearthbrush tidily by the coal-scuttle.

Shaking the bedcurtains free of dust: the fourposter went out of fashion by the middle of this century and the half-tester came in. Polishing the furniture of the bedroom, which included the bed, chairs, table with jug and basin, table with standing mirror and wig-stand, tallboy, wardrobe and chest of drawers, and tall swinging mirror. Shaking the feather mattresses and the down pillows (in lace-edged covers for fashionable ladies). Sweeping carpets and rugs with a dustpan and brush.

In 1760, Chinese furniture and ornaments became popular and needed care and attention from the servants.

Late 18th- and Early 19th-Century Occupations

For Household Servants

All those on the preceding page and:
Brushing with a soft brush the Chinese furniture and hangings that the Regent had made fashionable.
Carrying in dishes of food to be put on the side table: vegetables include potatoes, asparagus, peas, cabbage, French beans, carrots and a variety of salads, and celery. Fruit includes apples, melons, oranges, cherries, currants, gooseberries, strawberries, raspberries, plums, mulberries, apricots and pears.
Meat includes venison, bullocks' hearts, ducks, pig's-face and vast rounds of beef and legs of mutton, raised pies and small pasties.
Servants laid out cards and score-cards with pencils and set out dice in ornamental boxes. Sometimes the gentlemen carried their own dice in their waistcoat pockets or their personal servants carried the dice and produced them at the right moment.
All servants, such as footmen, butlers and major-domos lined up in the hall after a dinner-party in a private house for tips from the guests. (This should surely be counted as an occupation.)
Collecting and giving back the hat, stick and cloaks of the guests. Holding the toy dogs of the ladies and brushing and feeding them.

Occupations 1688–1810

For Cottage-Dwellers

Dipping rushes in bowls of tallow or fat to make rushlights. Putting rushlights in a bark container hung on the wall or in a stand which could either be set on the floor or fixed into a rod, which could be screwed up or down to whatever height was needed.

Washing the earthenware bowls and plates and heavy china mugs.

Polishing the pewter tankards and jugs used for ale and beer.

Straining the milk through a piece of muslin for cheese and buttermilk.

Sorting the goose-feathers for pillows and mattresses.

Sports and Amusements

From 1688 *to* (*approx.*) 1730

Hawking—Heavy gauntlet worn on left wrist for bird to clutch. Bird was hooded with little bells on its legs.

Wrestling, leaping, tossing the hammer, pitching the bar, riding, fighting with quarterstaff and cudgel play were all part of country and town fairs and festivities.

Archery competitions and running races with one man sitting on another's shoulders or, at night, the runner brandishing a flaming torch, can all be useful material for pageants, as well as see-saws, leapfrog, battledore and shuttlecock, Blindman's Buff, Prisoner's Base, and ball games of skill.

Quoits was played by rustics—not by the gentry—and indoor tennis was played by the townsman and not by the countryman.

Skittles was played with a stick thrown at the skittles, and ninepins with a ball thrown at the pins.

Golf and football were played: golf and hockey sticks were practically the same size—rather smaller than modern hockey sticks, larger than modern golf clubs. The ball was made of dark leather. Footballs were melon-shaped and made of dark leather. Cricket was played with two stumps only a foot high and two feet apart, with a hole the size of the ball between the stumps where the batsman rested his bat.

After 1730

Fly-fishing came in. (Useful for comedy business of fisherman getting tied up in line.)
Hunting the fox with hounds grew in popularity.
Roller-skating. (Ice-skating was popular from an earlier date but this cannot be presented on the stage although, if the character is meant to be athletic, he can come on carrying his skates.)

Indoor Games for Periods 1688–1800

Chess, cards, dice games.
Marbles, whipping-tops, skipping-ropes, building blocks, rattles, dolls and musical-boxes for children were all popular.
Nine Men's Morris—a game played with a flat board with coloured pegs which had to be fitted into holes in a certain pattern.
Masquerade Costumes—The men wore animals' heads and cloaks, the ladies wore ornamental masks and brightly coloured dominoes.
At Christmas, the servants would make a Kissing Bow. Hoops were arranged in the form of a crown, covered with leaves and ribbons and with apples, candles and mistletoe at the points. Presents were hung from it by long ribbon streamers.
Early Eighteenth-Century Christmas—Food was richly decorated with leaves and gilding and can include mince-pies, boars' heads, turkeys, swans and peacocks complete with feathers and gilded beak. (A good property master essential.) Hot spiced possets can be served—like hot punch from a bowl with a ladle—into each goblet.

18th-Century Occupations to be Used in Pageant or Crowd Scenes

Tanner wearing an apron of fleecy skin.

Firemen with heavy coats and axes.

Chimney-sweep with black face and long stick with flat circular brush.

Milk-woman with double yoke holding wooden pails of milk sling over her shoulders.

Lamplighter with ladder, jug of oil and wick.

Women bootblacks with brushes, jars of blacking and polishing-cloths.

Woman selling rabbits and pheasants slung on a long stick balanced on one shoulder and protruding in front and behind her. (*See* Fig. 30.)

Women with shrimping-nets and baskets selling shrimps.

Men butchers with a tray shaped like a modern butcher's tray filled with meat covered with a blue cloth.

Baker's boy with basket of loaves on his head or arm.

Billstickers carrying posters, brushes and jar of paste.

Washerwomen carrying tubs and wooden spades to beat their washing. (*See* Fig. 31.) (In Scotland and the north of England two women stood in the washtub and trod the clothes clean.)

Country fair showman, with two bells on his hands, his head and his feet, blowing a Herald's trumpet and waving a small flag. (*See* Fig. 32.)

Dustman with a basket like a modern log-basket on his back, ringing a bell for customers to hail him to collect their rubbish (other people could throw in their orange-peel, etc.)

Watermen with tubs with handles on each side filled with water.

FIG. 30. Woman Selling Rabbits and Pheasants

FIG. 31. Washerwoman

FIG. 32. Country Fair Showman

List of Useful Reference Books

Decorative Furniture G. L. Hunter (Lippincott)
This is a picture of the beautiful forms of all ages and all periods.

Period Furniture for Everyman W. G. Menzies (Duckworth)
This is a useful book for selecting the most important points to show the audience in a period setting.

A History of Everyday Things in England M. & C. H. B. Quennell (Batsford)
Volume II covers from 1500 to 1799 and includes unusual items such as shops, work-places, etc., which are not normally used on the stage.
Volume III, 1800–1850.

English Home Life Christina Hole (Batsford)
A most fascinating book, full of the detail and information about the subject of its title from 1500 to 1800.

CHAPTER XVI

MANNERS AND DANCES

Manners and customs—Bows and curtsies—Dances for each period, Gigue, Allemande, Gavotte and Minuet—List of suggested dance music and reference books on dances

THE manners of all these periods were formal. Husbands and wives bowed and curtsied to each other, as did sons and mothers and fathers and daughters. The usual greeting of a man to a woman was a bow and then he kissed her hand. Only servants bowed with the heels together, to give a message, and bowed again before leaving the room. Maids curtsied on speaking to their employers or to anyone else of superior social standing. Tradesmen bowed on being given an order, innkeepers bowed on receiving visitors who were noble and, on the stage, it is always better to have too many bows than too few.

If a meal was served, all the dishes were put on the table and either the host served or the guests helped themselves. If, however, tea (late eighteenth century), coffee or chocolate were the only refreshments, then they were handed round on a tray, each person receiving his cup already creamed and sugared. The lady of the house poured out at a small table placed by the servant in front of her chair. If the scene was a ball, the gentlemen fetched the ladies glasses of wine but if it was in a private house, then the servants did all fetching and carrying.

A gentleman could offer his arm to escort his lady and she could put her hand on his sleeve, but only the lower classes actually went arm-in-arm. This of course was partly because the hooped skirts were so wide that it was not possible or comfortable to link arms. The maids, skirts were not wired, only very full, and the soft little caps they wore made it even possible for them to drop their heads on the shoulders of their young men. They had not such rigid corsets and were able to run at a pace impossible to their mistresses. All this adds up clearly in a production to differentiate between the gentry and the others and helps the audience to understand the complications of plots that were often based on the substitution of man for valet or vice versa.

The bow *en passant* is useful for reception or ball scenes. It was used to acknowledge or greet people when one did not wish to pause and have a conversation. It consisted of bowing from the waist while dragging one foot from behind to in front without quite stopping the onward movement of the walk. If the person to be greeted was on the right of the greeter, the bow was on the right and the dragged foot was the right foot with its toe pointed; this was all reversed if the person to be greeted was on the left. It was quite a difficult bow to perform successfully, as the momentum was not actually lost and yet a pause was indicated. If a lady and gentleman were walking together, the same bow was used by both and the lady added a gentle wave of her fan. The supporting leg was slightly bent to allow the dragged leg to swish through. The gentleman had to warn the lady slightly beforehand that he was about to bow *en passant*, otherwise she was not able to do her part smoothly enough and it looked like a hiccup.

Snuff-taking was a general habit among men and is most expressive for characteristic stage business. Snuff was extremely expensive; therefore the top of the box was tapped so that any grains that had clung to the lid would drop back into the box. The box was held in the left hand, tapped with the right, and the spring in the lid pressed with the left thumb. A pinch of snuff was taken with the right thumb and second finger, the box was closed with the left hand and the snuff was placed on the back of the left hand which was carefully (so as not to spill a grain) lifted to each nostril in turn. The cuff and shirt frill were then flicked with the handkerchief, as snuff stains were difficult to remove if the snuff was allowed to settle on the clothes. Sometimes a small pinch of snuff was taken and applied directly to the nostrils. It was not considered correct to sneeze afterwards, so if it is necessary to convey an effect of bad breeding, a lavish and disgusting sneeze would do admirably. The box can be kept in the waistcoat pocket or in the coat pocket, according to its size. Snuff was offered as a social gesture, but many men had their own blends mixed and would not accept anyone else's. Ladies did not use snuff until the beginning of the eighteenth century, when it became the fashion amongst rather fast young ladies to do so.

Smoking as well as snuff-taking was a normal habit of the men. Tobacco was smoked in long pipes; it was kept in a jar or carried in a box, and the pipe was lit by a taper. Snuff-taking was an art.

Older people used the manners of their own generation, which does not always mean that they were more formal. Restoration manners were freer than Georgian and the Regency manners were formal to the point of dullness. Country people's manners were very often old-fashioned but in the smart Spas, London customs were observed.

After the intricate flourishes and precise footwork of the late eighteenth century, the Regency manners seem quiet and uninteresting. The curtsy was very simple but needed grace and finish and extreme smoothness. The long stole, which was draped over the forearms (not around the shoulders) was very difficult to manage gracefully. It had a habit of twisting into a bedraggled string or looping itself unkindly underneath the seat of the dress or sliding off the arms so that it fell underfoot. The Regency bow was taken from the waist with the right hand held on the heart with the palm upwards, while the feet were placed in the third position of dancing. This was done by placing the right heel, slightly raised, in front of the left instep. Shaking hands did not come into fashion until after 1830, but men could greet each other with a handclasp. The lady's hand could be kissed either as a ceremonious gesture or as a sign of affection.

All gentlemen rose to their feet if any lady not a servant entered the room, or even stood up from her chair. Younger ladies always rose when an older lady entered, and remained standing until she was seated. There were always chaperones at every dance and the young ladies sat beside them. A gentleman wishing to dance approached the chaperone with a bow, then bowed again to the girl and asked her to dance. If she accepted, she rose and curtsied to him, he offered his arm, and led her to the dance floor. After the dance he led her back to her chaperone and bowed to both of them before seeking his next partner. He was also responsible for bringing either of them a cool drink or a glass of wine, and if he wished he might stay beside the lady of his choice and fan her.

Period dance is far too apt to become a bogey for actresses and actors. By the time they have rehearsed the play sufficiently to be at home in the period movement they should be able to enjoy doing the right dances. When dancing is introduced into a play, it is to give a feeling of festivity; it is therefore much more important that this feeling comes across than that the players crawl correctly through the dances with harassed faces. The producer usually has three choices: he can import pupils from a local dancing school to do the dance, or he can send his cast to the teacher to learn the dance. The third alternative, to arrange the dance himself, is often the best. If he has qualms, he would still do better to try; as the dance of any period springs from the spirit of that period and is a great help in assessing the quality to be aimed at in the play. The floor pattern and the partners' hold are the things the audience mostly notice and it is not at all necessary to do many elaborate steps. There are only a few dances for which it is really essential to have an expert's tuition, and these are stated when they are described in this chapter. The others can be arranged by the producer with the help of the cast and will, therefore, give the impression of unity of production.

The descriptions have been purposely kept to the simple basic qualities of the dances; the music all has clear beats and phrasing and players have no conception (until they have tried) how enjoyable it can be to work out a dance successfully. The style in acting that they have worked so hard to achieve suddenly takes a spurt forward when they are moving to music, and they get so exhilarated by the rhythms that when they return to the script the whole thing falls into place. They gain a new mastery of their material and added confidence in their powers. Some casts will not believe this statement and will refuse to try: they will miss a great opportunity to enlarge their scope and will miss an enchanting experience—and it will serve them right!

The English Country Dances were so popular all through the seventeenth and eighteenth centuries that it is a waste not to make use of them in the plays. The Court dances became increasingly difficult, culminating in a Minuet that required the control and precision of a professional dancer to do it justice. This was due to the influence of France which, under Louis XIV, formed the "Academie Royale de Danse". This body, under the guidance of the King's dancing-master, laid down the law on the dances, the steps, the figures and formations that polite society must accept. French Court society did accept them, as the French Court was nearly always cooped up with the king and did not spend much time, if any, on its estates. English society accepted them for use at Court, but the English have always spent a great deal of time in the country, and balls with the tenantry for celebrations of every kind have always taken place. Therefore, the French rules were used for all the Court dances, which the country thoroughly enjoyed seeing, but the major part of the evening would be given up to English Longways dances.

It was the period of the great English Spas, Bath, Harrogate and others, where the country gentry came as well as the town gallants. The Assembly Rooms, where most of the balls took place, were halls in which the Longways dance showed to good advantage: it gave the chaperones sitting round the walls a wonderful opportunity to see and gossip about the various couples. As time went on, most small towns and even villages had their Assembly Rooms where select dances were held.

The Country Dances were favourites for several reasons. They could be danced with as many couples as the room would hold, whereas the French dances usually specified a certain number of couples; the music was often to the taste of country people, with its gay tune and rollicking rhythm. Lastly, whereas in the French dances each person stayed with his partner during the whole dance, in the English dances all the couples in turn danced with all the other couples and met everyone on the floor. One can instantly see the advantages from the point of view of a matchmaking mamma.

The Sarabande was known at the beginning of the seventeenth century but it became very fashionable in the time of Charles II, as he liked it himself and the Court followed suit. This is a dance that *is* better learned from a professional teacher, as it involves the use of the whole body and both arms in a graceful and exacting way. It is slow, stately, dignified, and written in triple time which demands careful attention. One form that a producer might like to introduce into his play is that of a Sarabande performed by ladies only, who would recite a poem while they danced and be accompanied by guitar, flute and harp. This was the fashion for the talented ladies of the Court and could be very charming if done well. The music of the dance was usually played on the guitar. For a larger modern theatre this might sound rather thin, and a discreetly amplified gramophone record would probably be more effective. The gallants on the stage could pluck their guitars as if they were playing for their ladies.

The Gigue, which includes tunes named after both Charles II and Anne, was gay and lively and was done in a very rowdy version by the country men and women. It was quite a free-and-easy affair even at Court (which was perhaps why King Charles liked it), with a simple hopping step alternating with little tripping runs. The backs of the hands were held at the waist, with the fingertips resting on the lower ribs both for the lady and the gentleman, and they danced without holding each other's hands as they travelled. There was one figure, when the lady turned under the hand of her partner several times and then dropped him a curtsy, which is easy and effective for the stage. The character of the dance is lightness; the hop should be more of a light bounce than a high hop if it is done at Court. If it is done at a Harvest Party they can all leap to their hearts' content and the boys can swing the girls round to happy shrieks. In this case the man's leg can be raised for the hop until the foot is level with the knee, and the girl's until it is level with her calf. The producer can use his own version; for instance, the dance could start with tripping steps, with all the dancers travelling in a circle, then the hopping step could be used and the lady turned under her partner's hand, and finally the hopping step could be used to travel in the opposite direction.

The Allemande was a popular eighteenth century dance

of simple steps, and can be effectively done in a balancing walk throughout and a special way of holding the partner. Both lady and gentleman put their right hands behind their own backs and clasp their left hands behind their partner's backs for a turning step. The gentleman faced one way and the lady the opposite way. When they had paced round in a circle, they turned in the reverse way; thus they had to move backwards. When they moved into the next figure, the gentleman raised his right hand and the lady raised her left hand and turned under the hand of her partner. The music is in duple time and usually has a charming melody. It should be played at a sprightly pace and the dance should be lively in a decorous way. In style and character it lies between the Country Dance and the Gavotte.

For stage purposes it can be arranged in a circle with couples joining in after the dance has started. Each couple can work as an individual pair and do different steps from the others. If all the performers are taught the step and the hold, they can combine them as they wish. This means that this dance is particularly suitable for a team that are not very good dancers. They can concentrate on the steps that they have fully grasped and not be bothered by having to synchronise with the other dancers. It is also useful for the producer who wants to have a dance in the scene with certain points of dialogue brought out significantly. The circle of the dance can mean that the characters who speak can be brought nearer to the footlights whenever the producer wants to make a point, and taken up stage whenever he wants them to fade out. This is yet another argument in favour of the producer taking the trouble to arrange the dance himself.

There were many Gavottes, and the dance seems to have inspired the composers to write gay and charming music for it. In one form of Gavotte the couples took it in turn to perform the steps by themselves, which gave the standing couples a chance to talk to their partners. In an age when young girls never went out alone, this was a heaven-sent opportunity for private conversation; even an elopement could be planned. After the solo performance of each pair, the gentleman kissed the lady. This should be done gracefully but it can also include a certain amount of fervour if the role demands it. The lady does not return the kiss but she may show her feelings on the subject by the way that she accepts it.

The Gavotte can be danced on the stage with any amount of couples and they can either be placed in a line, as in a Country Dance, or they can be arranged in sets of two couples dancing as a team of four. The Gavottes have a totally different feeling and effect from the Minuet. The Gavotte step has a little spring on one foot and another one which lands on both feet, so that the dancers look most sprightly. It gave the young people a little chance to let off steam, even when they were encased in Georgian costume and a wig. The dance was popular from the time of Charles I to the end of the Regency, but it was probably more often danced from the beginning to the end of the eighteenth century. The Gavotte step mainly used was called the *Contretemps* and consisted of a hop and two walks and a pause. This sequence of steps was counted as a 4-beat bar—one beat for each movement and one for the pause. The hop, therefore, came on the same foot each time. If the man began to hop on his right foot, the lady began on her left foot, and they continued to hop on the same foot when they repeated the *Contretemps*. As this gets very tiring, the dancers will soon want to learn the next step which releases them from this treadmill.

When they have done one *Contretemps*, as described, they will be left with the outside foot in the air ready for the next hop. Instead of hopping, they give a little jump and land on both feet with the heels together. They count one for this. They then step backward with the inside foot, counting one, and point the outside foot and count one, so that now they have added another four counts to their *Contretemps* and filled two bars of Gavotte music. It may look simpler if it is written like this:

1. Hop on right.
2. Walk on left, rising on to the toe.
3. Walk on right, rising on to the toe.
4. Pause.
5. Spring on both feet.
6. Step back on right, rising on to the toe.
7. Point the left toe.
8. Pause.

The Hop continues to come on the right foot, but the extra four beats rests the leg.

The partners stand side by side and start with the outside foot lifted so that they are ready to do their first hop on their inside foot. The bows and curtsys (or "Honours") can be the same as the Minuet ones in its steps and movement. The difference lies in the fact that instead of the first bow being made to the company, it is made to the opposite pair of dancers and the second bow is then made to the partner. There is a precise Gavotte Honours, but for stage purposes the foregoing is enough. The gentleman still takes off his hat for the bow and puts it on again before the actual dance begins, and the hand movements both for the lady and the gentleman are the same as in the Minuet. The figures can be very simple variations of the corner-to-corner type. The gentlemen can do their sequence of eight steps into the centre of the square made by the two couples, while the ladies do the step turning in their own corners. The gentlemen then do their steps returning to their partners still travelling forwards, while the ladies turn in the other direction still in their own corners. The ladies can then do the step to the centre while the gentlemen turn in their corners. The gentlemen then do their step simultaneously with the ladies, but this time dancing to the opposite lady, passing her until they have exchanged corners and finally returning to their own corners. It leads to less confusion if only two people dance this and then the other two, rather than all four doing it at once. If a bright quartette have managed to follow all this and are so flushed with triumph that they are prepared to go still further, they can do the whole eight steps travelling backwards. It is still counted in the same way, with the hop on one and the spring on five, but the walks are taken back instead of forward. If this defeats them, they can always fall back on a stately walk, placing the toe on the ground first, instead of the heel, counting one beat of music to each step; or three walks and a pause, while the toe is pointed on the fourth beat of the bar.

Almost any variation the producer can think of can be introduced, as the dancing-masters kept on inventing new figures. The essential thing that must be borne in mind is the style and spirit of any period dance, and in the case of the Gavotte it must be spirited but never, in any circumstances, rowdy or romping. An air of courtesy and gallantry must be apparent from the gentlemen and an air of graciousness and dignity from the ladies. It is much easier than the Minuet, so it is a strongly recommended choice if the cast is diffident, irresolute or frankly obstinate in its attitude towards dancing in public. (*See* Fig. 33.)

One word of warning to producers: it always takes much longer for the cast to learn any dance than seems reasonable, so rehearsal time must be carefully arranged. The dancers should be encouraged to go into another room and rehearse by themselves. If they have not all come punctually, those who have can listen to the music and learn the moments when the steps have to change and a new figure starts.

There were many different Minuets, but *The Minuet* was

FIG. 33. Gavotte

a set dance based on the old *Branle de Poitou*. It was the essential formal dance for balls from the middle of the seventeenth century until the end of the eighteenth century. It was based on the ballet technique of turned-out feet and legs, and included steps which demanded difficult control of the instep and posed problems of balance. The dancing-masters brought out Fancy and Birthday Minuets every year and the debutantes had to dance an intricate solo Minuet at their first ball while the dowagers criticised. All this took a great deal of practice and it is not possible for anyone but a trained dancer to do it nowadays.

It is reasonable to use a simplified form of steps for the stage, but it is vital to catch the spirit of the dance and its basic quality of movement. The usual effort of One-Two-Three and a droop over a relaxed leg is enough to make an eighteenth century dancer beat *entrechats* of pure fury. If a step is described as being taken on the toe, it means that the dancer is to step forward on to his toe with the instep fully arched and the whole body drawn up and braced. In this way the weight is lifted so that the dancer can stay comfortably poised for a full beat of the music before dropping on to his heel for the next beat. The trouble usually comes when the foot is allowed to slip down from the toe without taking its full musical beat. It should be a clean movement, almost staccato, with a definite pause while still poised on the toe. This gives the air of lightness and decision to the dance which is destroyed by woolly footwork.

The Minuet music is in 8-bar phrases and 12-bar phrases and there is a special little flourish played at the beginning for the first bows and curtsies, which are done in time to the music. Before the flourish, the lady and gentleman stand side-by-side in the centre of the room, the gentleman on the lady's left. He takes his hat off with his left hand and sweeps it round to his left. He then makes a gracious movement towards the lady with his right hand

and she puts her left hand in his. This is the cue for the flourish. The couple are now going to make two bows and curtsies, one to the dowagers and one to each other. They both point the inside foot. The gentleman takes three counts to draw his pointed right foot back until he is standing on both feet, which are slightly apart, and to bow. Then another three counts to close his left foot to his right and to straighten up again. Meanwhile the lady has drawn her left foot back to her right foot and curtsied by bending both knees. This takes her first three counts. On the second three counts she rises from the curtsy slowly. All this is done facing the audience. The second bow starts with the gentleman stepping across with his right foot and to the side with his left, turning so that he faces the lady (three counts). He bows to her and rises (two counts) and puts on his hat again (one count). During this time the lady has stepped across with her left foot and to the side with her right foot, so that she faces the gentleman, and curtsied (three counts), then risen slowly and held out her left hand for him to take (three counts). They are now ready to start the dance. Strictly speaking, these bows belong to the dance but they can be used in a play if a very formal atmosphere is needed.

The Minuet is more effective if figures are introduced as only the Minuet step is used throughout. The dance could begin with the dancers in two long lines behind the first couple who face the audience. The ladies are on the right of the gentlemen, they all point the inside foot and each new figure begins with the right foot for the gentlemen. The line can break up into circles of four (two couples) and this can either revolve as a whole circle or the dancers can loose hands and each dancer revolve in a circle on his or her own (*see* Fig. 34). If the Minuet is being danced in a pageant or an arena, the first two couples can do the figure and then stand still, and then the next two couples until everyone has danced. This is a life-saver to

FIG. 34. Minuet

the shaky dancers who have not come to all the rehearsals. They can be put at the end of the line and by the time it comes to their turn they will have had their memories refreshed. This figure needs space to show it off: on a small stage it will merely look as if all the cast had not remembered the step at the same time. The "Oranges and Lemons", or going under the arc of arms, is not advised, as the costumes can get fatally tied up with each other. The dance should always finish with the same two bows and curtsies with which it started. The lady is then led off the floor in the Minuet hold, her left hand resting lightly on the right hand of her partner and both held at about the height of the gentleman's shoulder.

This is a very simplified Minuet step. (If the dancers are interested in the absolutely correct one, they are advised to go to a qualified dance teacher and be prepared to spend six months at least in learning how to do it.)

Gentlemen—

1. Step forward on the right toe.
2. Drop on the right heel.
3. Step forward on the left toe. } No heel-drop on these steps gives the lifted look to the dance.
4. Step forward on the right toe. }
5. Step forward on the left toe.
6. Drop on the left heel.

Ladies—The lady does exactly the same, using the opposite foot. "Exactly" is the operative word as, if they rise and fall at odd moments like wanton corks, the dance is ruined. They must not use their arms as pump-handles: the top half of the body must remain superbly unmoved by the changes of toe and heel going on below.

Sometimes a character in a play has a stage-direction "Does a few steps of the Minuet . . ." In this case it looks rather dull if they just do the steps repeated two or three times. Little variations such as pointing the toe in front and to the side before the step, pointing the right toe to the side and taking the foot behind, stepping to the left and bringing the right foot back again in front, or taking the right foot over the left until a complete turn has been made, can all be done.

Some Suggestions for Dance Music

Bach French Suite No. 5 for Sarabande and Gavotte
Bach French Suite in E major for Gavotte, Minuet and Gigue.
Bach Suite No. 2 in B minor for Sarabande and Minuet.
Bach Suite No. 3 in D for Gavotte and Gigue.
Haydn Divertimento in F for two Minuets.
Handel "Berenice" Minuet and "Fireworks Music" for Minuet.
Beethoven Minuet in G.
Boccherini Minuet.
Mozart Minuet in D and Minuet from Sym. No. 39 in E flat and from Sym. No. 41 in A major and "Don Giovanni", Act I, Finale.
Bach Gavotte in E from Sonata No. 6 in E major.

The following can be used if the producer wants to keep the spirit of the dance but is not concerned with historical accuracy:

Elgar Gavotte in "Contrasts". Op. 10, No. 3.
Prokofieff "Classical Symphony" in D major, or Op. 25, Third Movement.

17th and 18th Century Folk Dance Tunes

Epping Forest, Christchurch Bells, Hit and Miss, If All the World Were Paper, Shepherd's Holiday, Sellengers Round, Black Nag, Black Jack, Pleasures of the Town, First of April, Mary and Dorothy, The Spaniard, The Dressed Ship, Draper's Maggot, Shrewsbury Lasses.

Morris Dances

Beansetting, Hunting the Squirrel, Constant Billy, Country Gardens, None So Pretty, Lumps of Plum Pudding.

Useful Reference Books

Historical Dances from the 12th to the 19th Century Melusine Wood (Cyril Beaumont for The Imperial Society of Teachers of Dancing)

English Men and Manners in the 18th Century. Ed. A. S. Turberville (O.U.P.)

This is a helpful book but concerned with much that is not stageable.

Country Dance Book
Ed. Douglas and Helen Kennedy (Novello)

This contains airs and descriptions of 30 dances from the famous "Dancing Master" by Playford, which was published in 1637.

English Folk Song and Dance F. Kidson and M. Neal (C.U.P.)

The Country Dance Book Cecil Sharp (Novello)

This has descriptions of 18 traditional dances from country villages, suitable for arena and pageants.

The Imperial Society of Teachers of Dancing, Historical Dance Branch, Euston Hall, Birkenhead Street, London WC1H 4AJ, will supply a list of teachers qualified in this subject.

CHAPTER XVII

MUSIC

Musical forms of the periods—Instruments used and modern stage equivalents—Lists of composers, instruments and useful reference books

MUSIC was not now the normal necessity that it was to the Elizabethans but it was still a social duty. Pepys mentions singing in a way that shows that people in the same circle knew the same songs and could take parts without hesitation. Songs crop up in all the period plays to be sung by *actors*: clearly it did not happen that an actor might not be able to sing. Instruments used in this era are mostly familiar: violins, violas, violoncellos, oboes, flutes, bassoons, trumpets and organs. It is mainly the form of music that developed and changed during this period. The Scarlattis, father and son, are an endless mine of incidental music for any plays. They wrote Cantatas, Operas, Sonatas, and the music has a delicate wit that makes it invaluable to any producer. The Anthem and the Choral Ode, Duets, Sonatas for Harpsichord, Violins and Organ, and Chamber-music of all kinds were increasingly written. Incidental music, both for actual occasions (weddings, coronations, celebrations) and for creation of mood, abounds and is infinitely varied.

Many Public Libraries have a store of forgotten music of the Georgian songs which could be used. The producer should be ingenious enough to link them with narrative, for an entertainment in connection with some appropriate centenary or civic occasion. There would be no royalty to pay and it would arouse pleased surprise among an audience steeled, probably, to watch yet another performance of "The Rivals". There are also operettas, which certainly need a little editing but which have the charm of novelty and are not too difficult, assuredly, for a group accustomed to tackling Gilbert and Sullivan.

If a period instrument, or part of it, has to be seen on the stage and the producer is a stickler for accuracy, he should consult the list at the end of this chapter but must bear in mind that not everyone possessed the latest type of instrument. Any family might have an out-of-date spinet: the point to grasp is that they could not acquire a shape that had not yet been invented. The custom of writing music in dance-suites lingered on long after the composers really bothered about the dances. Minuets, Bourrees, etc., were written because it was a useful way of dividing a number of short pieces. It does not by any means follow that they are suitable to use for those dances. The actual phrasing may even be the same but they may be very difficult for the dancers to work with: all sorts of unexpected trills, where a smooth phrase is needed for a curtsy, and a long chord where the dancer is doing a series of little steps and would like help on every beat. Care must be taken, if music is chosen from a list by its title only, that these snags do not occur.

There is a strong feeling among amateurs that it is best to find the incidental music used in the original production or, failing that, in the last professional West End production. The choice of music is such an individual one that it is more likely that the producer's own choice will suit his production style better than any other. He can always consult a musician on the quality of the music, but slavish copying of another person's ideas without knowing the reasons for the original choice may defeat its own end. Each producer has his own style and music is one of the strongest ways of underlining it: the man who directs the play, controls the dances and chooses the music has far more chance of achieving an integrated production. He will also have far, far more fun.

FIG. 35. Georgian Lady Playing Harpsichord

Recorders and lutes would still be used in country districts, just as even now old country houses have harpsichords and virginals (*see* Fig. 35). There is no necessity to try to provide modern equivalents for these instruments as there are so many excellent recordings of period music played on the correct instruments. If real recorders or spinets or harpsichords are used they will probably sound far too faint. They were meant to be played in drawing-rooms, not in large halls or theatres. It is easy to have four recorders played at the same time to increase the volume, but it is not so simple to get four keyboard instruments and almost impossible to find performers. A record, carefully amplified, is much the best solution to this difficulty.

Composers of the Periods

Purcell	1659–95
Alessandro Scarlatti	1660–1725
Gasperini	1668–1727
Couperin	1668–1733
Caldara	1670–1738
Rameau	1683–1764
Handel	1685–1759
Domenico Scarlatti	1685–1757
Bach	1685–1750
Tartini	1692–1770
Daquin	1694–1772
Pergolesi	1710–36
Arne	1710–78
Boyce	1710–79
Gluck	1714–87
Alcock	1715–1806
Pugnani	1731–98
Haydn	1732–1809
Gretry	1742–1813
Boccherini	1743–1805
Cimarosa	1749–1801
Clementi	1752–1832
Mozart	1756–91
Beethoven	1770–1827
Field	1782–1837

List of Instruments for the 17th and 18th Centuries

Virginals—a keyboard instrument, from 1610, rectangular shape.
Spinet—a keyboard instrument, from 1680, wingshaped.
Harpsichord—a keyboard instrument, from 1798, pentagonal.
Pianoforte—from 1700 to 1747 popular, small, shaped like a modern upright, but not so high.

All the following instruments are like the modern except for slight details that would not show on a stage: Bassoons, Flutes, Kettledrums, Trumpets, Oboes, Organs, Violins, Violas, Violones, Violoncellos.

List of Useful Reference Books

Music of the 17th and 18th Century	Leo Smith	(Dent)
A List of Music for Plays and Pageants	R. Holt	(Appleton)
The Foundations of English Opera	E. J. Dent	(C.U.P.)
Essays on Opera	E. Wellesz	(Dobson)
Music and Society	W. Mellers	(Dobson)
English Folksong	C. Sharp	(Novello)

The Rural Music Schools Association have offices all over this country and give advice on period music to their members, lend gramophone records and can recommend teachers, choirmasters and singers, and performers on most musical instruments. The Secretary's address is: Little Benslow Hills, Hitchin Herts., SG4 9RB.

The English Folk Dance and Song Society, 2 Regents Park Road, London NW1 7AY, has photographs of period instruments.

CHAPTER XVIII

PRACTICE SCENES

Suggested scenes from plays for practice in period acting—Mime scene for Restoration movement with music and poetry

SO many people would prefer to have lived in another century than the one into which they were born that it is more than fortunate when they can be cast in a play of their chosen century. They need not wait for this moment idly, they would be well advised to explore their pet period of drama for small scenes and work their way up to performing in a full-length play. The phrase "a typical Restoration" or "a typical Mediaeval" character often occurs and it is a fact that dramatists of a particular period seem to choose the same sort of characters to describe. Therefore, if the actress really wants to understand the art of playing period parts she needs much more practice than the usual amount of time allowed for rehearsals.

There are always occasions when a short piece of entertainment is wanted for a bazaar, a festivity or a club evening, and yet no one wants to pay a royalty. Period plays provide a vast fund of such scenes of infinite variety: comedy, farce, fantasy, whatever is most suitable for the occasion is there at hand. There are two great advantages to this method; the first is that the audience is unlikely to have seen the play and make unkind comparisons, and the second is that the play chosen may have only this one good scene and could not be done in its entirety. Another point to consider is that of the group which has never done anything except modern comedy and is unsure if its audience will take a costume piece. It can try out the reaction of its supporters in this way quite painlessly: many an audience has been softened-up with a small extract before the whole play is unleashed on them.

The following scenes are intended to give some idea of the variety possible to be found in the three periods already dealt with, and to give some suggestions for pointing the characters even if the scenes are only used for practice.

Miss in Her Teens by David Garrick
Act 2 *Scene* 4

This is an excellent scene to practise as it includes the manners of an elderly lady and gentleman, those of a valet and lady's maid and those of a well brought up young lady. The relationship of all five characters must be shown and there is a little plot between two of them which must not be overheard by the other three, so that some tricky moves are involved as well as some asides.

Love's Riddle by Abraham Cowley
Act 2 *Scene* 1

This play was originally written for a Young Ladies Academy so there is clearly nothing that is impossible for a beginner to attempt. The scene needs concentration on mood and character and is a good test as to whether the players have really absorbed the period atmosphere and are ready to convey it to an audience.

Everyone Has His Own Fault (1793) by E. Inchbald
Act 1 *Scene* 1

Here is a scene of quiet conversation between two gentlemen which is redolent of its period; it needs such a feeling for its age that it can be played slowly yet still put across its points and grip the listener.

Speed the Plough (1800) by Thomas Moreton
Act 4 *Scene* 3

This is an early melodrama and must be played with complete sincerity, however strong the temptation to shriek with laughter. The relationship between the two men is clearly one of deep affection and respect, so that Handy Junior is not a mere feed. He must listen with rapt attention and show the effect the awful revelations are having on him.

These scenes will all be more useful if they are worked with hand props. It is one thing to understand that the fan can be used as a weapon and quite another to be faced by a beau intent on rapid seduction (in Act 2) with nothing to keep him at bay but a handful of gilded gauze and ivory sticks. It takes two people working together to achieve the stage direction "A pinch of snuff offered and taken".

Restoration Scene from *The Relapse* by Vanburgh (1678)
Act 1 *Scene* 3

This scene should be played for the contrast between the foppish voice and manners of Lord Foppington, the superior condescension of the valet who identifies himself with his master's standards, and the struggle between the tradesmen's servility and their craftsmen's pride. It is an excellent exercise in teamwork, as everyone must react violently in character if the full comedy is to be extracted from the scene. The moment when the new wig is actually placed on the head should take place in breathless silence and then be broken by the fop giving a short, sharp scream.

The Clandestine Marriage (1766)
by George Colman and David Garrick
Act 4 *Scenes* 1, 2, 3

This takes place in a garden such as is described in Chapter XV, with great opportunities for eavesdropping. This scene should be played for movement and lightness of the comedy. Lord Ogleby has a series of asides as he confides to the audience that one after the other of the young ladies has fallen in love with him. This old rake should be played in a mellow way very different from the full-blooded Restoration gallants; although Lord Ogleby is an old man he is not a nasty old man.

Twelfth Night, or King and Queen (1591–1674)
by Robert Herrick
Scene with action, improvised speech and a poem

The scene is a room of the period furnished with small round table placed stage right, an entrance through looped curtains centre back, at each side of which is a five-branched candelabrum on a pedestal. There are two small chairs by the table on the wall side and another two on the other side of the stage to balance. These chairs are optional, they help to dress the stage, but if space is limited they may be omitted. The candlesticks may be replaced by tall vases of flowers. The general effect should be of a charming, light and formal reception-room.

There should be seven ladies: it could be done with only four, or it could be done with more than seven. One man, Herrick, is necessary, others can be used if wanted.

Music is Purcell's First Harpsichord Suite in G.

The curtain goes up on an empty stage with music heard off-stage.

The characters enter in ones and twos, chatting to each other, loud enough to hear there is speech but not loud enough to distinguish the words. Herrick enters last with ladies on each arm who are clearly enjoying themselves and flattering him. The audience should be given time to take in a charming period group with only one or two back views of the cast. Ladies flutter their fans and a general air of gaiety pervades the party. Herrick has a manuscript tied with a ribbon sticking out of his pocket. First Lady pulls this out while he is talking to the Second Lady, and comes a little downstage leaving Herrick and Second Lady stage right. She unties the ribbon and looks at the paper. She then calls out to everyone—"Oh, Mr. Herrick has written a new poem" (or words to that effect) and all turn to face her with interest and excitement. Herrick is delighted but pretends to protest (using what words he likes). They all move into centre of stage, pleading with Herrick to read his poem to them himself. He accepts and they rearrange the group, ready to listen to him. All the speech is meant to be heard by the audience and will give the cast the chance to use the language of the period themselves without the stiffness of a script. As all the speeches are straightforward statements, this should not be too difficult for them if the producer holds a watching brief to see that no slang anachronisms creep in.

Herrick now takes the centre of the stage and reads the poem, explaining first that he wrote it because the day of this party *is* Twelfth Night. When he finishes they all applaud and compliment him.

Then the Third, Fourth and Fifth Ladies suggest a further plan: Third Lady suggests he should read it again, Fourth says why not act it, Fifth agrees, adding they will bring in the real cake from the other room. Sixth Lady says that would not be acting, it would be more amusing to imagine, and see if they act it well enough for people to guess what they were doing while listening to the poem. Seventh Lady backs her up with other arguments (only not mentioning the word "mime") and then the two carry this point. The other ladies all agree.

Herrick now stands to left of the table with six of the ladies in a semi-circle facing him. The other guests group themselves stage left. The entrance must be left quite clear. The Seventh Lady has run off-stage. (All the ladies' work is now in mime: cake, beans, etc., are imaginary.) Herrick begins to declaim with a great deal of manner and vitality:

Herrick:

Now, now the mirth comes,
With the cake full of plums

Seventh Lady poses holding cake in the entrance.

Where bean's the king of the
sport here;

Sixth Lady runs to cake and picks bean off top holding it up in her fingers. All the guests bow and curtsy to Sixth Lady.

Besides we must know,
The pea also
Must revel as Queen in the
Court here.

Third Lady now runs to other side of cake, picks up pea and runs downstage right holding it up in her fingers. All guests now turn and bow or curtsy to Third Lady.

Begin then to choose,
This night as you use,
Who shall for the present
delight here;

Guests turn first to Sixth Lady then to Third Lady, obviously deciding which to choose.

Be a King by the lot
And who shall not

They all bow to Herrick who bridles. (If there is another man he can be chosen.)

Be twelfth-day queen for the night here.	All curtsy to Seventh Lady.
Which known, let us make	Seventh Lady brings cake and sets it on table.
Joy-sops with the cake;	First Lady runs out and returns with tray which she hands round, each taking a glass ready.
And let not a man then be seen here,	Fifth Lady waves away the drink but Herrick frowns at her so she hurriedly takes one.
Who unurged will not drink	All poise their glasses.
To the base from the brink	Raise them first to Seventh Lady, drink, and then to
A health to the King and the Queen here.	Herrick. First Lady goes out and brings in bowl which she holds, standing stage centre.
Next crown the bowl full *With gentle lamb's wool;*	Second Lady brings in lamb's wool and puts it into the bowl.
Add sugar, nutmeg and ginger	Fifth Lady sprinkles sugar from a sifter, Fourth Lady adds pinches of nutmeg. First Lady adds ginger.
With store of ale, too; *And thus ye must do* *To make the wassail a swinger.*	Third Lady brings jug and pours ale into the bowl and Sixth Lady stirs.

Give them to the King *And Queen wassailing;*	All file past bowl and Sixth Lady dips ladle into bowl and fills each glass.
And though with ale ye be whet here,	All drink.
Yet part ye from hence, *As free from offence* *As when ye innocent met here.*	All spin round finishing their drink, and curtsey deeply to Herrick, who strikes a noble attitude.

Music is heard again, the cake is cut by Seventh Lady and held aloft in triumph by Fifth Lady. She makes a sweep around the front of the stage from left to right followed by Sixth Lady holding up bowl. Other guests then follow in line, passing round behind table to put down their glasses, then coming in front of table, crossing stage from left to right and going out at centre exit. Herrick waves them past and makes his final exit laughing and talking to Seventh Lady.

Any gay music of the period may be used if the suggested ones are difficult to obtain. If it is wanted to present the scene as a short item in a period entertainment, real props would look effective, although as the words of the poem are said with the action, mime can well be used.

This not a suitable scene for a pageant as there must be the suggestion that the guests have come from another room and the action is, in any case, not broad enough. It could well be done in a small arena indoors. The cake should then be placed one end of the arena and the bowl of wassail the other end, and it would be as well to have two exits. The properties should be real and be fetched from the opposite end from where they are to be taken, so that the flow of period dress is fully seen.

The dresses would be charming if the scene were placed about 1640.

It was the custom of the period to draw lots for the first piece of cake, which was supposed to bring luck, so this could be done if it is necessary to make the scene play a little longer.

PART FOUR

THE VICTORIAN AND EDWARDIAN PERIOD

CHAPTER XIX

THE SPIRIT OF THE PLAYS

Spirit of the periods—Development of plays and places of performance—Style of acting—Conventions of setting—List of reference books, playwrights and modern period plays, both three-act and one-act

A SNOWSTORM with a heroine clasping a small bundle to her bosom is the picture most people have of Victorian Drama. The Dramatists of this period, however, classified their plays under far more headings than Melodrama. They had Domestic, Historical, Realistic, Satirical, Fantastic and Comedy Drama as well as various classifications for Farce.

Although no great drama has survived from this period, the theatre, as entertainment, has provided a great mass of material on which the modern producer may draw. The Theatre of Early Victorian days still had a vociferous audience which had to be appeased and wanted its money's worth. The programs were packed: the curtain-raiser, the after-ballet and the interlude were expected as well as the play proper, to fill an evening's entertainment.

The Age of the Machine was coming into its own, but actors cannot be mechanised and triumphantly asserted their personalities and dominated the theatre of Victoria. Producers, as such, did not exist and playwrights were sinking to the level of hacks. The French plays were the fashion and all the managers wanted were translations of established successes from France. Shakespeare was altered and added to, stock situations were taken and a star vehicle was built, but it was a dire time for dramatists of any serious talent. Sentimental and fantastic plays were popular. Infant Phenomena and stage effects were more important than the playwrights, who found it paid better to translate French Farces than to do original work. The audiences of the times were vocal and brutal in their comments on the fare offered and were used to the actors publicly apologising (sometimes on their knees) for anything in the acting that might have offended the mob. A performance might be stopped entirely while the audience clamoured for this apology (and threw things while they clamoured). An actor of those days must have courage as well as talent if he was to survive, and it is worth speculating if as many people were stagestruck then as nowadays. Plays from 1830 to 1850 fell almost entirely into two categories: the French Farces and the Victorian Melodramas. The latter, as has been stated in Part Three, were very watered-down affairs from the original Georgian Melodramas. They wallowed in sentimentality, had rigid moral values and painted everything in dense black or pure white. A happy ending was essential for the good characters and the bad ones were foiled with unfailing regularity. The audience had barely time to digest this play before the curtains would swing open on the "Ballet of the Spring Flowers", introducing the small lady who had played the dying child now leaping about as the "Spirit of Spring".

Pantomime flourished to a tremendous degree, as it was obviously the best medium for both the stage effects and the Infant Phenomena. These pantomimes abounded in rhymed couplets and puns and are neatly contrived to show a complete picture of their age. Planché, the king of pantomime writers, also turned out many Extravaganzas for Spring and Autumn, all well worth considering by the modern producer. The Victorian Melodramas are not nearly such strong meat as their predecessors. They turn on wild coincidences and well-worn themes of long lost wills, heirs, or mothers.

Later in the century (1865 onwards) "tea-cup and saucer" dramas came into fashion, usually played by players who were married and these plays are mild enough for the most prudish audience.

The Farces are worth disinterring, as the situations are usually genuinely funny and the correct costume adds piquancy to the modern eye. Farce always has to rely a great deal on the actor, and here he can embroider happily on the script without feeling that he is desecrating great drama.

The Victorian Playhouse was an ornamental affair of red plush, bobbles and gilt. The pit, which had always been directly below the footlights, had by now been firmly pushed back behind the stalls. The audiences grew steadily quieter, or more apathetic, whichever way one likes to look at it. The crowd which was accustomed to demand an apology on his bended knees from an actor who had displeased them, changed into the crowd who hissed the villain and cheered on the hero and finally became the intellectual audience who watched the play in silence and kept their arguments for outside the theatre.

The Victorian Music-Hall is so well known that it seems unnecessary to describe it. (*See* Fig. 36.) The genial Chairman, song-sheets and communal choruses would make an ideal entertainment for an amateur club evening that was off the beaten track. It would help the actors to broaden their attack, help the audience to participate, and undoubtedly swell the club receipts. It is essential to have a drink licence: it cannot be done successfully on lemonade.

During the 'nineties new theatres were being built and

FIG. 36. Victorian Music Hall Artiste

Oscar Wilde was writing his scintillating comedies, while Gilbert and Sullivan were enchanting audiences with their brilliant series of Comic Operas. Towards the turn of the century the intellectual theatre was stirring and soon plays were to be written about social problems, politics, prostitution and even drainage. Realistic dialogue and commonsense could not exist in the world of Melodrama and came into its own in the new century.

The spirit of this century, it is obvious, changed from the start to the finish, and this change is mirrored in the plays. The rise of a large new middle-class, full of the wealthy merchants of the Industrial Revolution, brought a different audience into the theatre. There was still a remnant of the Puritanical attitude towards the actors and the popular plays had excellent morals all laid out in convenient black and white. That is partly why Wilde's plays made such a terrific impact: they were among the first plays to laugh at respectability. They opened the way to the New Drama and allowed Shaw, Galsworthy and Granville-Barker the wide range of subjects that led to the modern play. The Edwardian Court was so much more sophisticated than Victoria's that society comedies and dramas now join the earlier classifications.

It is the fashion now to burlesque all Victorian Melodramas. It would be interesting to see a straight production. The player who wishes to preserve the style of acting certainly has to use a broader method than normally nowadays used, but it is still possible to be sincere. The asides should be taken straight to the audience: the soliloquies may be either to the player or to the audience according to the scene. All Comedies and Farces need considerable agility and variety of movement, as the actors were accustomed to lend a hand with the song-and-dance interludes when they began their careers. Only when they became established could they appear in the play alone. The sophisticated comedies of the nineties need a strong feeling for style. Normal etiquette was so precise that the actors had to play in a way that is practically stylised. Everyday people placed themselves in suitable attitudes for grief and joy and horror, therefore the actors had to exaggerate if it was to be effective in the theatre. A modern must get this feeling mainly by studying pictures of the period and then observing himself in a looking-glass, otherwise the play will lack the visual polish that will carry it across the footlights.

The Social Dramas, on the contrary, need to be played with the utmost sincerity and passion, and everything that the player has used in modern plays can be of service, except the habit of throwing the line away. Lines were not written to be thrown away at this time and if the actor persists he will find that the audience are not able to follow the next speech. In all these periods it was taken for granted that all the speeches would be clearly and easily audible and this is the hazard that must be faced bravely by modern players and overcome. It is useless to pretend that there are no puns; they are there to get a laugh, and get a laugh they must, even though it is much more difficult now than it was then. Diction and timing will always do it, if the players will only take the trouble.

The settings of the plays allow the producer to choose a wide range of style. He can aim at authenticity, or he can merely suggest the period. When a Victorian play says, "A Room in Mr. Smith's house", it need not be a living-room as a modern family knows it. Victorian houses had a variety of rooms. There would be, in a wealthy middle-class house, a dining-room used only for eating, with a table taking up so much room that no other occupation than eating could be carried on. There would be a drawing-room, very formally furnished, a breakfast-room or morning-room, where probably the young ladies had their needlework and sketching materials; Papa's study, lined with books with an easy chair for sleep, and a library lined with more books, and perhaps a billiard-table and a writing-table for visitors. Ladies had boudoirs, all frills and satin, with a chaise-longue and a cage of love-birds. Kitchens were utilitarian, with scrubbed floors and tables, hard chairs and benches. The decorative aspect was the beautiful copper and brass pans hanging round the walls and the dresser filled with vast plates and serving-dishes. Rows of bells hung against the wall. Nurseries were merely filled with cast-off furniture from the rest of the house, a high brass fireguard, and bars at the window. There was no attempt to make the nursery attractive or suitable for small people to use.

The conservatory was large and tended to have stained glass round the top. This was a favourite place for the heroine to retire to for a good cry; it was also chosen for proposals of marriage. It should have a variety of plants and flowers in it and could have a domed roof. It could also have a set of glass dangles, so that draughts could be detected, and basket chairs.

Garden sets should be meticulously tidy. Victorians did not really approve of Nature. The wheel had spun round from the Gothic ruins beloved by the Regency, and flowers were regimented into concentric patterns of red, white and blue, or red, white and yellow. Roses had to be standard, not ramblers, and while weeping-willows were allowed by the bank of a river, a monkey-puzzle tree found more favour in a garden. Lawns were superb as there were unlimited gardeners. Verandahs had hanging baskets of maidenhair fern and geraniums and probably clematis neatly trained up the pillars.

Although it helps the illusion if a number of ornaments can be got on the stage, the main thing to aim at is the effect of variety of shapes, no clear surfaces or plain colour. This can be gained by using as many patterned materials as possible trimmed with fringes and bobbles. This also helps with the problem of transport, if the play is going in for a Festival. Hand props, such as workboxes, tobacco-jars, smelling-salts and embroidered bell-pulls add immensely to the lived-in look of the room and could be brought by the actor who has to use them. The theatrical effect on the audience is all-important—Victorian detail is often so niggling that it is waste of time for a producer to recreate it; he must select what will arouse an instant recognition from the audience, something that will instantly evoke the spirit of the period.

List of Useful Books

Early 19th Century Drama 1800–1850 — Allardyce Nicoll (C.U.P.)

A History of late 19th Century Drama 1850–1900 — Allardyce Nicoll (C.U.P.)

Modern English Playwrights: A Short History of the English Drama from 1825 — J. W. Cunliffe (Harper, N.Y.)

Ring Up the Curtain — E. & A. Short (Jenkins)

The stage of English entertainment, covering half a century.

The English Stage — Lynton Hudson (Harrap)

This covers general entertainment in the nineteenth century.

Clowns and Pantomimes — M. W. Disher (Constable)

Fairs, Circuses and Music-Halls — M. W. Disher (Collins)

The Early Doors — Harold Scott (Nicholson & Watson)

All Right on the Night — A. Clinton Baddeley (Putnam)

The last two books give a vivid picture of the audiences and general management of the show business of the nineteenth century.

Blood and Thunder: Mid-Victorian Melodrama & its Origins — M. W. Disher (Muller)

Playwrights of the Period

W. T. Moncrieff	1794–1857
J. R. Planché	1796–1880
G. D. Pitt	1799–1855
J. B. Buckstone	1802–1879
C. H. Selby	1802–1863
G. H. Rodwell	1802–1852
Alexandre Dumas (*Père*)	1802–1870
N. Gogol	1809–1852
J. P. Simpson	1807–1887
J. M. Morton	1811–1891
J. Oxenford	1812–1877
T. Taylor	1817–1900
J. E. Carpenter	1820–1885
D. Bouccicault	1822–1890
A. N. Ostrovsky	1823–1886
J. P. Wooler	1824–1868
Alexandre Dumas (*Fils*)	1824–1875
T. W. Robertson	1829–1871
V. Sardou	1831–1908
Sir W. S. Gilbert	1836–1911
S. Grundy	1848–1904
H. A. Jones	1851–1929
Sir A. W. Pinero	1855–1934
A. Schnitzler	1862–1931
D. Marshall	1863–1910
Oscar Wilde	1856–1900
W. G. Robertson	1866–1948
L. Pirandello	1867–1936
J. Galsworthy	1867–1933
S. Phillips	1868–1916
H. Granville Barker	1877–1946

The British Theatre Association, 9 Fitzroy Square, London W1P 6AE, has a play library, and gives advice and information to all its members; books can be borrowed singly as well as in sets for play-reading.

Some Modern Plays About these Periods

Three-Act

Title / Author	Publisher	Period
Victoria Regina L. Housman	Cape	(1837–1902)
The Brontës of Haworth Parsonage J. Davison	Garnet Miller	(1840–60)
Wild Decembers C. Dane	French	(1840–60)
The Brontës A. Sangster	Constable	(1840–60)
The Lady with a Lamp R. Berkeley	French	(1848–1903)
Milestones A. Bennett & E. Knoblock	Methuen	(1860–1912)
She Too Was Young A. Vaughan & L. Lister	Constable	(1873–6)
The Two Bouquets (with Songs) E. & H. Farjeon	French	(1878)
Another Part of the Forest L. Hellman	Viking Press N.Y.	(1880)
Parnell E. T. Schauffler	Steele (Garnet Miller)	(1880–90)
The Little Foxes L. Hellman	English Theatre Guild	(1900)
The Damask Cheek J. Van Druten & L. Morris	French	(1909)

One-Act

Title / Author	Publisher	Period
The Language of Love E. Percy	Best One-Act Plays of 1934: *Ed.* Marriott Harrap	(1840)
Mrs. Fry has a Visitor G. Daviot	Duckworth	(1840)
The Chartist S. Schofield	French	(1848)
Mid-Victorian Trifle B. Shaw	French	(1865)

Spinning Jenny M. Facey	Rylee (Evans)	(1769)
The Apple Tree E. Richardson	Deane	(1850)
Battles Long Ago C. Bax	Eight New One-Act Plays of 1936† *Ed.* W. Armstrong Lovat Dickson	(1870)
The Impromptu Magazine J. Hayes	Garnet Miller	(1880)

CHAPTER XX

MOVEMENT IN COSTUME

Outline of costume from 1827 *to* 1910*—Movement in costume—List of costume accessories for movement and hair-style for each period—List of costume and other books—List of artists who sum up the visual aspect of each period*

THE nineteenth century began with its ladies draped with little more than damped chiffon and only two layers of that. It ended with its ladies heavily upholstered, strapped and girded, balancing more weight on their heads alone than the whole costume of their great-grandmothers. It is one of the most striking examples of the adaptability of the female form to fashion.

The outline of the lady of 1837 was triangular above the waist and below, with the two triangles meeting with their apexes at the waist. The outline of the lady of 1910 was like a stem with an outsize hat on the top. From 1840 to 1860 the crinoline held sway and from 1860 to 1890 the shape of the bustle lurked behind the ladies. There really seemed no fashion too silly for the Victorians to adopt and cling to for ten years at a time. From 1900 onwards, although small waists caused unnecessary anguish, the outline is comparatively that of the human body. Utterly ridiculous hats always were and always will be in fashion, but the Edwardian hats were so large that they could only be worn for everyday by the leisured classes. The gradual emergence of practical clothing for women of all classes has been achieved only in the century that has seen all classes of women doing practical work. In other centuries there has been a noticeable difference between the clothes worn by "working" women and the clothes worn by the leisured women; it is only since the 1914–18

War that there has been a difference, merely of expense, not of outline or detail.

The men, too, threw away their gorgeous Georgian plumage and sobered down, through fawns and greys to a universal black as the new offices swallowed them up into industry. The swiftly drawn sword dwindled into the long black, tightly rolled, umbrella which no-one ever thought of using for a duel. The swaggering outline of the brocade coat drooped down into the limp fall of the frock-coat, and glittering garters gave way to pearl-buttoned spats. Clothes were still used for display but now they showed whether women were useless or men were busy. They were seldom worn for their own beauty. The men's clothes changed from the elegance of tight-fitting trousers and a high stock to drainpipe trousers and a wing-collar. Perhaps the most significant development was the emergence of special clothes for sport. Bicycling, golfing, shooting and river picnics, and tennis, all had their special outfits and hot and cold weather was catered for in a way that had not happened in other centuries. On the debit side colour was disappearing from men's clothes: black, brown, snuff-colour, pepper-and-salt and shepherd's plaid reigned supreme by the end of the century. The last stronghold was the brilliant blazers in gorgeous colours which were repeated in the ribbon band round the hard straw hats, or in scarves that dashing young men wore round their waists. Army, Navy, Legal and Court uniforms, of course, still continued to display vivid colours on ceremonial occasions.

The women's clothes all pose special problems of movement. By 1845, petticoats were becoming a bugbear; as many as ten had to be worn to hold the skirt out to the fashionable width. It is obvious that this slowed down the walk, so a gliding movement was cultivated, with the top half of the body held very erect to balance the weight of the skirts.

The crinoline, although it seems cumbrous, was hailed with cries of joy, as it took away the awful weight of all those petticoats and made a nice cool draught around the legs in hot weather. The walk which shows it off well is taken with small smooth steps. The crinolined lady aimed at sailing along without visible means of propulsion. The actress must manage to guide her crinoline with her hands and always have it lightly under control. It can hitch on furniture, tilt up behind and in front unless carefully handled. When sitting, the hands rest gently on the front of it so that it behaves. When going through a door, one shoulder and hip should lead the way so that the actual crinoline turns sideways and thrusts through the door. It was considered most illbred to let a crinoline sway about wildly. Poise and serenity are the effects to be aimed at. The crinoline went out by 1870 and the bustle appeared. This in turn led to the top half of the body being thrown forward to balance the erection behind. Skirts became more and more tightly draped across the front of the legs and the attitude known as the "Grecian bend" was the correct posture. Difficult as it may be to believe, these costumes were considered dangerously seductive. They showed the shape of the legs from the thigh to the knee quite clearly and this, to a generation of men who only knew that women were bell-shaped (until they married them), was madly exciting. So the walk capitalised this feeling and became swaying and seductive. The ladies bent forward to show the bosom, and swayed to show their hips, and moved one leg in front of the other to show their legs, and thoroughly enjoyed the sensation they caused. There have always been old gentlemen who deplored the New Woman—now they really had something to puff about. In 1900 the line became trimmer and shorter skirts were worn for bicycling and lawn-tennis. (*See* Fig. 37.) The normal skirt was still long and flowing—when walking in the house it could trail, but when walk-

FIG. 37. Edwardian Tennis Player

ing in the street it was held up, gathered in the hand at about thigh level, with a graceful turn of the wrist. It was essential to hold the dress close to the body and to show as little of the ankle as possible. When a teagown or evening dress with a train was worn, the train helped to make a picture. As it lay on the ground its owner could turn from the waist and the train made a decorative comma round her feet. If she wished to walk to and fro at a reception, she paused on the turn and gently raised the train with her foot just clear enough off the floor to replace it behind her. This movement was never a sharp kick (unless in the privacy of her home or when she was in a hurry or in a temper) and was almost imperceptible. The sporting types who wore aggressively athletic costumes for their activities had movements to match.

The feather boa and the muff are useful and elegant movement accessories and a specially period gesture is that of rolling the face veil out of the way to drink tea. This was done slowly, as the raised arms showed off the trim line of waist and bust.

All the accessories at the end of this chapter are intended to be used to help the characterisation of the part. So much can be done to build up the picture of the period if all these little intimate objects show what kind of woman the actress is portraying.

Ladies did not work outside their homes and so they did not have to consider whether it was worth carrying something about all day; they only had to think if it was pretty enough to take on an afternoon call. The actress will find so many opportunities of pointing period dialogue if she has, at an early stage in rehearsals, the correct accessory. The style of the late nineties and on to 1910 was more forthcoming and brisk, although certain people affected a languid air of boredom at everything. It was quite possible for women to be intelligent, as long as they were pretty as well, and an adventurous spirit was encouraged as the automobile became popular.

The bicycle had rather unkindly killed off the chaperone as far as outings were concerned, although she still held her own in the ballroom. Therefore, in a crowd scene of an Edwardian picnic the young people could wander away from the older ones in a way that was not done in Victorian days. (*See* Fig. 38.)

The Edwardian hat was large and top heavy and it had to be balanced on top of an elaborate coiffure. It could not be flipped off as a modern hat can; it had to be removed with extreme care, both for itself and for the hair underneath. Large hatpins held it in position and had to be removed, the hat lifted high to clear the coiffure and then placed in the lap while the hatpins were carefully put back in the same holes from which they were taken, so that the material of the hat was not covered with pinpricks. This is a particularly period piece of business which is too often slurred over, as the modern actress is so used to small hats that she does not at all realise the difference in the gestures then and now.

Pince-nez often lived on a chain attached to the bosom of the dress. They were pulled out with a sharp click, poised on the nose to read a letter and then decisively snapped back again. Men sometimes wore them threaded on to a wide black ribbon fixed in the buttonhole of the waistcoat.

Period movement for women means that they combined the best way of showing off the clothes. It must be in keeping with the woman's place at that particular period, plus the clothes' own special characteristics. It is the last point that must always come first for the actress. It is far more important to show character than period, but it should be perfectly possible to do both. There are certain qualities that have been admired in women at certain periods, such as meekness, camaraderie or coyness, and

FIG. 38. Edwardian Picnic

in a social crowd scene all the women should convey this general effect if they are crowd actresses. The star character will probably provide the contrast.

When Victoria was young, it was the fashion for young ladies to be gay, lighthearted and slightly silly, and the costume helped all this. The shorter, wider skirt could swing giddily, the curls could be tossed coquettishly and little feet could patter to and fro in flat slippers. The bonnet ribbons could be tied with much fluttering, the full frilled sleeves could swell with excitement, and muffs or nosegays could be clasped to the heart in moments of ecstasy. Deportment was carefully taught and all girls were made to spend hours on a steel backboard (a useful prop for a scene) every day. The walk was done with an absolutely straight back but the head droops becomingly when talking to older people or to "the gentlemen". Never, in any circumstances, were the knees crossed when sitting, or the legs straddled when standing, and the waist was never allowed to slump. Corsets held the middle rigid even when the flesh was weak. The hands could be clasped in front when speaking to an older person and used for gestures (pretty, fluttery ones) when speaking to contemporaries. Handkerchiefs, fans, parasols, embroidery, sweetmeats, cups of tea or glasses of cordial were handled gracefully and lightly.

Great stress was laid on being "ladylike", which meant self-control and politeness, from the stage viewpoint, although it also meant a tradition of *noblesse oblige*. Ladies could shriek at a mouse or faint at the sight of blood, but they must not shout in anger or faint when the hostess had the room too hot, as that would be rude to her. It is impossible to cover all possible actions that may be needed in a play, but if the actress understands the spirit of the age and why people behaved as they did, she can apply the rules to any situation.

The gentlemen were now entering their heyday of

being masters of the earth, including home and society. They had a swaggering walk, they stood at ease with legs straddled in front of the fire, they eyed the ladies through quizzing-glasses before they chose a dance partner, but they also had, when in company, a protective attitude. The position of the hands varied: either the hand belonging to the front foot could be placed, palm up, by the heart, or it could take the hand of the lady and give it a kiss, or it could hold the lapel of the coat. The other hand could be held behind the back, with bent elbow, or it could hang at the side. There was still a hangover from the dashing style of the Regency. Grace of movement was a sign of good breeding, and a dandy could add a few flourishes to his bow if he wished. It was still the mode to dance well, and movement of this period needs style and finish if it is to look real.

From 1845 onwards Respectability became important, and the whole atmosphere got duller and heavier. The young men strove to give an impression of steadiness and responsibility—not to say pompousness. Now the custom had come in of shaking hands, of ladies walking arm-in-arm, not with any gentleman but with their husbands and families, which included dozens of cousins. A favourite sitting position of this time can be seen in family portraits, where the man sits well into the chair, his feet planted firmly far apart, his back bolt upright, one hand on his knee with the elbow bent outwards and the other fingering his watch or the fob at his waist. One hand can grasp the coat lapel while the man is arguing or laying down the law, while the other saws the air. Great play was made with putting on and taking off eyeglasses for a professional man, spectacles for anyone, and monocles for gentlemen and dandies. All these had ribbons which could be twirled and fingered. Watches all had heavy chains and lived in the waistcoat pocket. Long thick canes for day added to the heavy effect, and short slender canes showed that it was going to be a frivolous evening.

The following lists have been arranged in rough divisions of period, but it must be remembered that some people's clothes would be very smart and in the latest fashion, and others—the poorer and older—would be behind the times. People who lived in the country would not wear the more exaggerated styles. Young people wore the paler or brighter colours and older people wore dark, rich colours. It is as well to try to get the right materials and patterns if the costumes are to look convincing. The muslins and gauzes for evening, the brocades and heavy reps and woollens for day wear, and the stiffened petticoats, so that the skirts hang properly. Some sort of tight foundation that approximates to corsets must be worn and the producer must override all protests about this. The shoes also affect the walk so directly that they should be worn from the early stages of rehearsals. Shawls and long scarves need practice, as they have a life of their own and have evil habits of swathing themselves in a way that is unbecoming to their owners. The top-heavy hats are a menace: some travesty must be arranged for rehearsals, or there will be disaster at the performance.

The players should try to enjoy wearing their costumes and convey their pride of bearing and elegance throughout the play as this is a large part of the charm for the audience looking at these period plays.

Costume Accessories for Movement for Each Period

1827–45

Ladies

Huge balloon-like sleeves, with trimmings of little capes, frills, bows and flowers, and a wide gored or gathered skirt to the ankles if the wearer was young, to the floor if she was older.

Scarves and long stoles, and rich Cashmere shawls all with fringed ends.

Hair taken up into a knot with side curls, or parted in the middle and smooth at the sides. A band of jewels could be worn round the forehead, and a short gauze veil behind, or a wreath for evenings.

1836—High tortoise-shell combs worn in the hair, which was plaited and arranged to look like a wicker basket on top of the head.

1845—The hair was parted in the middle and bunches of curls were arranged at the sides and shaken winningly at every opportunity.

By 1850 hair was done hanging down the back, like "Alice in Wonderland", banded with a snood, and either a pork-pie hat or a graceful, wide Leghorn hat, with a ribbon round and streamers down the back.

Caps were for indoors, or turbans and poke-bonnets, with lofty plumes for outdoors. Cloaks were thrown over the full sleeves.

Mittens, long gloves, fur boas, fans, parasols, nosegays, handkerchiefs and little handbags, square and flat or like an inverted candleshade, could be carried. Silk aprons were popular for indoor wear.

Earrings and sets of brooches worn at intervals, spaced across the neckline of the bodice, were in fashion. Garnets, turquoises, seed-pearls, mosaics and amethysts were used for lockets and other jewellery.

Narrow slippers with blunt toes were worn with white stockings.

1830—Pantalettes were always worn both by the *girls* and by little *boys*.

Poke bonnets, and the hair parted in the middle, was the universal style for girls.

After 1840, boys wore plaid trousers, full at the hips, and

they were starting to wear sailor-suits, kilts and tunics. The girls wore their hair knotted into a chignon, in a net, ring-striped stockings and aprons over their dresses.

Men. In 1827 men wore black trousers in the evening, but breeches and chapeau bras were worn at Court and at the opera. The coat had a high collar with spreading lapels, which were grasped while the gentleman was thinking what to say. The satin waistcoat had brilliant buttons which were fingered at moments of worry. The pale-coloured nankeen trousers were shown off by striking, elegant, attitudes. Men also showed a great deal of shirt-front, which was frilled or pleated above a richly-coloured or flowered waistcoat, with a stock tied round a high collar. The outdoor coat had a high collar too, and huge silver buttons, or elaborate braid frogs down the front, and was worn with a high hat of white or grey beaver, with black beaver the correct wear for evenings. Hair was brushed up off the forehead into a pompadour and side-whiskers were luxuriant. Canes, gloves, snuff-boxes, gaiters, eyeglasses, signet-rings, were all favoured accessories.
1844—Whiskers were proudly caressed, and in 1855 a moustache was stroked.

1845–70

Ladies could wear:
Waistline coming to a V in front with a tight ribbon belt with buckle, and a basque frilling out below it.
For evening, the bodice dropped off the shoulders with a lace bertha, or puffed sleeves and a nosegay tucked into the neck centre front, or a circle of roses or violets edging the neckline.
Skirts looped up with flowers, tassels, bows, rosettes or lace.
Crinolines from 1855.
Cloaks and shawls of cashmere, or black, white or red

lace which could be draped mantilla-fashion. Sealskin capes and toques.

White stockings and ankle-boots, laced up for day with low curved heels, sometimes elastic-sided boots with tassels at the top.

Hair with a long chignon in a net, or a fringe on the forehead and curls over the shoulders. For evening, ribbon bands or feathers or flowers, or a high Spanish comb.

The poke-bonnet, small, and worn at the back of the head, tied with long ribbons under the chin. Flowing veils at the back. A Leghorn hat with wide brim and ribbons for young woman.

Accessories: Muffs, sunshades, reticules, lockets, cameos, corals, jet, garnets, wide heavy bracelets, necklaces, brooches and rings.

Men could wear:

Coats with wide lapels and fitted waists, rather low; breast pockets. Shepherds plaid trousers, checked, plain, quilted or flowered waistcoats of a variety of materials. Shirts with tucks or well-starched pleats. High collar for formal and low collar for informal wear (*see* Fig. 39).

Dress trousers still looped under the foot. Striped socks for dress wear and low slippers with bows: usual shoes low heels and blunt toes.

Hair parted at the side and down the back, with curls over the temples. Small moustache, or cleanshaven with side-whiskers, or a short beard or a long heavy beard.

Dressing-gown of elaborate brocade or quilting, with a small round cap to match, with a button on its top.

Accessories: Canes, signet-rings, watches with chains looped across the waistcoat, gloves and monocles.

1870–1890

1870–80 *Ladies could wear:*

A bustle and train edged with a pleated frill.

An over skirt looped up either in panniers at the sides or

FIG. 39. Victorian Dandy

a puff at the back. A bodice buttoned down the front, and a pleated frill tucked into a V-neck, finished with a small ribbon bow at the front.

Shoes or boots with high heels and scalloped tops.

Long earrings and necklaces made with coins and little bells, jet or coral bracelets, earrings and short necklaces and cameo brooches, bracelets and earrings and lockets of gold, silver, jet or ivory.

Coloured or white gloves, usually short for day or evening, although really long gloves, buttoned, could be worn.

A lace cap with ribbon bows, if she is elderly, or thirty and unmarried; knots of ribbon, if she is young, for indoor wear.

White grosgrain, with bouquet and veil, for her wedding.

A high hat with feather, tilted well forward, for outdoors, and a muff of sealskin in winter, and an umbrella. A parasol, small with a long handle and tip, for summer. In 1870 she can part her hair in front and pile it up into a pompadour, with curls down the back: later on she can cut a fringe and loop her braids at the back and show her ears.

A fan may be of satin, gauze, or embroidered and edged with fringe.

Bags may be carried of any rich material trimmed with tassels.

Only a widow may wear a white crêpe ruching inside her bonnet, and a long black veil reaching to the knees.

1875–80—*Boys* wore reefer coats and Norfolk suits and, for the country, navy jerseys and scarlet fishermen's stocking caps.

Fashionable colours were: puce, purple, bottle-green, plum and navy.

After 1890, the smock became smart for young *boys and girls*, who were also dressed in sailor blouses and pleated skirts.

After 1885, the bustle stood out a yard at the back from the figure, but by 1890 it had dwindled.

1890–1910

Ladies: 1890—The Princess line, with wasp waist was worn. The petticoat fitted in front but was ruffled at the back so, when it was gathered up to go upstairs or cross the road, the ruffles showed attractively.

A high neck was daytime wear and low neck, with flowers, was evening wear.

The skirt followed suit: it cleared the ground by day and swept the floor with a train at night.

The hair was combed into a fringe, curls piled on top and the hat poised quiveringly on top of that. The hat itself had flowers, fruit and /or birds' wings, and a spotted veil to keep it all together.

Accessories: Belts with large buckles, card-cases of mother-of-pearl, silver, tortoiseshell or ivory, muffs with velvet bows on them, small rosette earrings, a choker or looped gold chain, a parasol or umbrella, which was long and striped, and a small reticule.

Fans were very large, painted with flowers or landscapes, or Chinese, circular with bamboo handles.

1895—The fashion was for the hour-glass figure, with a gored skirt and leg-of-mutton sleeves. A jacket and skirt and shirt blouse was worn by the ultra-modern, and this needs a brisk walk, while the ultra-feminine wore hip-pads and pliable hoops to hold out the hem of a skirt that had eleven gores. There was a slight bustle and a slight train for daytime, with a loop to hold it up.

The bicycling skirt was short, with full bloomers and gaiters and a man's straw hat held on with a cord attached to the lapel by a button. (This is the costume that would be worn by H. G. Wells's "Ann Veronica".)

Boudoir scenes had tea-gowns which gave the girls a rest

from tight-lacing, although the hair was always faultlessly arranged.

HAIR (1905): Ladies' hair was piled in a pompadour and waved all round the head, with a knot in the centre. Ornaments or birds and butterflies in jewels were perched on top of the knot for evening wear.

Motoring clothes were taken seriously and consisted of a duster coat or cape, large gauntlet gloves, a large hat tied with a veil right over both hat and face, several bracelets, and a feather boa.

1890–1900 *Men could wear:*

A morning-coat in the morning, but must change into a frock-coat for the afternoon.

For bicycling and for picnics, or the country, a blazer was worn or a Norfolk jacket with a high stiff collar and a waistcoat.

For an evening at home, a quilted smoking jacket of velvet in a dark colour, heavily braided round the sleeves and pocket, was the fashion.

Bow ties (or "Ascot Puffs") for young men, and a string tie for elderly men may be chosen, and knickerbockers., stockings, an Inverness cape and mackintoshes were the garments for this period.

Hair, was worn fairly short and the moustache full and drooping, or sharply turned up in the style of the German Kaiser. Mutton-chop whiskers or side-whiskers were worn by the older men. Pointed Vandyke beards show that the character is a doctor or an artist.

Summer wear included a straw hat with a narrow brim and a cord looped about the crown and attached to the coat lapel.

Accessories showing individuality were Tam-o'-Shanters, chest-protectors, and buttonholes of carnations or rosebuds.

1900—Evening Dress for Stag Parties: A dinner-jacket.

For formal parties, black broadcloth tails, white vest, white tie, and buttonhole.

The hair was parted at the side and brushed over the forehead and a small pointed moustache was waxed. Older and professional men wore beards.

1900–1910 *Men could wear:*

Single-breasted coats buttoned with three or four buttons. By 1905, a sack coat, or a double-breasted coat and matching waistcoat, shirt and stiff collar with deep turnover or wide wings, and bow tie.

Evening dress did not alter: dinner-jackets were not worn when ladies were present.

A black or grey waistcoat, with a frock coat, and a black or a white pique waistcoat with a cutaway coat. Creased, rather wide, trousers were coming in; knickerbockers buttoned below the knee for bicycling and golf, with stockings, while otherwise socks of any colour were worn.

Shoes: buttoned or laced—patent leather for evening.

Hair, parted on the side or in the middle and worn fairly long over the forehead.

Straw hats, Panama hats and top-hats and bowler hats for formal occasions.

1905–1910 *Ladies could wear:*

Chemises, long corsets, knickers, petticoats, and pads on the hips and behind. Petticoats were gored and had ruffled frills at the hem of taffeta. An ankle-length skirt for bicycling, lawn-tennis and ping-pong. In 1909, an Empire line in dresses and in tailored suits of coat-and-skirt.

A long straight coat buttoned down the front and a large flat muff. Black stockings for day, coloured and openwork for evening: shoes with pointed toes and medium high heels. Lace-up shoes for walking.

Hair, a pompadour in an even pile all round the head. A black taffeta bow could be at the nape of the neck, or on top of the head from 1905 to 1907: after this, a velvet band round the hair was more popular.

Long green veils tied right over the hat for motoring, worn with goggles and gauntlet gloves.

Accessories: Large flat handbags, with a chain and clasp parasols, link charm bracelets, brooches, rings, and necklaces worn in profusion.

Clothes for servants and tradesmen are given in the next chapter. (Pages 283–4 and 289–92).

Brief Summary of Main Points

Ladies:

1835–40	Wide shoulders, longer skirts, mittens and embroidered handkerchiefs.
1840	Velvet, embroidered with coral, seen everywhere.
1844–50	Flounced taffeta, and velvet or satin.
1850–60	Ribbons, hair nets with strings and tassels of pearls, carved and inlaid fans made of gauze with gold and silver spangles.
1860	Largest crinolines.
1860–5	Pork-pie hats.
1865–70	Skirts looped up over underskirts.
1870	Crinolines go out: gloves are important.
1875	Dresses made of combined plain and patterned material and plaid taffeta: bustles and draped skirts, hats tilted forward.
1875–80	Dresses plain at front, draped at back, tight at hips.
1880	Bustles out, but bow still at back of skirt. Vivid colours.
1885	Bustle back again: heavy materials.
1889–95	Leg-of-mutton sleeves, wasp waists.
1895–1900	The shirt blouse, with skirt, and hat placed flat on head.
1900–1905	High necks for daytime, very low for evening, when long gloves essential; broderie Anglais

and dotted net popular. Tweed and serge for daytime.

1907–1909 Skirts shorter and narrower.

1910 Skirts are slit and hats like coalscuttles.

List of Costume and Other Reference Books

Elegant Modes in the 19th Century from High Waist to Bustle (with illustrations) — Angus Holden (Allen & Unwin)

Fashion and Fashion Plates 1800–1900 (Penguin Books 1943)

Taste and fashion from the French Revolution to to-day.

English Costume of the 19th Century — James Laver and Iris Brook (A. & C. Black)

This has coloured plates and short descriptions of the details of dress.

English Costume, 1900 *to* 1950 — Iris Brook (Methuen)

This is extremely useful, with drawings of every kind of costume.

Dress: How and Why Fashion in Men's and Women's Clothes has Changed in the last 200 *Years* — James Laver (John Murray)

The title explains itself but gives no hint of the delightful text and illustrations.

Dressing the Play — N. Lambourne (Studio Publications)

A practical handbook showing how the costumes were cut and made.

A History of the Uniforms of the British Army — C. C. P. Lawson (Peter Davies)

Very helpful.

Two books on Make-up that are helpful are:

The Dramatic Student's Approach to Make-Up — C. Thomas (Garnet Miller)

Guide to Greasepaint — A. Stanley (French)

Adaptable Stage Costume for Women Elizabeth Russell (Garnet Miller)
Basic bodice and skirt with additions and accessories for each period from Saxon to Victorian. Detailed patterns and sewing instructions.

Artists Who Sum Up the Visual Aspect of Each Period

These artists are mostly portrait-painters and their pictures help immensely in showing how the costumes were worn. The figures are usually shown standing beside an article of furniture that is typical of its period. There are many other artists of this century but some of them specialised in pictures of a fantastic kind and so they have not been included in this list.

Franz Winterhalter	1806–73
William Frith	1819–1909
Holman Hunt	1827–1910
Dante Gabriel Rossetti	1828–82
Sir John Millais	1829–96
Edouard Manet	1832–83
Sir Edward Burne-Jones	1833–98
William Morris	1834–96
J. A. M. Whistler	1834–1903
Hilaire-Germaine Degas	1834–1917
Claude Monet	1840–1926
J. S. Sargent	1856–1925

Cartoons by George Cruikshank (1792-1878) and Phil May (1864–1903) and George Du Maurier's (1834–96) drawings may be studied with advantage.

CHAPTER XXI

OCCUPATIONS

Occupations and amusements of the periods for stage, arena and pageant production—Classified list for men, ladies, servants, tradesmen, etc.—List of useful books

IN the genuine period plays situation follows situation with such dramatic rapidity that there is little time for the characters to do more than catch their breath before the next abyss yawns in front of them.

Modern authors are more merciful and in the plays written about these periods there are many occasions when the producer will want to introduce some occupations or amusements.

The plays of this period deal almost entirely with the life of the leisured classes, so that the occupations are based on the fact that there were plenty of servants to do the work and it was the business of their employers to be elegant and unhurried. When scenes take place in which the working-classes are present, they are treated as comic relief or as stark tragedy (humble girl betrayed by young Lord). When Shaw made a flower-girl his heroine (in "Pygmalion") he was breaking new ground in treating a working girl as a serious human character. Pinero, in "The Gay Lord Quex" certainly has a manicurist in an important part, but Sophie knew her place in a way that Eliza never did. Ann Veronica, in H. G. Wells's play of that title, pinpoints how difficult it was for a girl of the middle classes to earn her own living and how few jobs were open to her.

Domestic servants were very much at the mercy of their employers, who could refuse the reference which would get them another job, and this attitude must show when acting such a part.

Soldiers were not encouraged to "walk out" with the maidservants, as is clearly shown in Barrie's "Quality Street".

The furnishing of the Early Victorians still kept the clean lines and graceful curves of the Regency, but as the century progressed, so the rooms became uglier. The chairs were stuffed fatter and had more cushions, the curtains and tablecloths burgeoned bobble and fringe, the wallpapers sprouted roses and crysanthemums, and the carpets followed suit. Dark, heavy colours were fashionable and if they could clash, so much the better. Maroon, magenta, mustard, peacock-blue and bilious green were freely employed. Everything that could be draped heavily, was: even the statues had skirts, if decency demanded it. Marble busts loomed on topheavy pedestals, and potted plants dripped lugubrious leaves over swollen brass and china pot-holders.

The producer should beware of making his set so revolting that it would be impossible for a modern audience to face it. Lighting is often the solution to this problem: he can ignore the fact that the Victorians kept the curtains closed in case the lovely colours faded. An atmosphere of stuffiness and of possessions crowding round should be achieved.

The poor homes were really poverty-stricken and should be a contrast by being very bare.

The lordly homes of England were very much the same as they are now, with beautiful antiques and lofty rooms.

In the 1860's the craze was for furniture inlaid with mother-of-pearl, and the chairbacks, cushions and hangings were embroidered with brilliant Eastern flowers and parrots and humming-birds. Love-seats were popular.

Towards the end of the century the fashion turned to bamboo and stools, whatnots and hall-stands were all made of this.

William Morris brought in the fashion for design in household things, and then drainpipes with sunflowers painted on them were made into umbrella-stands: but on the credit side, really lovely wallpapers began to appear. These had a close design of flowers and leaves in soft colours and the paper was often used to cover the screens that checked draughts from door and window. Japanese screens in black and gold or silver were also seen. The tea-tray was often a large round brass one, which stood on a four-legged stand. Ornaments and knick-knacks abounded.

Meals were a formal occupation. Afternoon tea was served with Mamma pouring out, using a tea-strainer. A kettle on a spirit-lamp was usually on the tray. The parlourmaid—or in wealthy houses the footman—passed round the cups on a tray which also held milk and sugar and the guests helped themselves. Then bread-and-butter and cake were handed round by the parlourmaid. The curate, if present, did his share of the handing-round, and if it was an informal party, all the gentlemen could help.

Servants were rung for to put coal on the fire, sweep up the hearth or draw the curtains, and this can sometimes provide useful business if the producer wants to prolong the agony while the heroine makes up her mind about some ghastly alternative. The hostess rang for some servant to show any guest to the front door, whether they were being thrown out or merely escorted.

Wealthy households employed a butler, footmen, parlourmaids, housemaids, cooks, between-maids, kitchen-maids, coachmen, grooms and gardeners. There might also be bootboys, gardeners' boys, valets, ladies-maids, sewing maids and stillroom maids.

Cooks would wear gingham dresses buttoned up to the neck, a gingham apron with a bib, and a cap with a frill round the edge. Parlourmaids would wear print dresses with a white apron with a bib, and a white cap in the morning, and so would housemaids. In the afternoon, parlourmaids would wear a black dress with a small lace-trimmed or frilled apron. In Edwardian times, the apron would be much smaller and the cap a flat triangle of muslin edged with lace, or a small starched cap edged with a frill, or lace, and shaped like a snood, only standing upright.

Organ-grinders, crossing-sweepers, flower-girls, chair-menders, knife-grinders, paper-boys, lavender-girls, lamp-lighters, sweeps, men selling hot chestnuts or hot potatoes or crying the claims of patent medicines, or men selling trays of bootlaces or strings of onions slung over their shoulders were seen in the towns. Drivers of horsebuses wore a long coat and a top-hat, and walked about carrying their whips. Beggars in ghastly rags were often seen in large cities, and very ragged tramps on country roads. Every fairground and common had gypsies in caravans.

Amusements

1827–1910

Sports and Games: Fly-fishing, archery, polo (from 1863), golf, croquet, lawn-tennis, football, cricket, billiards, roller-skating, ice-skating (actor could carry skates), quoits, skittles, battledore-and-shuttlecock, rounders, basket-ball, "touch", hide-and-seek, hunt-the-thimble, pick-up-the-handkerchief, charades, blind-man's buff. (These last "party games" have been included as there are so many party scenes in the plays.) Card games of all sorts. Draughts, chess, cribbage, dominoes, solitaire (played on a polished board, with glass marbles fitting into holes in the board.)

Fly-fishing, polo, golf, football and cricket were usually only done by the gentlemen; the others were done by both sexes.

Pastimes included sketching (both indoor and outdoor),

practising and performing on various musical instruments, cup-and-ball, diabolo (consisting of spinning rapidly, throwing up and catching again, a small double-cone-shaped piece of wood suspended on a string stretched between sticks held in each hand). (*See* Fig. 40.)

Hypnotism was a party game, done in a very amateur way, and this could very amusingly be used for an impromptu sketch.

Paper games, jigsaw puzzles, acrostics and cards whiled away the long evenings at home.

Billiards was played by the men, while the ladies admired and marked or kept the score. By 1902 ladies were allowed to join in this game in a mild way. Cribbage was the stand-by of the elderly, and the sticking-in of the little pegs in the cribbage-board can be an effective way of pointing dialogue.

In Victorian and Edwardian periods there was a suitable time for each kind of handwork. Plain sewing and knitting was done in the mornings, embroidery, crochet, lacemaking and beadwork in the evenings. It could vary according to the materials used: for instance, they might knit a woollen sock in the morning but they would prefer to knit a silk purse in the evening.

Men's Occupations through the Periods 1827–1910

The gentlemen rarely did anything with their spare time in the evenings except smoke, play cards or billiards. Their days were devoted to either business or sport, according to their incomes.

Ladies' Occupations through the Periods 1827–1910

Watering potted plants from a small watering-can with a long spout. (*See* Fig. 41). Cutting flowers in the garden,

FIG. 40. Victorian Child Playing Diabolo

FIG. 41. Lady with Watering Can

using scissors, gloves and a wide basket to carry them in and arranging the flowers in vases stood upon newspaper. An apron was worn for this type of work.

Cleaning jewellery, using liquid in a saucer and a little brush, set out on newspaper or a thick cloth. (Gloves and an apron essential.)

Cleaning out the bird-cage (never risk having a live bird on the stage).

Combing and brushing the lapdog and tying a bow of ribbon on his topknot.

Threading ribbon through the embroidery on petticoats was a job that was only done in privacy (in a bedroom or nursery scene) never in public reception rooms and only by ladies so poor that they had no maid to do it for them. (*See* Fig. 42). Such ladies can also sew new braid round the edges of their skirts: as late as 1906, this had to be done every two weeks as the skirts brushed the pavements and the braid frayed. Embroidery, knitting, crochet, tatting and beadwork.

The games were played by the ladies in a very gentle way, as it was not considered correct for them to excel in either physical or mental strength. Accomplishments were highly prized in all womanly works, and no actress must bungle her sewing in a Victorian play; but when it came to a game played by both sexes, then there was no question of competing with the men. It is difficult for moderns to grasp this. They will swing their racquets expertly instead of toying with them gracefully. The croquet mallet lends itself very well to a drooping stance—and an upward glance at the nearest male. It must not be gripped as if it could be used as an instrument for murder. (*See* Fig. 43).

The men can afford a pleasing swagger that would seem the essence of side now, and they can show off to their hearts' content and still remain exquisitely in period. The special clothes for sports and games all emphasise

FIG. 42. Lady's Maid Threading Ribbon in Petticoat—
Late Victorian or Edwardian

FIG. 43. Victorian Lady Playing Croquet

this and should be displayed to their full. Any scene in which a game of skill or sport is used should have its quota of men kindly teaching the helpless females how to do it in a protective, if patronising, way.

Crowd Scenes and Pageants

Occupations and Appropriate Clothes

1827–1910

In poor districts and in country markets up to the 70's, the *Street Doctor* was a familiar sight. He wore a billycock hat, black frock-coat and trousers. In front of him was a black tray of medicines supported on a folding stand. He sold large bottles of "Universal Tonic" with flaring labels tied to them, and pink boxes of pills.

The *Public Disinfectant Man* went round the slums in times of epidemics. He wore loose pale grey trousers and a belted tunic reaching to his knees: a leather bag containing disinfectant was slung over his shoulder.

The *Ginger-beer Seller* wore a brightly-striped shirt and a peaked cap.

Sandwich-men with large placards hung from their shoulders (back and front), advertising all kinds of wares, walked the streets constantly.

Flower Women wore full dark skirts with a huge pocket in the side, a knitted shawl around their shoulders and carried their flowers in (or, if they had a pitch, marketed them from) a large laundry basket. (*See* Fig. 44.) The old ones wore bonnets and the younger hats with, if possible, feathers.

Girl Flower-sellers went bareheaded and barefooted.

Muffin Men, wearing green baize aprons, walked the streets balancing the tray of muffins, which had a cloth over it, on their heads. They rang a handbell slowly as they walked. Sometimes they had a mouth-organ and played a little tune on it. They only worked in winter.

FIG. 44. Flower Woman—Late Victorian or Edwardian

The *Shrimps, Winkles and Mussels Man* called his wares while trundling a small barrow with two flags fixed to it.

Italian Street Vendors were often seen in London in 1870. They wore check shirts open at the throat, open waistcoats of a gay colour, with a brilliant scarf knotted at the throat and a peaked hat like a French gendarme. (*See* Fig. 45.) They often had small monkeys (it is better not to try to use real ones).

Coachmen, whether they drove private coaches or the public horse buses, wore a caped coat buttoned high at the neck, a high hat, and carried a whip. Bottle green, dark green or drab may be chosen, but the coat must have two rows of large buttons down the front. (*See* Fig. 46.)

Shop Salesmen wore frock coats if in a position of authority.

Shop Saleswomen wore a black sateen apron with a large pocket in the front. Similar aprons were worn by:

Sewing Women and Teachers.

Shoemakers, Blacksmiths and Harness-makers wore leather aprons.

Butchers and butcher boys wore blue aprons.

Workmen and Labourers wore loose coats, trousers tied with string at the knees and a shirt with no collar or tie but a handkerchief or muffler tucked in at the throat, and a cap.

Housekeepers wore a black dress and were allowed to wear a brooch and a watch pinned on the bosom.

Organ Grinders wore a velveteen jacket, red handkerchief round the neck, a broad-brimmed felt hat with a feather and gold hoop earrings.

Bailiffs wore square-crowned hats, leggings, boots, check waistcoats, scarf and a coat open to the knees.

Countrymen wore spotted scarves, leather gaiters or leggings and smocks.

Fig. 45. Italian Street Vendor with Onions

Fig. 46. Coachman—both Periods

List of Useful Reference Books

A History of Everyday Things In England: *Vol. III.* 1800–1850 *The Rise of Industrialism* *Vol. IV.* 1851–1934 *The Age of Production*	M. & C. H. B. Quennell	(Batsford)
Victorian Panorama—A Survey of Life and Fashions from Contemporary Photographs	P. Quennell	(Batsford)

CHAPTER XXII

MANNERS AND DANCES

Manners and customs—Bows and curtsies—Dances for each period, Waltz, Polka—List of reference books on dances

ETIQUETTE books flowed from the printing presses during this century, covering every hazard, from a morning call to "See, our postillion has been struck by lightning!" The manners are very formal from the beginning to the end of these periods. Lounging and lolling only takes place in the intimacy of the ladies' bedrooms or the gentlemen's clubs. Indeed, the only place where there were comfortable chairs were these clubs, where they had foot-rests and little shelves which clipped on to the arms of the chair to hold glasses and refreshing drinks.

Greetings were exchanged whenever anyone entered the room and again if they entered it after any lapse of time.

Curtsies and bows were used up to 1870, although men shook hands from about 1840. Ladies shook hands out of doors but retained the curtsy for indoors and formal occasions until the crinoline went out of fashion. The tighter skirts made a gracious bow and handshake easier. Royalty were always curtsied to, whatever the period.

Gentlemen raised the hat in greeting and held it in the air until they had passed the person they had greeted, took off the right glove to shake hands, and did not replace it until they had again shaken hands on parting. They could kiss the hand of a lady as a gallant gesture, or a gesture of respect or affection. Cousins kissed each other—if male, the opposite sex—and uncles kissed nieces and aunts kissed nephews. These kisses must all be on the cheek or forehead—except, of course, Mr. Barrett's kiss which so much upset poor Bella in "The Barretts of Wimpole Street".

Artists of every sort affected a freer manner, and should be differentiated in this way. Actresses were not welcome in Society until they had married into the Peerage. All foreigners were suspected of being disreputable—or at best careless—because they had not managed to be born British. They usually appear as comic characters in the plays.

All the plays set in Society need a certain amount of gushingness in the manners: a slight exaggeration of graciousness. The scenes which take place among the working-classes need simplicity—either a broad comedy attack or else a shining honesty, almost too good to be true. Some heroines are so innocent that they are practically half-witted. To get away with this, the actress will need great charm. The poise of the head and the position of the eyes are worth mentioning. Dowagers were awe-inspiring and terrifying creatures, and could gaze with beetling brows on anyone, even Royalty. Young girls were not supposed to look anyone straight in the eye. They sat with lowered eye-lids during tea and dinner parties and when they looked up it was with a submissively drooping neck. This trick of raising the eyes but not the head always came into play when talking to the gentlemen. The head might be bent coyly to either side, also, while the lashes were raised and lowered with telling effect. It must be remembered that gentleness was a trait highly admired and praised by the older generation and cultivated even by those of the younger generation to whom it did not come naturally. It is a mystery where they developed the ability to become fearsome Dowagers.

The gentlemen were obviously the "stronger" sex, and everything was done to bolster this idea. They fetched and carried for the ladies (whenever it was anything light, leaving the women-servants to lug along the heavy things).

The only burden the Victorian lady had to bear was her husband's temper. Men opened doors and allowed the ladies to pass through in front of them, and they never sat if a lady was standing. This protective attitude was preserved towards ladies but it was becoming increasingly patronising as Victoria kept on about women's place being in the home ready to bow to men's superiority. There was a complete change of manner if the man was talking to a maidservant or a Bad Woman—an ease and familiarity that he would never have used to his own family.

Gentlemen visitors had to leave their hats and canes in the hall when entering a house and they did not cross their legs or loll, except in the company of other men. They did not smoke in front of ladies until about 1903. They smoked cigars after dinner, when the ladies had departed, and in their own clubs, smoke rooms and studies. (Ladies did not smoke in public until 1912, although "fast" women smoked in the privacy of their boudoirs and among their friends: they always used a cigarette-holder.)

In the nineteenth century unemployment was so usual that the working-classes were more subservient as the fear of losing their jobs rose. Tradesmen, governesses, teachers, servants were mostly extremely civil, and even bordered on the cringing attitude. Nannies, cooks and old family retainers were the exception to this rule: they had a privileged freedom of speech and manner.

Maidservants dipped a quick curtsy when they were spoken to, and again after taking an order. If they had to announce a caller, they would enter the room ahead of the caller, curtsy, say the name, usher the visitor in, curtsy and exit. Butlers bowed from the waist, with their thumbs held down the side-seams of the trousers, and the backs of the hands showing and with their heels together.

What therefore has to be portrayed on the stage is the

difference in manner between the workers, when talking amongst themselves, and their subservient manner when talking to their social superiors. The sense of inferiority can be characterised by humility, servility or defiance, while the leisured class superiority can be either haughty, or condescending or gracious.

The Bow was used expressively, to denote the social standing of the recipient. A curt nod to inferiors, a deeper bow to equals and a really deep bow to superiors, older people (if worth it) and to ladies—not to women. One foot was placed in front of the other, with the front heel slightly raised, and a bow from the waist was made. Gentlemen always bowed to the assembled group when entering any room. If the greeting was to someone of whom they were fond, they kissed them on the cheek, or advanced with both hands outstretched and clasped the hands of the greeted. Passionate embraces only took place when the lovers were entirely alone. A firm handclasp was permissible between two men who were fast friends or who had not seen each other for some time.

The Curtsy was simple: one foot was placed slightly behind the other and both knees bent, while the skirt was picked up with both hands in front and held away from the legs without showing too much ankle.

For a more elaborate curtsy in crinoline or Edwardian dresses, the great secret of graceful performance is to take the same amount of time to come up as to go down. It is best to practice this in counts of equal number going down and coming up. First try it in three counts each way, then in four, six, eight and then twelve, which is a grand curtsy, suitable for Court occasions. The full count must be taken in actually coming up and standing erect on the very last count, no-one must cheat by merely waiting still for the last bit.

When a man asked a girl to dance, he came over and bowed first to the chaperone and then to his partner. He then asked her to dance, with another bow. She rose, he offered his arm, they both bowed to the chaperone and moved away to dance. When he returned her to the chaperone, they bowed and curtsied to each other, he bowed to the chaperone, bowed again to his partner and walked away. He could stay and fan her, or he could bring her (and the chaperone) refreshments. Dance programmes were always used. The girl could dance, with her bouquet in a bracelet holder or she could leave it with her chaperone, and she could do the same with her programme. "Curtsy while you're thinking what to say" is quite a useful rule to follow, as they curtsied in all the cases where a modern would say "Well . . ." before saying goodbye.

All this tends to slow up a production, so it must be worked into the texture of the scene early in rehearsals.

The dances were surprisingly vigorous. In spite of tightlacing, the Victorians managed to leap in a sprightly way for hours on end. The Quadrille, the Waltz, the Polka and the Gallop figured on the dance programs with now and again a Country Longways Dance left over from the previous century or a Jig or Reel, if the Ball was held in the country. Edwardian balls consisted mostly of Waltzes, but with the Valeta, the Military Two-Step and other novelty dances for each new season.

The Waltz, which had caused shocked horror to the Regency ladies, had become respectable by Victoria's time. The scandal had been caused by the fact that it was the first dance to be seen in Society in which the gentleman put his arm round the waist of the lady instead of chastely holding her hand. The dresses took up so much space that the gentleman was kept at a respectful distance, so all was ultimately in order and the mammas stopped their worried cluckings.

The main object of the waltzers was to turn smoothly,

practically on the same spot. They did not try to travel, as the crinolines crushed easily and the corsets of the ladies were so tight that they could only take small steps. Unlike the modern waltz, it had a lilt, and is not difficult to do as long as it is not rushed. For stage purposes it is most effective if not all the couples keep turning. There is an attractive little balancing step that was used when the lady felt giddy or when the couple wanted to indulge in a private conversation. They had so few chances to get to know each other that any seconds of privacy were doubly precious.

There are six steps in the Waltz which take two bars of waltz music. The lady and the gentleman do precisely the same steps but her first three steps are the same as his second three because she starts by travelling backwards and he finishes by travelling backwards. If the gentleman starts with putting his right foot forward while turning to the right, then puts his left foot to the side and closes his right foot neatly to the left, he will have made a half turn and now be in the position in which the lady started, while she is now facing forward. She now does the same steps that have just been described while the gentleman does the steps with which the lady started. The lady starts by putting her left foot back, then her right foot behind across her left foot and turning on her toes until she is facing front, when she repeats the first three steps that her partner did.

For those who find this difficult to follow, here is a tabulated list.

	Gentleman	*Lady*
(1)	Right foot forward turning to right	(4)
(2)	Left foot to side	(5)
(3)	Right foot up to left	(6)
(4)	Left foot to back	(1)
(5)	Right foot behind across left foot	(2)
(6)	Left foot close to right	(3)

These six steps make one right turn, but the steps must be small—really small—or the partners will not manoeuvre around each other. If any difficulty is found in learning, it is certainly because the dancers are taking good modern strides. If they take as small steps as they think they can and then halve that, they will find the steps fit in easily to the music. The lady puts her hand on the right elbow of her partner and he holds her at the waist with his right hand. His left arm is bent and the hand is level with his shoulder while her right hand rests within his hand. There should be space clearly visible between their bodies and the lady should lean back slightly so that she can look up at her partner. If she is taller than he is, then she must use feminine guile to give the general effect at her partner. The little balance step consists of a step to the side and a hovering for two counts, or one waltz bar, and then a step to the other side, and hovering for two counts. In this way quite a long chat could be had without bothering about the turn, so long as they were on the side of the room away from the ever-watchful eye of the chaperone.

Everyone, of course, wore gloves and the lady could leave her fan or bouquet with her chaperone while she danced or she could hang them from a ribbon or bracelet at her wrist.

The Waltz was still done by the Edwardians and it was considered rather "fast" to reverse. This is not quite as silly as it sounds, because, in order to reverse (or turn to the left) the hold round the waist had to be very firm and close.

The Edwardian lady could gather up her train or dress slightly but had to try not to show any ankle. Sometimes she did not try hard enough, and there were mutterings among the dowagers.

In both periods, a smooth gliding lilt was admired, although for family parties the dance can get rather rowdy. If a young lady was no lady, she showed it in an abandoned and voluptuous waltz movement.

Other dances were the Quadrille, the Lancers, the Gallop and the Polka.

The Lancers and the Quadrille were figure-dances and not suitable for the stage as they take too long and there is so much repetition. In other centuries such dances can be used effectively in Pageants, but Edwardian dress is so rarely seen in Pageants that these dances are not worth describing.

The most popular among the young people was the Polka. The Prince Consort had brought this over from Germany and there are numberless variations and sequences which were full of the party spirit and easy to learn and perform. These adapt themselves gaily to stage, arena or pageant work as they can have any number of dancers who can work as couples in sets of four, or as a procession round the dance space. It can be danced in the period 1837–1907.

The basic step is simple, but it must be danced lightly and gracefully if it is a ballroom scene. If it is done at a family party, there can be a certain amount of romping. Even so, it must be the young men who romp, not the young ladies.

The Polka step takes one bar of 4–4 music and consists of three steps and a hop. The step can be done forwards, backwards, sideways and turning. The easiest way to start learning it is forwards.

The couple stand side-by-side holding hands. They both start with the outside foot: the lady with her right and the gentleman with his left, so that when they move into the ordinary dance hold to do the step turning, they are already using the correct feet. The steps are the same for both all the time. A step forward, close the other foot up to the first one, another step forward and the foot which closed is brought to the front with a pointed toe in the air, while the other foot gives a hop. So the lady does —Forward right foot, close left foot, forward right foot, hop right foot, and bring the left foot through in the air with pointed toe. When the step is done to the side the timing is exactly the same but the first and third steps are taken to the side. When the step travels backwards, the first and third steps are taken to the backwards. The style is given to the dance by the way that the lifted foot is brought to the front with the body bending towards the lifted foot. When the step is done turning, two Polka steps are taken to complete one turn which takes two bars of Polka music. The dance hold is the same as that used for the Waltz, but many of the Polka variations are done with the couple side-by-side for the greater part of the dance and the hold and turn are only used for a few bars at the end of a figure. Producers who have not much time to rehearse the dancers can arrange a dance on the simplest lines, which can still be charming and effective, by making the actors and actresses dance alternatively and only letting them dance together for the last figure. By that time not much is likely to go wrong.

In the Clap Polka man and girl stand side by side holding hands—not high, but just clearing the crinoline. The man's left hand is on his hip, the girl's right hand holds bouquet or fan. The couples form up behind one another and travel round the dance floor in procession. All point the inside foot (the foot nearest each other) in front and then behind and do one Polka step forward, taking two bars altogether, or eight counts. They repeat these eight counts using the outside foot. They go on doing all this until they have done it sixteen times and used thirty-two bars of music. Strauss' Polka "Sans Souci" is recommended, as if they cannot dance to that they are hopeless and the producer can cut out the dance.

The man then stands still and the girl polkas round him in a small circle eight times one way and eight times going back the other way. The man holds his right arm up with the girl's left hand in his and lets it go when she has travelled to behind him, catching it again as she comes round to the front again. The girl can use her fan very coyly in this step. They then do one polka step facing each other but travelling to the side without holding hands and another with the other foot. (This means that all the dancers move to the right towards the way they originally travelled and then back again with the girls backing to the centre of the room and the men facing it.) Standing still, they then clap both hands together and then clap them against their partner's hands: again clap both hands together and clap first the left and then the right against the left and right hand of their partner (like "pat-a-cake"). (*See* Fig. 47.)

(The only tricky part is that the clapping of single hands is done twice as quickly as the clapping of both hands, so it can be counted in one bar in four—clap, clap, clap, clap—while when both hands clap, the clap takes two counts and there are only two claps in the bar.)

Repeat the two sideways polka steps and all the claps four times. This will take sixteen bars. Then the man catches the girl into a loose dance-hold and they do eight polka steps, turning, travelling round the floor.

This dance can be shortened by halving all the numbers of times the steps are done, or it can all be repeated until the dancers are exhausted.

The Imperial Society of Teachers of Dancing, Historical Dance Branch, Euston Hall, Birkenhead Street, London WC1H 4AJ, will supply a list of teachers qualified in this subject.

FIG. 47. Victorian Polka

Useful Reference Books

Old Time Dancing Victor Sylvester (H. Jenkins)
No. 1 includes the Waltz, Valeta, Military Two-Step, Barn Dance, etc., in simplified form for modern dancers.

Country Dance Book ed. D. and H. Kennedy (Novello)
English Folk Dance Society, New Series I.
This has music and descriptions of thirty country dances suitable for Victorian or Edwardian country scenes for stage plays or pageants.

CHAPTER XXIII

MUSIC

Musical forms of the period—Instruments used—List for each period of composers, instruments and suggested music for atmosphere

VICTORIAN music soars to the divine and drops to the ridiculous.

Every young lady learned to play the piano and most of them learned to sing, not so much with a view to performing solo, as to prepare for duets. The accompaniment of Victorian ballad songs demanded a formal ritual of manners. For serious songs, the silver photograph-frames and other ornaments were removed from the top of the piano and the handpainted or embroidered velvet cover was folded back carefully. The piano-stool was wound up or down by the gentleman under the coquettish guidance of the lady. She then took off her jangling bracelets and any heavy rings and put them beside her at the end by the keys. The gentleman gallantly pulled out the music-rack and opened the music for her. If the lady was playing alone, he stood by and turned over the pages; if she was playing his accompaniment, she turned over the pages herself although he could make a gesture of helping her. When all was ready he pulled down his waistcoat and she shook her skirt and her curls, they flashed a smile at each other and the audience, and rollicked away. If the performers were amateurs, the assembled company stopped talking, but if they were professionals, the conversation continued unabated as music was considered a pleasant background for conversation.

The harp was the chosen instrument for any girl with beautiful arms, as it showed them off to advantage. Its only drawback was that it was difficult to take to parties and produce with surprise, as was the habit of the young ladies who always accidentally brought their songs with them.

Contraltos were allowed to choose songs with the guitar to play at parties, but it was considered a shade theatrical.

The older ladies and gentlemen rendered dramatic monologues which had a stirring piano accompaniment; this came under the heading of music, although most of them were more like stage-effects.

Families would each learn a different instrument so that they could form a string-quartet or a trio, and the flute was also popular. The bass instrumental parts were mainly the prerogative of the gentlemen, as the posture for cello or double bass playing called for an unladylike disposition of the skirt, which was of course unthinkable.

From 1830 every home of any standing had a piano and grand ones had grand pianos from 1860.

The form of music was set and every possible variety flourished: opera, operetta, ballad-songs, oratorios and symphonies filled the concert-halls and theatres.

The music-hall songs are in rather a different category: they were sung in the Halls and at stag dinners, they were whistled by butcher-boys and played on barrel-organs but were never heard in the drawing-rooms. The Salvation Army pioneered the idea of fitting the words of their hymns to popular tunes, coining the phrase that they didn't see why the Devil should have all the best tunes.

Military bands were very much the same as they are now and made a brilliant spot of sound and colour in the parks of seaside places.

Dance-bands consisted of strings and piano with discreet percussion, but a Hunt Ball would have a posthorn.

In Edwardian times, standards of amateur accomplishment were under heavy criticism: too many people were forced to listen to too poor performances. In country districts, however, where they had to make their own music or go without, the amateur tradition still lingered and families practised together and played at the village concerts and at their neighbours' dinner-parties. The Italian school was favoured and songs with trills were the most popular.

The music for dances were usually the most recent musical-comedy selections. The "Blue Danube" was still the favourite but other Strauss waltzes were often heard. The Strauss polkas and gallops, the "Washington Post", various waltz-quadrilles, the "Valeta" and (for 1910) the waltz "Destiny" are all suitable for use for incidental music for Edwardian plays.

This type of music is so often needed that some suggestions for light music are in a list at the end of this chapter. Although to modern ears it all sounds vaguely "Edwardian", in reality popular music was changing very much, and it is worth while choosing the music that is actually of the right period for the play.

Some Composers of the Period

Paganini	1782–1840
H. Bishop	1786–1855
Weber	1786–1826
Meyerbeer	1791–1864
Rossini	1792–1868
Schubert	1797–1828
Donizetti	1797–1848
C. A. Adam (Composer of the ballet-music for "Giselle")	1803–56
Berlioz	1803–69
Schumann	1810–56
Liszt	1811–86
Verdi	1813–1901

Wagner	1813–83
Gounod	1818–93
Offenbach	1819–80
César Franck	1822–90
Smetana	1824–84
Johann Strauss	1825–99
A. Rubinstein	1829–94
Borodin	1833–87
Brahms	1833–97
Saint-Saens	1835–1921
Delibes	1836–91
Bizet	1838–75
Moussorgsky	1839–81
Tchaikowsky	1840–93
Chabrier	1841–94
Dvořák	1841–1904
Sullivan	1842–1900
Grieg	1843–1907
Rimsky-Korsakov	1844–1908
Fauré	1845–1924
Messager	1853–1929
Elgar	1857–1934
Puccini	1858–1924
Leoncavallo	1858–1919
Albeniz	1860–1909
Mahler	1860–1911
Debussy	1862–1918
Delius	1862–1934
Bela Bartok	1881–1945

Instruments Used

Spinet—Out of date by 1837 but would be seen in old fashioned homes.

Piano—with violin, 'cello and double bass for dance orchestra. No drum until 1880.

Harp—Popular for lady solo player from 1870.
Banjo—Popular for gentleman solo player from 1890.
Guitar—Popular for lady solo player from 1880.

Light Music and Ballad Songs

Scott Gatty's "Plantation Songs"	1880
"The Wolf" "Oh that We Two were Maying" "Daisy, Daisy give me your answer"	*c.* 1890
Selections from "The Belle of New York" and "The Quaker Girl"	*c.* 1898
"Soldiers of the Queen" and "Tommy Atkins"	*c.* 1902
"Lily of Laguna"	1903
"Glorious Devon" Selections from "Miss Hook of Holland" "The Chocolate Soldier" and "The Merry Widow"	from 1905–7

CHAPTER XXIV

PRACTICE SCENES

Suggested scenes from plays for practice in period acting—Mime scene for practice in period movement, with music

The New Planet. PLANCHÉ. *Period* 1847.

Spirited attack must be used and the rhyming couplets be given their full value. Fantastic movement may be introduced and in certain speeches a fantastic pose may be struck and held for the whole speech. Above all, the actors must enjoy the fun and frivolity of the scene.

Colleen Bawn. D. BOUCCICAULT. *Period* 1860. *Act* 2 *Scene* 3

This scene must be played seriously and sweetly, giving full stress to the sentiments and not playing for laughs. The actresses should aim to give the whole thing charm. This is not an easy task but the exercise must continue until the flavour of the period is attained.

The Importance of Being Earnest. OSCAR WILDE *Period* 1895. *Act* 2

The long duologue between Cicely and Gwendoline is specially recommended from this Act. The young ladies must not sweep to and fro too much; the varying emotions must be conveyed by changes of positions of the body with turns of the waist and head. A parasol may be used effectively as an accessory to point certain lines and the manner of speech must be in keeping with the formal manner of movement.

The Voysey Inheritance. H. GRANVILLE-BARKER

Period 1903. *Act* 2

This is a dinner-party scene which gives an opportunity for manners between the men and women and for the handling and invention of business with properties on the dinner-table. The family are together, so the manners should be formal yet familiar. It is important to show the relationships between the various husbands and wives.

The Twelve Pound Look. SIR J. M. BARRIE

Period 1910.

This is an important exercise to bring out the difference in manner between the sheltered wife and the New Woman who has chosen to earn her own living. As both their scenes are with the same man, he has to show his ability to deal with the wife who knows her place, and his baffled bewilderment when confronted with the typist (his ex-wife) who does not know her place.

Mime Scene for Practice with Period Movement with Music

ST. VALENTINE'S FLUSTER

Music — "Voices of Spring" by Johann Strauss
Time — 1850
Place — A garden. (This can be represented by a sky cloth, two flowering plants in pots placed on pedestals, a rustic bench and cushions on the ground.)

Characters

Sophie, Melanie, Louise	Daughters of the house, aged 17–25.
Aunt Maria	Aged 37 (approx.)
Miss Moxey	Governess, aged 40 (approx.)
Jane	The Maid

(1) Sophie enters carrying sketch-book and pencil with Jane in attendance with folding-stool. They select a view for Sophie to draw, she sits down and Jane exits. Sophie fusses with her pencil and book and then starts to sketch.

Melanie enters with a box of beads, needle and thread, escorted by Jane carrying scissors. Melanie sits on a cushion and starts to sort her beads, Jane exits.

Louise enters carrying her small embroidery-frame, escorted by Jane carrying the book of silk and patterns. Louise sits on a cushion and starts to embroider, Jane exits.

The three girls continue to work but they are all listening for the postman so they work for four bars of the music and pause to listen for two. Each in turn gets up, crosses to where Jane went out and peers across hopefully, then with a shake of the head returns disconsolately to her work.

(2) Aunt Maria and Miss Moxey enter, girls get up and drop a curtsy. Aunt Maria makes a little tour, inspecting each girl's work carefully and critically, making suggestions for improvement. (This is an opportunity for comedy, to be developed by each actress in her own way and may take up a good deal of music.)

The girls react in character.

Aunt Maria and Miss Moxey sit on the bench and Miss Moxey holds wool for Aunt to wind.

(3) Jane enters with a letter on a salver which causes wild

palpitations among the girls who all think it is a Valentine for them. Jane exits. Aunt Maria opens it but it is a bill for new shoes. She considers it exorbitant and each girl is called to her, has to display her shoes and is scolded for extravagance and then sent back to her work.

(4) Jane enters with another letter at which the girls look hopefully, and presents it to Aunt Maria, who opens it watched breathlessly by the girls. It is clearly a letter which makes her furiously angry. She reads it (three pages should be in the envelope) getting more and more furious, then springs to her feet, crumples the letter and throws it violently away. She glares at the girls, daring them to ask questions, gestures to Miss Moxey to pick up the letter and give it to her, then storms off stage.

The girls mime enquiry of each other, but no one knows what the letter contained.

At this moment a loud postman's double knock is heard off stage. The girls freeze in their positions with all heads turned towards the exit.

(5) Jane enters, they all rush to her but she has no letter. Each girl reacts differently but makes it clear that she is bitterly disappointed. They pick up their work and exit despairingly. Jane then takes a letter from her pocket and, handing it to Miss Moxey, waits with a knowing smile on her face to see what it contains. Miss Moxey draws herself up with great dignity, places the letter on the bench, sits down and starts tidying up the wool. Jane, thwarted, flounces off.

Miss Moxey watches her go, then swiftly runs across to make sure she really has gone, looks all round to see there are no spies and comes to the centre of the stage with the letter. She carefully draws it out of the envelope and it is a large, lacy Valentine. She looks at it, then inside it, and her face breaks into a radiant smile as the curtain drops.

Production Note: This mime is not intended to be done in strict time with the music, although the producer can arrange to do so if preferred and if enough time is allowed for rehearsals. The music has various different melodies and it is better if each little section of the mime starts with a different melody. The sections are marked with numbers to indicate where this takes place. Sometimes it is found that one part of the mime develops amusingly and needs more time in which case the melody can be repeated. The girls may use waltz steps for all their moves and Aunt Maria and Miss Moxey may use one walk for each waltz-bar if the producer wishes.

INDEX

A

Amusements, 39–41, 124–9, 211–213, 284–9.
Artists, lists of, 33, 113, 198, 280

B

Books, lists of General Reference, 10, 42, 91, 129, 177, 216, 256, 293

C

Children's clothes, toys, manners, 34, 44, 90, 115, 118, 119, 124, 126, 132, 193, 198, 205, 217, 270, 274
Clergy, 16, 28, 32, 102, 283
Clowns, 136
Colours, Period, 28, 106, 193, 261, 269
Courtiers, 15, 18, 24, 35, 36, 43–50, 84, 86–7, 100, 104–6, 117–19, 131–7, 140, 147, 148, 153, 183–5, 203, 218, 221–3, 225, 229, 261, 267, 281–3, 294–5, 301, 307
Costume Accessories, 24–32, 99–101, 108–12, 191–8, 269–79
Composers, lists of, 67, 158, 238, 308
Country, habits in, 16, 22, 36, 52, 101, 109–12, 129–36, 138–40, 147, 153, 156, 187, 193, 200–4, 206, 221–3, 238, 269, 291, 305, 306–7

D

Dances, books on, 60, 152, 234, 305
Dances, in chronological order,
Farandoles, 51
Caroles, 51
Branle or Brawl, 54
Estampie, 56
Salterelle, 56
Almain, 56
Basse Dances, 56
Pavane, 57, 138
Galliarde, 57, 138–43
Tordion, 57
La Volta, 57, 143
Coranto, 57, 144
Courante, 148
Country Dances, 138, 140, 147, 221, 233, 298, 305
Canaries, 144
Siciliana, 150
Chaconne, 150
Passe Pied, 150
Mattachins, 150
Bourree, 150
Rigaudon, 150
Sarabande, 222
Gigue, 223
Allemande, 223–4
Gavotte, 224–7
Minuet, 226–33
Quadrille, 298
Waltz, 298–301
Polka, 298, 301–303
Gallop, 298, 301
Valeta, 298
Lancers, 301
Military Two-Step, 298
Décor, 7, 8, 37, 85–7, 115–22, 173, 203, 204, 254, 282

F

Food, 37, 40, 121, 122, 126, 128, 134, 201, 207, 210, 283, 291
Fools, 106, 136
Furniture, 26, 28, 38–40, 115, 119–128, 135, 200–4, 211, 282–3, 294, 306
Footwear, 15, 18, 30–2, 97, 100, 102, 108–12, 185, 192–8, 267, 269–77

G

Games, 35, 39–42, 117–19, 124–8, 211, 212, 284–7
Gardens, 37, 114, 204, 255

H

Hair Styles, 26–32, 91–9, 109–12, 192–7, 260, 270–7
Headwear, 15, 16, 26–32, 96, 101–102, 107–12, 135, 180–2, 187, 191–7, 260–1, 265, 270–9

I

Illumination, methods of, *see* Occupations, lists of

J

Jesters, 50, 106, 136

L

Lepers, 17

M

Make-up, styles of, 31, 32, 38, 110, 135, 194–6, 205–6, 210–13
Manners, 22, 36, 43–59, 89, 99, 101, 119, 121, 130–50, 183–7, 190, 201, 203, 217–33, 250, 253, 261–9, 281–4, 294–306
Masques, 86–90, 102–4, 138, 153
Mimes, 75, 162, 243, 312
Music, lists of, 60, 67–72, 160, 233–234, 310
Musical Instruments, lists of, 67–9, 155–9, 239, 309–10

O

Occupations, lists of, 38–41, 122–9, 204–13, 284–91

P

Plays, Genuine Period, lists of, 11, 93, 178–9
Modern Period, lists of, 12, 13, 93–4, 179, 258
Playwrights, lists of, 11, 92, 178, 297

R

Ruffs, 96, 99, 123
Rulers, 26–31, 107, 191, 195

S

Servants, lists of work, 38–42, 101, 106, 115, 117, 122–9, 206–13, 283–91
Stomachers, 99

T

Tradespeople, lists of, 16, 38–41, 101–2, 124–6, 136, 193, 201, 213, 284, 289

W

Widows, 107, 193, 197, 274